STAGING FASHION, 1880–1920
Jane Hading, Lily Elsie, Billie Burke

1900   NOVEMBRE – I   N° 45

LE THÉATRE

DIRECTION ET REDACTION :	PUBLICITÉ :	CONDITIONS DE L'ABONNEMENT :	ABONNEMENT ET VENTE :
24, Boulevard des Capucines.	DUHAMEL et COMMUNAY, seuls concessionnaires 15, Boulevard Montmartre.	PARIS : 1 an ...... 40 fr. DÉPARTEMENTS : 1 an 44 fr. ÉTRANGER (Union postale) 1 an .. 52 fr.	Librairie du FIGARO, 26, rue Drouot.

Cliché P. Nadar.

THÉATRE DE L'ATHÉNÉE. — Mme JANE HADING

STAGING FASHION, 1880–1920
Jane Hading, Lily Elsie, Billie Burke

MICHELE MAJER, EDITOR

LENARD R. BERLANSTEIN
MARLIS SCHWEITZER
SHEILA STOWELL

with contributions by BGC Graduate Students
MAUDE BASS-KRUEGER
WILLIAM DEGREGORIO
REBECCA PERRY

PUBLISHED BY THE BARD GRADUATE CENTER: DECORATIVE ARTS, DESIGN HISTORY, MATERIAL CULTURE
DISTRIBUTED BY YALE UNIVERSITY PRESS, NEW HAVEN AND LONDON

This catalogue is published in conjunction with the exhibition *Staging Fashion, 1880-1920: Jane Hading, Lily Elsie, Billie Burke*, held at the Bard Graduate Center: Decorative Arts, Design History, Material Culture from January 18 through April 8, 2012.

Curator of the Exhibition and Editor: Michele Majer
Project Coordinator: Ann Marguerite Tartsinis
Coordinator of Catalogue Photography: Alexis Mucha
Copy Editor: Barbara Burn
Catalogue Design and Production: Laura Grey with Ben Tuttle
Media Team: Kimon Keramidas and Han Vu
Exhibition Designer: Ian Sullivan

Acting Head of Focus Gallery and Executive Editor of Gallery Publications: Nina Stritzler-Levine

Published by the Bard Graduate Center: Decorative Arts, Design History, Material Culture, New York, New York

Cover: Foulsham & Banfield (English, 1906-20). Postcard of Lily Elsie as Angèle Didier in *The Count of Luxembourg*, ca. 1911. Photograph. Private collection.
Back cover, left: Reutlinger Studio (French, 1850-1937). Postcard of Jane Hading in *La Pompadour*, ca. 1901. Hand-colored photograph. Private collection.
Back cover, center: Foulsham & Banfield. Postcard of Lily Elsie in *The Merry Widow*, ca. 1907. Photograph. Private collection.
Back cover, right: Dover Street Studio (English, active ca. 1906-12) Postcard of Billie Burke, ca. 1907. Hand-colored photograph. Private collection.
Frontispiece: Paul Nadar (French, 1856-1939). Jane Hading in *Les Demi-Vierges.* Cover of *Le Théatre* (November 1900). Private collection.

Exclusive trade distribution by Yale University Press, New Haven and London
ISBN (Yale University Press): 978 0300 18113 5

Library of Congress Cataloging-in-Publication Data
Staging fashion, 1880–1920 : Jane Hading, Lily Elsie, Billie Burke / Michele Majer, [curator of the exhibition and] editor; Lenard Berlanstein, Marlis Schweitzer, Sheila Stowell ; with contributions by BGC graduate students.
    p. cm.
Catalog published in conjunction with the exhibition, Staging Fashion, 1880-1920: Jane Hading, Lily Elsie, Billie Burke, held at the Bard Graduate Center: Decorative Arts, Design History, Material Culture, from January 17, 2012, through April 8, 2012.
 Includes bibliographical references and index.
 ISBN 978-0-300-18113-5 (alk. paper)
1. Costume—History—19th century—Exhibitions. 2. Costume—History—20th century—Exhibitions. 3. Hading, Jane, d. 1941—Exhibitions. 4. Lily Elsie, Miss, 1886-1962—Exhibitions. 5. Burke, Billie, 1885-1970—Exhibitions. 6. Theater—France—History—Exhibitions. 7. Theater—Great Britain—History—Exhibitions. 8. Theater—United States—History—Exhibitions. 9. Fashion—History—19th century—Exhibitions. 10. Fashion—History—20th century—Exhibitions. I. Majer, Michele. II. Berlanstein, Lenard R. III. Schweitzer, Marlis. IV. Stowell, Sheila, 1954- V. Bard Graduate Center for Studies in the Decorative Arts, Design, and Culture.
PN2067.S83 2012
 792.094109'034—dc23
    2011042506

Printed by GHP, West Haven, Connecticut

Contents

Foreword

This timely volume examines the cult of the celebrity through the intriguing lives of three stage actresses: Jane Hading, Lily Elsie, and Billie Burke. Their careers in Europe and America, which spanned the years 1880 to 1920, paralleled, indeed epitomized, the increasing acceptance of the stage actress as a figure to be admired—not the woman of questionable character disdained and distrusted by previous generations but a personable, attractive individual whose elegant wardrobe and lifestyle reflected the highest aspirations of the general public. The way in which these three women overcame the disreputable role played by the stage actress to become admirable international celebrities has a fascinating, if somewhat troubling, aspect, especially when one reflects on the sensationalist celebrity images that overwhelm our lives today. Once stardom on the stage brought these actresses into public view, they became fodder for an emerging mass media that literally dismantled the social boundaries between public and private life. Through an unprecedented proliferation of photographic images that appeared on widely distributed postcards and in newspapers and magazine articles, these actresses were shown wearing the latest fashions and endorsing the newest consumer products. Composed with great precision, exceptionally beautiful photographs of these actresses enabled a yearning public to satisfy an insatiable appetite for images of celebrities. This publication and the exhibition it accompanies consider the effects produced by the photographic images, fashion designers, and ephemera that helped to construct the public personas of these alluring actresses.

Curated by Michele Majer, BGC assistant professor and research associate at Cora Ginsburg LLC, who served as the overall content editor of this publication, *Staging Fashion* was developed in a seminar on fashion and theater that Michele offered and in a tutorial dedicated to the exhibition. I am grateful to her for organizing such an intriguing project and for bringing together cultural historian Lenard Berlanstein, and theater scholars Marlis Schweitzer and Sheila Stowell,

LEFT: Richard Brown (British, active ca. 1890). Postcard of Billie Burke, ca. 1907. Photograph. Private collection.
CENTER: Postcard of Jane Hading in *La Châtelaine*, ca. 1902. Hand-colored photograph. Private collection.
RIGHT: Foulsham & Banfield (English, 1906–1920). Postcard of Lily Elsie, ca. 1907. Photograph. Private collection.

who contributed essays that elucidate the geographic scope and social complexity of celebrity culture at the turn of the twentieth century in France, Great Britain, and the United States. With great dedication, Michele collaborated with three BGC graduate students—Maude Bass-Krueger, William DeGregorio, and Rebecca Perry—who prepared the fascinating in-depth case studies of Jane Hading, Lily Elsie, and Billie Burke. I am also grateful to everyone who participated in this outstanding research effort and to all the authors for their important contributions.

The generosity of both institutional and private lenders was of utmost importance to the realization of this exhibition. The Museum of the City of New York, the New York Public Library's Performing Arts Library, the Philadelphia Museum of Art, the Metropolitan Museum of Art, Jan Glier Reeder, Marlis Schweitzer, and an anonymous individual provided the loans. Phyllis Magidson of the Museum of the City of New York, Karen Nickeson of the Performing Arts Library, Dilys Blum of the Philadelphia Museum of Art, and Harold Koda of the Metropolitan Museum of Art provided assistance with this important process.

The production of this catalogue involved a wonderful group of talented people: Laura Grey, the BGC art director, created the beautiful design; Bruce White photographed many of the period postcards, magazines, and other materials; Barbara Burn provided critical copyediting skills; and Charmain Devereaux served diligently as proofreader. Ann

Marguerite Tartsinis, assistant curator at the BGC, was an essential contributor to coordination of the publication. I appreciate the work that Alexis Mucha, BGC coordinator of catalogue photography, did on the complex task of researching and acquiring illustrations. The following individuals offered assistance with obtaining photography from our institutional lenders: Tom Lisanti and Stephan Saks of the New York Public Library, Robbi Siegel and Jean-Luc Howell of the Museum of the City of New York, and Giema Tsakuginow of the Philadelphia Museum of Art.

We are fortunate to have a remarkable team of creative and knowledgeable staff members who worked closely with Professor Majer and Nina Stritzler-Levine, chief curator at the BGC, on the exhibition. Ian Sullivan, exhibition designer, orchestrated the installation, integrating the diverse components of the checklist in a beautiful and engaging design. Han Vu, digital technology designer, and Kimon Keramidas, assistant director of the digital media lab at the BGC, provided invaluable knowledge of and assistance with the various technological components of the exhibition, including the film and touch screen used for the scrapbook. Ms. Tartsinis assisted with the exhibition interpretation. The complex task of organizing the loans was undertaken with great professionalism by Olga Valle Tetkowski, our administrator of curatorial projects, and Eric Edler, BGC registrar.

Lastly, I would like to thank Dean Peter Miller and Dean Elena Pinto Simon for their ongoing support of and contributions to the Focus Gallery projects.

Susan Weber
Founder and Director

Editor's Note and Acknowledgments

The topic of the stage actress and fashion in France, Britain, and the United States at the turn of the twentieth century is clearly vast and, of necessity, we present only a partial picture of its complexity and a selective use of methodologies in our approach and interpretation. My own expertise as a clothing historian is in the area of fashionable "street" dress, and both theater history and fashion on stage were entirely new subject matters for myself and the students. For our purposes, we relied on the enormously helpful scholarship of Lenard Berlanstein, Sheila Stowell, and Marlis Schweitzer, whose various publications were crucial in providing us with an intellectual foundation for our endeavor and who have contributed essays to this catalogue. Their chapters offer important evidence and insights into the broader history of the theater, the actress, and society, as well as the more specific story of the actress, fashion, celebrity culture, and consumption in these three countries during this particular period. In the catalogue section proper, each of the students worked on all three of the actresses, and while I guided them both in discussions and in the editing process, I also encouraged and have allowed them to use their individual "voices" in their essays.

Although *Staging Fashion* occupies a single gallery at the Bard Graduate Center, the multiple aspects of its realization would not have been possible without the support, contributions, and dedicated efforts of many colleagues, whom I would like to thank here. I am deeply grateful to the Bard Graduate Center's founder and director, Susan Weber, whose enthusiasm for the exhibition and especially the catalogue was instrumental to their success. I also thank Dean Peter Miller, who encouraged the project from the outset.

I am greatly indebted to the entire staff of the Exhibitions Department for their guidance, expertise, and professionalism offered with patience and good humor throughout: Nina Stritzler-Levine, chief curator and executive editor of gallery publications; Olga Valle Tetkowski, administrator of curatorial projects; Ann Marguerite Tartsinis, assistant curator; Ian Sullivan, exhibition designer and chief preparator; Alexis Mucha, coordinator of catalogue photography; Han Vu, digital technology designer; and Eric Edler, registrar and associate preparator. I also extend my sincere thanks to Laura Grey, art director, for her creative sensitivity in designing the catalogue; Kimon Keramidas, assistant director for digital media, for his much-needed help in developing media components for the exhibition; Doug Clouse, who assisted us in identifying printing techniques for the ephemera; and Barbara Burn, our scrupulous copy editor. Additional thanks are due to Elena Pinto Simon, dean for academic administration; Susan Wall, director of development; and Rebecca Allan, head of education. Additionally, I owe a debt of gratitude to my friends and colleagues Amy Ogata and Marilyn Cohen for their insightful comments on my introduction.

Staging Fashion is visually enriched by its loan pieces. The theme of fashion and the roles played by the individual actresses come to three-dimensional life through the inclusion of costumes and accessories, and I truly appreciate the generosity of Phyllis Magidson, curator of costume and textiles at the Museum of the City of New York; Dilys Blum, curator of costume and textiles at the Philadelphia Museum of Art; and Jan Glier Reeder for lending these important and beautiful objects. Marlis Schweitzer kindly lent a selection of her Merry Widow ephemera, which supplements our own material. The extensive collections of the Performing Arts Library were invaluable to our research, and I am very obliged to Karen Nickeson, curator in the Billy Rose Theatre Division, for arranging loans from their superb theatrical holdings.

The most personally rewarding part of this journey has been the collaboration between the BGC students and myself. I thank all those who prepared the groundwork for the exhibition during the Fall 2010 seminar: Maude Bass-Krueger, Sarah Brown-McLeod, William DeGregorio, Mellissa Huber, Katrina London, Gena Maldonado, Emily McGoldrick, Ruth Osborne, Rebecca Perry, Sara Spink, Kimberly Vagner, and Hampton Wayt. In particular, it has been a true pleasure and a privilege to work with my "A-team": Maude Bass-Krueger, William DeGregorio, and Rebecca Perry. These three students signed on for the long haul and continued to devote many hours to Staging Fashion during the Spring 2011 Tutorial and well beyond. I have relied on their passion for and indefatigable commitment to the project and welcomed their input regarding many aspects of the exhibition and its publication. Their exhaustive research on Jane Hading, Lily Elsie, and Billie Burke is evident in their excellent thematic essays. As exhibitions assistant this past summer, William undertook several painstaking and time-consuming tasks, for which he deserves special thanks.

Last but far from least, I thank my husband, Leslie, and I trust that he will think the end result of the many weekends and late nights his "e-babe" spent in her office was well worth it. It is a joy to share these women who have long fascinated me with a wider audience.

Michele Majer
September 2011

Selected Chronology: Theater, Fashion, and Culture
France, Great Britain, and the United States

1859   Jane Hading born as Jeanne Alfredine Trefouret in Marseilles (March 25 or November 25/26).

1861   Death of Prince Albert initiates a forty-year period of mourning for his wife, Queen Victoria of England (December 14).

1863   Lucile born as Lucy Christiana Sutherland in London (June 13).

1867   The first issue of *Harper's Bazar* (later *Harper's Bazaar*), edited by Mary Louise Booth, is published in New York (November 2).

1868   Formation of La Chambre Syndicale de la Confection et de la Couture pour Dames et Fillettes, a trade union created to govern the dressmakers of Paris, spearheaded by the couturier Charles Frederick Worth (1826-1895).

1870   France declares war on the Kingdom of Prussia, inaugurating the Franco-Prussian War (July 19).

1871   The Paris Commune and the Siege of Paris by Prussian forces end with the signing of the Treaty of Frankfurt (May 10), and the Third French Republic begins.

The Great Chicago Fire kills hundreds in Illinois (October 8-10).

1873   The Boyer photography studio in Paris publishes one of the first pictorial postcards in France, which features an image of the department store La Belle Jardinière.

1875   Charles Garnier's Opéra de Paris opens (January 15).

Arthur Lasenby Liberty founds his eponymous department store on Regent Street in London.

1880   *L'Art et la Mode* prints the first fashion photograph in a periodical.

Charles Reutlinger (1816-1880) hands over control of his photography studio to his brother, Émile Reutlinger (1825-1907).

1881   The Savoy Theatre in Westminster, London, opens, the first public building in the world to be lit by incandescent electric light bulbs, which were manufactured by the English inventor Joseph Swan (October 10).

John Redfern (1819/1820-1895) opens his first *maison de couture* in Paris.

The Rational Dress Society, which promoted the establishment of an alternative "aesthetic" mode of dressing over tightly corseted French high fashion, is founded in London.

American inventor Frederic E. Ives devises the first commercially viable form of halftone printing in Philadelphia; the method will be further refined, so that by the early 1890s halftones are used in most printed media.

Grand Opera House, Paris. ca. 1903-16. Card for Hignett's Cigarettes. George Arents Collection, The New York Public Library, Astor, Lenox and Tilden Foundations.

1883 Publication of Émile Zola's novel *Au Bonheur des dames*, about the modern department store; the book was translated into English the same year.

The Ladies Home Journal and Practical House-keeper is launched under the editorship of Louisa Knapp in Philadelphia (February 16).

New York society gathers to celebrate Mrs. W. K. Vanderbilt's Fancy Dress Ball at 660 Fifth Avenue in New York City; Mrs. Vanderbilt's sister, Alice Claypool Gwynn, comes dressed as "Electric Light" in a gown designed by Worth (March 23).

The Brooklyn Bridge is opened (May 24).

"A union of hearts and a union of hands [Finis coronat opus]." from *The Daily Graphic*; an illustrated evening newspaper. (May 24, 1883). The Milstein Division of United States History, Local History, and Genealogy, The New York Public Library, Astor, Lenox and Tilden Foundations.

Jane Hading creates her most memorable role, Claire de Beaulieu, in *Le Maître de Forges* at the Théâtre du Gymnase in Paris (December 15).

1884 Jane Hading marries Victor Koning.

Lucy Christiana Sutherland (Lucile) marries James Charles Stuart Wallace.

Laws prohibiting divorce in France are rescinded.

Billie Burke born as Mary William Ethelbert Appleton Burke in Washington, D.C. (August 7).

Liberty of London introduces its costume department, headed by architect and aesthetic theorist E. W. Godwin.

New York photographer Napoleon Sarony (1821-1896) sues the Burrow-Giles Lithographic Company for copyright infringement after it publishes unauthorized lithographs of Oscar Wilde; the Supreme Court rules in Sarony's favor, extending copyright protection to photographic images and awarding him $610.

1886 Lily Elsie born as Elsie Cotton in Wortley, Leeds, England (April 8).

Dedication of the Statue of Liberty on Bedloe's Island in New York (October 28).

1888 Jane Hading divorces Victor Koning.

Printemps in Paris becomes the first department store to install electric lighting.

1889 Sarah Bernhardt and Jane Hading star in *La Dame aux Camélias*, the former in Paris and the latter on tour in America; both wear gowns designed by Maison Laferrière.

Opening of the Exposition Universelle in Paris with the inauguration of the Eiffel Tower (March 31).

1890 American comic opera star Marion Manola obtains an injunction from the New York Supreme Court barring her management from using photographs of the actress for any purpose without her prior consent.

Émile Reutlinger passes control of the family photography studio to his son, Léopold Reutlinger (1863-1937).

Alfred Roll (1846-1919) exhibits his portrait of Jane Hading at the Paris Salon (March-May 15).

Lucy Christiana Wallace (Lucile) divorces James Wallace.

1891   Jeanne Paquin (1869-1936) founds her *maison de couture* on the rue de la Paix (near the Maison Worth) in Paris.

1892   *Vogue* begins publication in the United States.

1893   Joseph Byron, a British-born New York photographer, develops a successful system to photograph players onstage for the first time.

Mrs. James Wallace (née Lucy Christiana Sutherland) opens her first dressmaking business, located at 24 Davies Street in Berkeley Square, and adopts the trade name Lucile.

1895   Charles Frederick Worth dies in Paris (March 10).

Oscar Wilde is convicted of gross indecency and sentenced to two years of hard labor in London (May 25).

John Redfern dies on the Isle of Wight (November 22).

Alexandre Dumas fils dies in Marly-le-Roi, France (November 27).

Lucile designs costumes for her first play, a charity production of *Diplomacy* starring her sister, the writer Elinor Glyn. She is listed in trade directories as "Mrs. Lucy Wallace, court dressmaker, 24 Old Burlington Street."

1896   Paul Poiret (1879-1944) begins to design for Maison Doucet.

Napoleon Sarony dies in New York (November 9); his son Otto continues to run the Sarony Studio.

1898   Émile Zola publishes "J'accuse," an open letter to the government condemning its anti-Semitism in the wake of the Dreyfus Affair, in *L'Aurore* in Paris (January 13).

The actress Réjane popularizes Paul Poiret's designs for Maison Doucet by wearing his cloak of black tulle and taffeta hand-painted with mauve irises in the play *Zaza* at the Théâtre du Vaudeville in Paris.

Goupil et Cie begins publishing *Le Théâtre* in Paris (January 1).

Lucile moves her business to 17 Hanover Square; she is listed in directories as "dressmaker and court dressmaker."

1899   Macmillan publishes Thorstein Veblen's book *A Theory of the Leisure Class* in New York.

1900   *La revue illustrée de la carte postale* begins publication in France (February 15).

Twenty *maisons de haute couture* present their creations at the Exposition Universelle in Paris, including Jeanne Paquin, president of the fashion section of the exhibition and designer of the ensemble worn by *La Parisienne*, a 15-foot-tall statue on top of the Porte Binet entrance arch (April 15-November 12).

"La Porte Monumentale" from *Le Panorama, exposition universelle, 1900*. Paris: Librairie d'Art Ludovic Baschet, [1900?]. Library, Bard Graduate Center: Decorative Arts, Design History, Material Culture; New York.

The Picture Postcard Magazine begins publication in London (July).

Lucile marries Sir Cosmo Duff Gordon at the British Consulate in Venice (May).

1901   Goupil et Cie begins publishing *Les Modes* in Nancy, France (January 1).

Queen Victoria dies on the Isle of Wight (January 22) and is succeeded by Edward VII.

Femina begins publication as a bimonthly fashion magazine in Paris (February 1).

President William McKinley is shot by anarchist Leon Frank Czolgosz at the Pan-American Exposition in Buffalo, New York (September 6); he dies eight days later and is succeeded by Vice President Theodore Roosevelt (September 14).

1902 Greening & Co. begins publishing *The Play Pictorial* in London (April).

The United Kingdom's postal service permits the publication of postcards with a "divided back," allowing senders to legally include a personal message on the reverse of picture postcards for the first time.

Macy's flagship store on Herald Square in New York City opens; by 1924 it will be the world's largest department store.

1903 The French postal service allows the publication of "divided back" postcards.

Selfridges department store opens its flagship store on Oxford Street in London (March 15).

Approximately 450 million picture postcards (and 613 million postcards in total) are sent in Great Britain, according to the Postal Union.

1904 Lucile London Ltd. is incorporated and listed in the trades directory as "Dressmakers, Lucile Limited, 23 Hanover Square." The house stages a private viewing of a mannequin parade.

1907 Lily Elsie debuts as Sonia in *The Merry Widow* at Daly's Theatre in London (June 8).

The United States Post Office allows the publication of "divided back" postcards.

Pablo Picasso completes *Les Demoiselles d'Avignon* in Paris; couturier and collector Jacques Doucet (1853-1929) will purchase the painting in 1924.

Billie Burke signs contract with Broadway producer Charles Frohman.

The C. M. Clark Publishing Company in Boston publishes Judge J. Albert Brackett's legal treatise *Theatrical Law*, establishing a distinct difference between private and public individuals; the latter group surrendered the right to control images of themselves in the press because they sought public recognition.

1908 "The Battle of the Hats," a riot at the New Amsterdam Theatre in New York City, erupts as 1,300 women vie for 1,200 Merry Widow hats distributed free to celebrate the 275th performance of the play (June 13).

The United States Post Office reports 677,777,798 postcards delivered in the country for the year 1907 in its annual report dated July 30 (at the time, the total US population is 88,700,000).

1909 Condé Nast purchases *Vogue* and shifts its primary focus from society to fashion coverage.

1910 Paul Poiret introduces the hobble skirt.

Gabrielle Chanel (1883-1971) opens her first millinery shop on the rue Cambon in Paris.

Lucile opens a branch of her dressmaking house on West Thirty-sixth Street in New York; the house will move to West Fifty-seventh Street in 1912.

Fashion design from "Lucile" Sample Album Book, 1904. Watercolor on paper. Victoria and Albert Museum, London, T.89-1986.

French photographer Gaspard-Félix Tournachon (b. 1820), known as Félix Nadar, dies (March 23).

La Chambre Syndicale de la Confection et de la Couture pour Dames et Fillettes is dissolved, and La Chambre Syndicale de la Couture Parisienne is formed the following year, officially separating the couturiers from makers of ready-to-wear garments.

King Edward VII dies in London and is succeeded by George V (May 6).

The New York State Forest, Fish and Game Law prohibits the collection or sale of plumage from certain species of birds for use in hats (July 13).

1911 Paul Poiret introduces the *jupe culotte*, or harem pant.

Lucile opens a branch of her dressmaking house in Paris at 11, rue de Penthièvre.

Lily Elsie marries Ian Bullough (November 7).

1912 At age 68, Sarah Bernhardt stars in *Les Amours d'Elisabeth, Reine d'Angleterre*, a major silent film success.

Billie Burke debuts in The *"Mind The Paint" Girl* at the Lyceum Theatre in New York (September 9).

1913 Florenz Ziegfeld divorces actress Anna Held (January 9).

Publication in Paris of Marcel Proust's *Du côté de chez Swann*, the first volume of his epic novel *À la recherche du temps perdu*.

1914 Archduke Franz Ferdinand of Austria is assassinated in Sarajevo, igniting World War I (June 28).

Billie Burke marries Florenz Ziegfeld in Hoboken, New Jersey (April 11).

Opening of the Gimbel Bros. flagship store on Herald Square in New York City.

1915 *The Birth of a Nation*, a film starring Lillian Gish and directed by D. W. Griffith, premieres at Clune's Auditorium in Los Angeles, California (February 8).

The *RMS Titanic* strikes an iceberg and sinks; Lucile and her husband, Cosmo, Sir Duff Gordon, survive (April 14-15).

Program cover featuring an illustration of Billie Burke for *Simple Simon* at the Ziegfeld Theatre, New York, March 31, 1930. Billy Rose Theatre Division, The New York Public Library for the Performing Arts, Astor, Lenox and Tilden Foundations.

Billie Burke dissolves her contract with Charles Frohman.

Charles Frohman dies in the sinking of the *RMS Lusitania* (May 7).

Lucile opens a branch of her dressmaking house in Chicago.

Billie Burke signs a five-week contract worth $40,000 with the New York Motion Picture Corporation; she is also paid a $50,000 advance on a three-year contract worth $150,000 (July 16).

1916 *Gloria's Romance*, a series of twenty movie serials starring Billie Burke, begins its run at the Globe Theatre in New York (May 22).

Patricia Burke Ziegfeld (later Mrs. William R. Stephenson) is born to Billie Burke and Florenz Ziegfeld in New York City (October 23).

1917 Sarah Bernhardt addresses a crowd of 50,000 in Prospect Park, Brooklyn, on behalf of Franco-American cooperation in the war effort during her farewell theatrical tour of America (July 4).

1918 Tsar Nicholas II and his family are executed by Bolsheviks during the Russian Revolution, begun the year before (July 16/17).

Germany signs an armistice agreement with the Allies, ending World War I (November 11).

1919 The Eighteenth Amendment to the U.S. Constitution prohibits the consumption of "intoxicating liquors"; the amendment will be repealed in 1933.

1921 *La revue illustrée de la carte postale* ceases publication.

The Chicago branch of Lucile Ltd. closes.

1923 Sarah Bernhardt dies in Paris (March 26).

1927 Lily Elsie makes her stage comeback in a production of *The Blue Train* at the Prince of Wales Theatre in London (May 10).

1930 Lily Elsie divorces Ian Bullough.

1932 Florenz Ziegfeld dies in Hollywood, California (July 22).

The New York branch of Lucile Ltd. closes (October); Lucile herself had been dismissed from the bankrupt company in 1922.

1935 Lucile dies in London (April 20).

1937 *The Great Ziegfeld*, the life story of Florenz Ziegfeld with Myrna Loy as Billie Burke, wins Best Picture at the ninth annual Academy Awards in Los Angeles (March 4).

Léopold Reutlinger dies (March 16), and the family's photography studio in Paris is closed.

1938 Billie Burke receives her first and only Academy Award nomination as Best Supporting Actress for *Merrily We Live* and is chosen to play the role of Glinda, the "Good Witch of the North," in the musical film *The Wizard of Oz*.

1941 Jane Hading dies in Neuilly-sur-Seine, France (February 18).

1962 Lily Elsie dies in London (December 16).

1970 Billie Burke dies in Los Angeles (May 14).

Staging Fashion, 1880–1920
Michele Majer

Through printed ephemera, clothing, and accessories, *Staging Fashion, 1880-1920: Jane Hading, Lily Elsie, Billie Burke* explores the phenomenon of actresses as internationally known fashion leaders at the turn of the twentieth century and highlights the mundane artifacts that constituted the primary means by which the general public—especially women—experienced the visibility and influence of these three particular performers in their everyday lives. Formerly ostracized as women of dubious morals, actresses were presented—and presented themselves—as respectable role models for women across the social spectrum. Postcards that circulated by the millions, thousands of magazine and newspaper articles, and print advertisements celebrated them as exemplars of fashion, youthful beauty, elegance, and modern femininity (fig. 1). These mass-produced forms of communication, instrumental in the creation of a public image and persona, both contributed to and reflected the rise of celebrity culture. During this period, the "staging" of fashion occurred not only within the physical space of the theater itself, but it extended well beyond, thanks to these new forms of mass media, in ways that had not been possible a few decades earlier, presaging our present-day fascination with celebrities.

Staging Fashion originated from two separate yet parallel avenues. A few years ago, I began to think about teaching a class on the relationship between fashion and theater. In reading French fashion periodicals from the late eighteenth through the early twentieth century, I was repeatedly struck by the significant role that the theater assumed in these publications and, by extension, in French social and cultural life. Along with regular references to the latest plays and to the stylish toilettes worn by women in the audience, there were detailed descriptions and illustrations of costumes worn by actresses that inspired new fashion trends. Indeed, throughout this period, both garments and accessories—particularly hats—were frequently named for women of the stage, titles of plays in which they appeared, or one

FIG. I Postcard of "Stage Favourites" including Billie Burke and Lily Elsie, ca. 1906. Composite photograph. Private collection. Cat. 83.

of their characters. In spite of their marginalized societal status, actresses were readily acknowledged as objects of sartorial emulation.

More recently, I discovered that one could buy postcards of turn-of-the-century stage actresses on eBay, and so my collection began. I had no fixed criteria; I bought postcards based on my own purely personal response to the images: in bust-length portraits, it was often the features, hairstyle, headdress, or expression of the subject that attracted me; in full-length portraits, it was the ensemble and pose. In addition to searching for a specific performer with whom I was already familiar, I browsed more general categories such as "artistes" and "Edwardian actresses."[1] In the case of the former, I quickly learned the name of one of the leading, Paris-based photography studios of the period, Reutlinger, which specialized in portraits of many different types of stage women (actresses, opera singers, and dancers) and whose work is well represented in the exhibition (fig. 11).[2]

These cheaply manufactured objects were produced during what has been described as the "Golden Age" of the picture postcard, and their size and intended use as a quick, practical means of communicating a short message meant that they would be closely handled.[3] The hundreds of thousands of actress postcards—both used and unused—

FIG. II Reutlinger Studio vitrine advertising photographs of actresses, ca. 1902. Photograph. Collection of William DeGregorio.

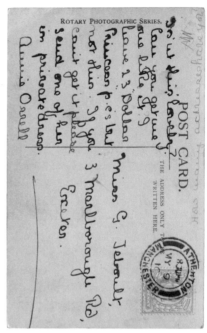

FIG. III Foulsham & Banfield (English, 1906–20). Postcard of Lily Elsie in *The Dollar Princess*, ca. 1909. Photograph. Private collection. Cat. 107.

FIG. IV Verso of the postcard in fig. III.

that have survived for a century are an indication of the intense world-wide interest in these women, the insatiable demand for and production of their images in Europe and the United States, the practice of collecting these ephemera and sharing them with friends and family members, and the degree to which they were cherished (figs. III and IV).[4] The women in these photographs cast a powerful spell; one is drawn into the glamorized world they inhabited and seduced by their beauty and elegant sophistication. Although in the twenty-first century we may experience these images in a very different context, they still impart a compelling aura and create an intimate connection between viewer and subject.

The seminar that served as the foundation for *Staging Fashion* covered France, Britain, and the United States from 1780 to 1920 and drew on the work of scholars of theater, history, gender, and consumption—including those who have contributed essays to this catalogue. The decision to concentrate on the turn of the twentieth century for the exhibition was based on my own intellectual interests in this later period, as well as on practical reasons pertaining to access to materials. In addition to a rapidly expanding celebrity culture, the end of the nineteenth and beginning of the twentieth centuries also witnessed a flourishing mass media and mass consumerism. The actress's role as a highly influential fashion arbiter and key figure in these manifestations of modernity is well established and provides a rich area of study. The availability of turn-of-the-century postcards, cabinet cards, and other publications relating to actresses not only situates them firmly within this larger context but also allows for a fully representative display. Although there is a paucity of extant theatrical costumes from the late eighteenth century and most of the nineteenth, those dating to about 1900 survive in comparatively large numbers. Even so, given the often fragile condition of these pieces because of their use on the stage, we are extremely fortunate to be able to exhibit two Lucile gowns—one worn onstage by Billie Burke and the other very similar to Lily Elsie's wedding dress by the same designer—as well as a spectacular evening dress by Redfern, a couture house patronized by Jane Hading (all three are from the collection of the Museum of the City of New York).

The choice of our three actresses was somewhat—though by no means entirely—arbitrary and depended in part on the availability of material. They serve as case studies for the project described earlier, although we could have easily selected three other performers from among many equally well-known French, British, and American actresses to illustrate the exhibition's ideas and themes.[5] Jane Hading (1859-1941), a relatively unknown actress today, was a major figure on the French stage in the late nineteenth and early twentieth centuries (fig. v). As a result of several tours that she undertook during her career, she was also popular in Britain and the United States. In 1910 an American newspaper declared the British actress Lily Elsie (1886-1962) "the most photographed woman in the world" (fig. vi).[6] She appeared in a number of critically and commercially successful operettas and musical comedies at fashionable theaters in the West End of London, particularly those managed by the savvy impresario George Edwardes (see fig. A.8).[7] Although her acting career was briefer than those of Jane Hading and Billie Burke and she never performed outside Britain, her popularity was enormous and extensive. In 1907 her breakthrough role as Sonia in *The Merry Widow*, costumed by the couturiere Lucile, made her an immediate sensation and launched the subsequent craze in Europe and the United States for the oversized "Merry Widow hat."[8] Lastly, Billie Burke (1884-1970) enjoyed a promising stage career in London before she came to New York in 1907 at the behest of the

MADAME JANE HADING

THE "VANDERWEYDE" LIGHT

182 REGENT ST. W.

FIG. V Henry Van Der Weyde (English, 1878–1902). Cabinet card of Jane Hading in *Sapho*, ca. 1886.
Billy Rose Theatre Division, The New York Public Library for the Performing Arts, Astor, Lenox and Tilden
Foundations. Cat. 13.

11501 A ROTARY PHOTO. E.C.　　MISS LILY ELSIE.　　FOULSHAM & BANFIELD

FIG. VI Foulsham & Banfield. Postcard of Lily Elsie, ca. 1907. Photograph. Private collection. Cat. 93.

FIG. VII Bassano Studio (English, 1850–1963). Postcard of Billie Burke and Farren Soutar in *The Belle of Mayfair*, ca. 1906. Photograph. Private collection. Cat. 148.

powerful manager-producer Charles Frohman (fig. VII). She quickly became a Broadway favorite and, as Marlis Schweitzer observes in her catalogue essay "Stylish Effervescence: Billie Burke and the Rise of the Fashionable Broadway Star," was well known for her expensive costumes and was frequently featured in high-end fashion magazines.

As with many other stage women at the time, the fame and appeal of these actresses were by no means based solely—or, in the case of Lily Elsie and Billie Burke, even primarily—on their thespian talents. Rather, the three exemplify the principal factors that contributed to widespread success and acclaim: a leading couturier (or couturiers) who regularly designed for the theater dressed each actress in gowns that were integral to the creation of a glamorous image; each of the women exhibits a type of physical beauty that conformed to elite notions of class and race; each had a distinct "personality" that was often conveyed by her stage roles and further underscored in photographic images as well as in the media; each appeared on postcards and in fashion and theater magazines, newspapers, and other periodicals. Finally, each of these women illustrates the phenomenon of actress-as-marketable-commodity, who promoted and depended on the consumption of her own image to create and maintain her celebrity status and whose celebrity, in turn, was used to market an array of goods.

Our four main organizing themes—the actress and fashion, the actress in the photographer's studio, the actress and the press, the actress and advertising—emerged from our study of the material. Although these themes are clearly interconnected and overlapping, each one constitutes a specific area that we have grouped and discussed separately in sections devoted to the three individual actresses featured in the exhibition and catalogue. We start with fashion, since the trendsetting actress exerted her influence long before the period bracketed by this exhibition. The advent of photography in the middle of the nineteenth century, however, firmly secured this role through the extensive diffusion of "real" likenesses of the actress in her expensive finery to an ever-widening audience. In the 1890s, when it became commercially viable to print photographs in newspapers and magazines, the press further propelled the actress into the realm of celebrity. And, at the same time, an increasingly sophisticated and aggressive advertising industry took advantage of her face and name recognition to sell a myriad of goods to an expanding consumer culture. Before providing a short context for the four themes, I will briefly summarize the profound shift in the public perception of actresses that granted them the status of respectability and allowed them to be so widely admired and imitated as fashion icons.

For centuries, actresses suffered much more than their male counterparts from social and religious stigmas that regarded the theater as an immoral profession and a degenerate lifestyle. Traditional middle-class expectations that obliged women to marry, have children, and lead a virtuous life out of the public eye, meant that actresses who regularly put themselves on display for the entertainment of others— and were paid to do so—flagrantly transgressed accepted codes of bourgeois behavior. The prevalent assumption that actresses were little more than—or the same as—prostitutes persisted until the late nineteenth century.[9]

Scholars have identified the turn of the twentieth century as marking an important moment in eradicating this age-old prejudice against actresses. A unique set of social, economic, political, and cultural conditions certainly existed in each of the three countries that Jane Hading, Lily Elsie, and Billie Burke represent, one that impacted changing attitudes toward women of the theater.[10] Yet significant transnational developments, including rapid urbanization and the growth of mass entertainment, mass media, and mass consumption, along with improvements in travel and communication, simultaneously contributed to effect a major turning point in the way that the public in Europe and the United States viewed and experienced the theater in general and the actress in particular.[11]

Further, the institution of the theater itself underwent important changes at this time that helped dispel the characterization of actresses as "notorious" women and instead fostered an increasing acceptance and recognition of them as worthy members of society. France, Britain, and the United States all witnessed a significant expansion of the theater industry in the latter part of the nineteenth century and a concomitant rise in female attendance (see fig. A.1). A marked regendering of theater audiences dramatically transformed these previously male-dominated, erotically charged spaces into sites of female spectacle and consumption.[12] As historian Susan Glenn has argued, the contribution of women as producers and consumers of urban spectacle was of greatest significance in the theater, and "the growing phenomenon of the female star went hand in hand with the rise in female spectatorship."[13] Managers actively targeted women theatergoers and emphasized in their productions high-fashion costumes as an important attraction—a development that was tied to the burgeoning fashion industry and fashion press. In fact, fashion itself became a topic on the stage with the "fashion play" constituting a popular theatrical genre that often functioned as a pretext to parade beautiful young women wearing the most recent styles.[14] As a result of these changes, the actress was constructed as a professional woman who shared the same middle-class values and concerns as ordinary women, but who, by virtue of her beauty and special appeal, was also the era's most visible fashion arbiter.

FASHION

The trendsetting position that actresses had enjoyed since the eighteenth century was reinforced by the establishment in the 1850s and 1860s of a couture industry that intensified and underscored the existing reciprocal relationship between fashion and theater. At the turn of the twentieth century, increasingly popular plays and musical comedies focusing on modern life served as perfect vehicles for showcasing the latest designs.[15] Indeed, the stage was readily acknowledged as the primary site for anticipating and launching new fashions with actresses "serving as living mannequins;"[16] as Florence Alexander, who was responsible for women's costumes at the St. James's Theatre, later recalled: "In those days people went to see the St. James's plays *before* ordering a new gown."[17] Actresses and couturiers both realized the benefits that accrued to each from this association: the former enjoyed the cachet of appearing in front of fashion-conscious audiences wearing au courant modes while the latter garnered publicity for his or her innovative creations.

Given the obvious commercial potential that the stage offered, many prominent European and American couturiers and custom dressmakers designed for the theater during this period. The "father of haute couture," British-born Charles Frederick Worth, whose clients included Empress Eugénie and other royal and aristocratic women, as well as wealthy socialites, created stage costumes throughout his career.[18] In December 1865, the Goncourt brothers noted in their diary that Worth, who had costumed the leading actress for their play *Henriette Maréchal*, was in attendance at the dress rehearsal just days before it opened at the Comédie-Française: "As for the audience, it was a very curious audience, [including] first of all Worth and his wife [former model Marie Vernet], without whose inspection Mme Plessy never goes on, and with them all the well-known milliners and dressmakers."[19] In addition to Worth, the houses of Laferrière, Jacques Doucet, Redfern, Lucile, Jeanne Paquin, and Paul Poiret, among many others, frequently dressed women of the stage.[20]

For the actress, a selection of eye-catching custom-made gowns was imperative in securing principal roles and in achieving and maintaining a fashionable position in the public eye. In 1881 Pierre Véron, a columnist for *Le Monde illustré*, pointedly noted that "today, a Rachel who does not have a wardrobe designed by Worth runs the risk of remaining disdained and ignored among the cheap chorus girls."[21] An actress's identity and public persona were inextricably tied to her fashionableness, which required that she constantly display herself in up-to-the-minute designs. Within the physical setting of the theater itself, she needed to take full advantage of her stage appearances as a crucial point of contact between herself and her audience. Whether an actress was performing in serious drama (like Jane Hading) or lighthearted musical comedy (like Lily Elsie and Billie Burke), she was expected to be well dressed. Indeed, the American periodical *The Theatre* encouraged a deliberate blurring of social boundaries between actresses and elite women stating that "the actress in make-believe drawing rooms must not only *appear* as richly dressed as the society leader she impersonates, but she must *actually* be as well dressed and wear, not make-believe gowns, but gowns costing the same and turned out by the same dressmakers as those worn by the millionaire dames of Fifth Avenue."[22] As Schweitzer has argued, "simultaneously acting and acted upon, the fashionably dressed actress *becomes* an actress both in and through the clothes she wears."[23]

Until the late nineteenth century, most actresses were obliged to provide their own costumes when playing contemporary roles. Véron cites this longstanding custom (in France) and the equally longstanding assumption that actresses relied on wealthy admirers to cover such expenses—a characterization that reinforced the morally suspect view of these women.[24] In the United States, aspiring young actresses were often in debt to theater managers who paid for custom-made costumes and then deducted the amount in installments from performers' salaries.[25] During this period, however, managers began to pay for or subsidize actresses' costumes. In 1881 Émile Perrin, administrator-general of the Comédie-Française, decided that the company would take charge of costuming its actors. However, in order to prevent excessive expenditures—especially by female performers—he stipulated price limits for their couture purchases.[26] In the United States, Charles Frohman first began to pay for his actresses' gowns in 1894 for a contemporary society play.[27] In her essay in this volume, Schweitzer discusses the generous costume allowance that Billie Burke enjoyed under Frohman, albeit she still managed to overspend.

FIG. VIII Seamstresses at work in one of the ateliers at Maison Redfern, Paris. From *Femina* (April 15, 1901): 127. Private collection. Cat. 6.

As part of their publicity strategy, couturiers often offered *prix de faveur* to theater managers and performers. The actress Béatrix Dussane, who joined the Comédie-Française in 1903, recalled that although historical costumes were commissioned from theatrical costumiers, those for modern plays were ordered from top designers, including Paquin, Doucet, Redfern, Drécoll, and Callot Sœurs. Even if their names did not appear in the programs, the couture houses considered this welcome advertising and discounted their prices to the theaters.[28] The British actress Mary Moore, who performed at Wyndham's Theatre, which she also co-managed with her husband, Sir Charles Wyndham, commissioned costumes from Paris couturiers and was delighted to be offered *prix d'artiste* by Worth for her offstage wardrobe. Moore's appearance in these French ensembles at exclusive social events such as the Royal Ascot Races was another important opportunity to "stage" fashion that reflected both her own sense of chic and the designer's creativity.[29]

Some designers were undoubtedly concerned that their society clients might be unwilling to patronize a couture house that cultivated an active connection with actresses and thus deemed it detrimental to their business. As Sheila Stowell notes in her catalogue essay, "Lucile and the Theatricalization of Fashion," a number of well-known London dressmakers, with the exception of Lucile, gave up their stage work after they received the "Drawing Room commissions that enabled them to call themselves 'Court Dressmakers.'" Redfern, however, who in 1888 received the royal patent "By appointment to Her Majesty the Queen and HRH The Princess of Wales," designed costumes for West End productions in the following decades and, as shown in this exhibition, regularly dressed Jane Hading—both on- and offstage— from about 1900 (fig. VIII).[30] Overall, the evidence in theatrical journals and fashion magazines aimed at an upper-class readership and in the records for surviving garments in museum collections indicates that many society women did not shy away from frequenting couturiers and dressmakers who designed for actresses.[31] For many women, the appeal of observing actresses in performance offered the excitement of seeing new fashions in motion and imagining themselves in the same—or similar—clothes. In fact, as Schweitzer has shown, upper-, middle- and working-class American women staged "copy acts."[32] Whereas those with lesser financial resources might only be able to approximate an actress's particular look, affluent society women could—and did— order faithful copies of stage gowns. In doing so, Schweitzer argues, "female audiences drew upon the cultural meanings associated with admired actresses to fantasize about alternative lives and make personal statements about themselves as modern women."[33]

IN THE PHOTOGRAPHER'S STUDIO

Actresses, photography, and celebrity were a "potent commercial mix" at the turn of the twentieth century.[34] From the introduction of the daguerreotype process in 1839, pioneered by Louis Daguerre and Niecéphore Niépce, to the small-format *carte de visite* patented by A.-A.-E. Disdéri in 1854, the larger cabinet card of the 1870s and 1880s, and the picture postcard, which emerged in greater numbers during the 1890s, the actress was one of the most popular and iconic subjects of the studio photographer.[35] Her renown, influence, and visibility were inextricably linked to her increasingly reproducible and accessible image. Carefully "staged" photographs represented a powerful self-promotional tool by which she asserted her status as fashion arbiter. Actress photographs from this period, such as those in the exhibition, emphasize an image of a beautiful, elegantly dressed and poised young woman who offers herself for admiration and scrutiny. And not only do the *images* of Jane Hading, Lily Elsie, and Billie Burke evince this deliberately contrived similarity in the mode of presentation of these three women, but they also share physical characteristics that reflect a narrow, upper-class definition of beauty: regular features, slender physiques, and white skin.[36]

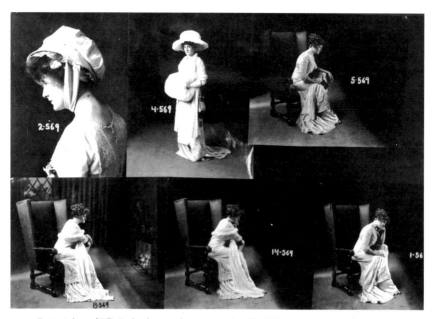

FIG. IX Contact sheet of Billie Burke photographs, ca. 1910 printed by Culver Service, New York. Private collection. The photograph in the upper left corner appeared in *The Green Book* in 1912, accompanying a short story by Billie Burke. Cat. 154.

Leading photography studios in Paris, London, and New York including, respectively, Reutlinger, Foulsham & Banfield, and Sarony (all represented in this exhibition) were eager to produce actress portraits. In some cases, performers paid the studio a fee that was based on the degree of their prominence and on whether their image might attract business, but in other cases—particularly for famous actresses— the studio offered a fee knowing it was a profitable investment in terms of sales to consumers.[37] The collaboration between actresses and their photographers required an extensive time commitment; the actress brought a large selection of her on- and offstage ensembles to the studio and was prepared to spend long hours in front of the camera. The American actress Margaret Illington Banes noted that the photographer "took hundreds of [negatives], all [of which] are discarded except those few which show the sitter at her best" (fig. IX).[38] Although these images took on a life of their own that neither the actress nor the photographer would control once they entered the public sphere, a scrupulous selection process clearly occurred before they left the studio.[39]

Photography historian Roger Hargreaves evokes the "almost innate magnetic impulse" that drew fame and photography together at this time.[40] Historians of both theater and photography have explored the symbiotic relationship between the actress, the photographer, and the public.[41] Like the association between actress and couturier, this also benefited all parties involved from producers to consumers: the actress who was ensured the circulation of her image, thereby maintaining a public presence; the photographer who created, sold, and often prominently displayed her image in his studio windows to attract business; the theater or management company that also exhibited these photographs, promoting interest in both the actress and their establishment; and the actress's far-flung male and female admirers whose constant demand for her newest image spurred ever more production of these highly sought-after commodities.[42]

Of particular importance to the shifting attitude toward actresses during this period were the rapid technological innovations in photography that resulted in the proliferation and "democratisation of the image" and "a new way of visual ordering."[43] The *carte de visite*, which was much cheaper and faster to produce than the daguerreotype, exploded in the second half of the 1850s and dominated the market for the next decade. It was a key factor in a social leveling that blurred class

FIG. X Reutlinger Studio (French, 1850–1937). Postcard of Jane Hading in *L'Alibi*, ca. 1908. Hand-colored photograph. Private collection. Cat. 12.

FIG. XI Foulsham & Banfield. Postcard of Lily Elsie in *The Dollar Princess*, ca. 1909. Photograph. Private collection. Cat. 106.

distinctions, since sitting for one's portrait was no longer the exclusive domain of the wealthy. Also, the common studio practice of displaying in their windows photographs of society's high-born alongside those of actresses and other celebrity figures inverted traditional hierarchies, as did the similar, indiscriminate arrangement of such images in family albums.[44] As a result, the public became increasingly familiarized with the actress as she was assimilated into mainstream society.

Drama historian Laurence Senelick argues that stage performers themselves made a significant aesthetic impact on the photographic portrait, functioning as "shape changers" in this particular genre of the new medium. Accustomed to appearing before an audience, they were considerably more comfortable in front of the camera than non-performers and contributed "a dynamic of spontaneity and topicality to portraiture."[45] The photography studio with its painted backdrops and props was a highly theatrical space that served as an extension of the stage where actors and actresses enacted role-playing and experimented with identity. The cabinet cards and postcards in the exhibition illustrate the actress's use of the studio as a place to amplify her performative role as fashion leader and alluring beauty and to communicate her distinctive "personality." Graceful comportment was an important attribute in achieving true glamour, and actresses' bodies were as much on view as their expensive clothes.[46] Through their various poses and expressions, Jane Hading, Lily Elsie, and Billie Burke created their individual personas and demonstrated an easy and knowing engagement with the camera and, by implication, the consumer-viewer (figs. x, xi, and see fig. 3.14).

THE PRESS

As noted earlier, actresses appeared regularly in fashion journals as the illustrated fashion press emerged during the late eighteenth century.[47] In the nineteenth century, the burgeoning periodical literature—particularly that relating to fashion and the theater—continued to provide substantial information about actresses' stylish costumes. The explosion of the press that occurred in the late nineteenth and early twentieth centuries in Europe and the United States was crucial in circulating the actress's image as fashion celebrity and, at the same time, in normalizing her social status through articles and interviews that featured her private life and insisted on its everyday domesticity. Like the ubiquitous photographs of actresses in *cartes de visite*, cabinet cards, and postcards, the rapidly proliferating magazines and newspa-

MISS LILY ELSIE.

FIG. XII Foulsham & Banfield. Lily Elsie in *The Count of Luxembourg*. From *The Play Pictorial* (July 1911): 49. Private collection.

pers that were aimed at a broad readership affirmed her influence and extended her reach as role model of high fashion and modern femininity to those who may never have seen—or might never expect to see—her on stage. And, like the relationships between actress and couture and actress and photography, that between actress and the press was mutually advantageous: her image boosted sales and her press presence augmented her celebrity. As Hargreaves contends, "the collusion of celebrities was essential to the whole enterprise of *published* photography" (emphasis mine) (figs. XII, XIII, and see fig. 1.27).[48]

Two technological advances were of paramount importance in this media surge: the introduction of the halftone process, which allowed photographs to be printed on the page (rather than pasted in by

FIG. XIII Sarony Studio (American, 1866–ca. 1930). Billie Burke. From *The Theatre* (October 1912): 111. Private collection.

hand) and the innovation of onstage flash photography, which made it possible for the photographer to work in the theater itself.[49] Although the halftone process was available as early as 1869, its commercial potential was not realized until the mid-1890s. In 1893 New York photographer Joseph Byron invented a method that enabled him to take cast pictures during final dress rehearsals.[50] Although these were not yet truly "live action" photographs, since actors were required to hold their poses, they nonetheless conveyed a much greater sense of immediacy in terms of recording theatrical performances. As a result of these two developments, magazines and newspapers increasingly

FIG. XIV Advertisement for bound issues of *The Theatre*. From *The Theatre* (October 1912): xvi. Private collection.

included photographs in their publications and new, often large-format, heavily illustrated theater journals—including those on view in the exhibition—flourished.[51] Clearly intended as collectors' items, some of the theater magazines regularly advertised earlier issues and special editions available for purchase, as well as handsomely bound volumes (fig. XIV).[52]

The intertwined relationship between fashion and theater is explicitly demonstrated in publications devoted to each; these provided extensive coverage of actresses, plays, and new styles named in their honor in specially designated columns and spreads, generously illustrated with drawings or photographs. In France, Britain, and the United States, fashion periodicals such as *L'Art et la Mode*, *Le Moniteur de la Mode*, *Les Modes*, *The Queen*, *The Lady's Pictorial*, *Harper's Bazar* (as it was called from its founding in 1867 to 1929, when it was renamed *Harper's Bazaar*), and *Vogue* all conveyed such information, and actresses also appeared on the covers.[53] The *Harper's Bazar* column "Gowns Seen on the Stage" featured actresses as fashion originators with access to the most beautiful clothes by the best-known designers, which they displayed to great effect.[54] *Les Modes*, first published in 1901 by the same firm that issued *Le Théatre*, regularly included full-length photographs of actresses with captions that identified the theater at which they were performing and summarized their toilettes, sometimes providing the name of the couturier or milliner as well (see fig. 1.8).[55]

Evocative descriptions of couture gowns that actresses wore onstage were an important component of many of the new theater magazines and served to transmit the latest fashion trends to eager (female) readers. Rita Detmold, author of "Frocks and Frills," and Mrs. Robert E. Noble, author of "Fascinating Fashions behind the Footlights," both columns in *The Play Pictorial*, rhapsodized over the luxurious gowns Lily Elsie and other actresses modeled.[56] In *The Theatre*, "Furs, Frocks and Footwear Fashions Fore-and-aft the Footlights" by "Mademoiselle Thespis" and "Footlight Fashions" by "Mlle. Manhattan" detailed "the newest thing in gorgeous garments" worn onstage as well as the "exceedingly smart," "radiant," and "chic" ensembles actresses were seen wearing offstage.[57] And in *Le Théatre*, Claire de Chancenay's full-page section titled "La Mode au Théâtre" highlighted the couture ensembles of actresses in current productions.[58] Further underscoring the pronounced commercial relationship between fashion and theater, these magazines published advertisements for high-end dressmakers and other purveyors of fashion, and *The Theatre* also offered readers a shopping service (fig. xv).[59] Both fashion and theater publications "helped naturalize the relationship between going to the theater and shopping" and promoted consumption that was sparked by what women saw on stage.[60]

The public's interest in the private life of the actress was certainly not new to the turn of the twentieth century; it had always been avid for information about her presumably "irregular" lifestyle offstage. What *was* different was the new portrayal of her lifestyle and the actress's active collaboration in that effort.[61] No longer a woman tainted by an aura of scandal, the actress was now a middle-class model of propriety who happened to operate—very visibly—in the public

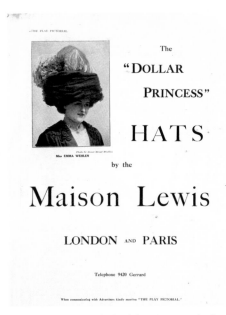

FIG. XV Dover Street Studio (English, active ca. 1906–12). Advertisement for Maison Lewis hats. From *The Play Pictorial* (November 1909): i. Private collection.

sphere. The earlier, tantalizing press accounts of the risqué behavior of actresses gave way to admiring reports and interviews that stressed the familiarity of their interests and pursuits. Photographs and accompanying stories showing them in their tastefully decorated homes, engaged in such ordinary activities as correspondence, gardening, and playing with their children, promoted a radically altered impression of actresses. Illustrated articles depicting Jane Hading *chez elle* in an elegantly appointed home in a Parisian suburb, Lily Elsie relaxing in the garden of her English country house, and Billie Burke on the terrace of her Hastings-on-Hudson, New York, residence are examples of the construction of this new image (see figs. 1.31, 2.29, and 3.22).[62] As Lenard Berlanstein asserts in his essay in this volume, "Dangerous and Influential Women: Actresses in Nineteenth-Century French Culture," the actress's dressing room—undoubtedly the most eroticized site associated with the female performer and frequently evoked in titillating detail in art and literature as a setting for private assignations—became a solidly bourgeois space. Rather than lovers, actresses now entertained family friends and attended to their waiting children as soon as a performance was over.[63] By the turn of the twentieth century, the "immoral" actress who had existed outside the boundaries of genteel womanhood became a *femme de foyer*.[64] She was, in effect, like and unlike other women: although her beauty, wealth, and fame set her apart, she was nevertheless someone with whom they could identify and, if provided with the right tools, could aspire to become.

ADVERTISING

The shift in the perception of actresses combined with their glamorous, highly public profile made them ideal figures to promote a range of commodities in a period of growing consumerism. Advertisers were keen to exploit the popularity of these women and trade in their recognizable faces on a host of goods. Images of Jane Hading, Lily Elsie, and Billie Burke were used to sell dress silks, knitwear, skin-care creams, soap, biscuits, chocolate, and cigarettes. The appearance of an actress in an advertisement, like that of her appearance in couture gowns, photographs, and the press, fulfilled a dual role: it both sold a product and added to her fame. In advertising especially, the actress participated in her own commodification and in the larger cultural discourse linking femininity with the commodity itself.[65] Although advertisers constantly had to contend with the degree and potential longevity of an individual actress's appeal—the waning of her fame and concomitant decrease of her usefulness as a spokesperson—women of the stage were eagerly sought after for their testimonials, which added an element of authority and a personal note to manufacturers' product claims.[66] Advertisers capitalized on the allure of actresses "primarily as a purchasable commodity," and on their side, actresses in their new role of respectable middle-class women "minimize[d] the visibility of the cash nexus behind the endorsement."[67]

As fashionable women, actresses were particularly in demand to endorse products for other women. Turn-of-the-century concepts about "personality" as related to stage performers, identity, transformation, and individual self-expression established a connection between actresses and female consumers that advertisers stressed to their advantage.[68] Drawing attention to an actress's personality rather her character was an important component in testimonial advertising because, as Schweitzer has observed, "it positioned the actress as a cultural performer *outside* the limits of her stage roles," making it possible for advertisers to reach a much broader audience.[69]

Whether selling clothes or other types of goods used by women, the actress was presented as a knowledgeable consumer and role model.[70] The copy in an advertisement for Klosfit petticoats that

FIG. XVI Advertisement for Klosfit Petticoats. From *The Theatre*
(October 1912): xxv. Private collection.

appeared in *The Theatre* in 1912, for example, conveys several strategic
messages (fig. XVI): "Actresses are admired as much for their style of
dress and grace of figure as for their talent or beauty. That they excel
in the art of dressing well, and are regarded as models in this respect is
a well known fact. Most, if not all of the popular stars wear the Klosfit
petticoat because of the stylish grace and symmetry it gives to the figure."[71] The advertisement gives equal significance to the actress's "style
of dress and grace of figure" and to her "talent or beauty"; it highlights
the actress's ability to select products that will enhance her appearance;
and it suggests that by imitating actresses and buying a Klosfit petticoat, consumers will acquire a similar "stylish grace and symmetry."

One of the most important areas in which the images and testimonials of actresses were prevalent was the expanding culture
of beauty that emerged at the turn of the twentieth century in the context of changing attitudes toward women and their appearance.
The nineteenth-century belief that true physical beauty resided in

and emanated from the soul was replaced by the idea that women were entitled to be, and in fact should, make themselves as (youthfully) beautiful as possible, and manufacturers' advertisements for beauty products clearly advanced this idea.[72] Our three actresses were all associated with skin-care products that promised a flawless, young-looking complexion—like theirs: Jane Hading promoted her own Eau de Jeunesse, Lily Elsie endorsed Helena Rubenstein's Valaze cream, and Billie Burke's testimonials extolled the wonders of Créme Nerol and Pond's cold and vanishing creams.[73] Like the Klosfit petticoat advertisement, these ads positioned actresses as women who were acutely aware of the importance of their physical appearance and its maintenance, and who were equally familiar with and availed themselves of beauty products. Female consumers who bought these commodities were thus assured of the justification of their purchases and encouraged to believe that, by following the regime of a particular actress, they might achieve the same results. Use of such products thus offered the potential for self-enhancement, for transformation, and, ultimately, for self-expression as women asserted their feminine agency as actors in the modern world.

The three essays in this catalogue address different yet complementary aspects of the exhibition and its themes. In "Dangeous and Influential Women: Actresses in Nineteenth-Century French Culture," Lenard Berlanstein examines the perception of actresses in the context of French politics and regime change. "Lucile and the Theatricalization of Fashion" by Sheila Stowell discusses the significance of this entrepreneurial British couturiere regarding her use of the theater to advertise her overtly dramatic fashions and her adoption of theatrical conventions (stage, lighting, music, and even scripts) in the couture house to sell her designs. Marlis Schweitzer's essay, "Stylish Effervescence: Billie Burke and the Rise of the Fashionable Broadway Star," analyzes the importance of fashion in Billie Burke's rise to prominence on the stage in the early decades of the twentieth century. Three BGC students, Maude Bass-Krueger, William DeGregorio, and Rebecca Perry, contributed the thematic entries. In addition to the four main themes discussed in this introduction, we have included a short biography that precedes the themed section for each actress.

Taken together, this catalogue and the exhibition explore the social, political, and cultural contexts in which the turn-of-the-century actress performed; the role of the couturier in the creation of the actress as fashion leader; and the actress who promoted herself through fashion. With the rise of the film industry in the 1910s and 1920s, the screen actress replaced her stage counterpart as an icon of modern fashion and beauty. However, there is a clear trajectory between these earlier adulated stage performers and today's leading film stars. One hundred years after Jane Hading, Lily Elsie, and Billie Burke captivated a public enthralled by beautiful and exquisitely dressed women of the theater, movie actresses, their lifestyles, and their fashion choices continue to fascinate a public increasingly overwhelmed by media that can now broadcast instantaneously their every move, whether on or off the stage.

1   EBay has undoubtedly given a new impetus to the interest in and collecting of "Golden Age" postcards. Of the three actresses featured in this exhibition, postcards of Lily Elsie and Billie Burke are readily available, those of Jane Hading somewhat less so.

2   Most of the cabinet cards and the great majority of the postcard images of Jane Hading were taken by Reutlinger. The wide availability of Reutlinger postcards today speaks to the large output of this studio, particularly when it was under the direction of Léopold-Émile Reutlinger (1863-1937). See Jean-Pierre Bourgeron, *Les Reutlinger: Photographes à Paris 1850-1937* (Paris: Jean-Pierre Bourgeron, 1979), 27-43. Léopold Reutlinger was married to the sister of the well-known actress Cécile Sorel, who appeared extensively in the periodical *Le Théatre* at the turn of the century; ibid., 27.

3   Victoria Kelly, "Beauty and the Market: Actress Postcards and their Senders in Early Twentieth-Century Australia," *New Theatre Quarterly* 20, pt. 2 (2004): 99. This article explores the increasing reach of theatrical images and celebrity made possible by the mechanisms of industrial mass modernity, the specific social purposes and contexts of postcard senders as revealed by their messages, and the ways in which the actress operated as an icon with multiple meanings within mass culture; ibid.

4   There is an extensive literature on turn-of-the-century postcards. See, for example, Aline Ripert and Claude Frère, *La carte postale: Son histoire, sa function sociale* (Paris: Centre National de la Recherche Scientifique, 2001); Benjamin H. Penniston, *The Golden Age of Postcards: Early 1900s: Identification and Values* (Paducah, KY: Collector Books, 2008); Bjarne Rogan, "An Entangled Object: The Picture Postcard as Souvenir and Collectible, Exchange and Ritual Communication," *Cultural Analysis* 4 (2005): 1-27; and Kelly, "Beauty and the Market," 99-116.

5   Examples of French celebrity actresses include Réjane (born Gabrielle-Charlotte Réju, 1856-1920), Cécile Sorel (1873-1966), Eve Lavallière (1866-1929), and Geneviève Lantelme (1887-1911). British actresses include Gertie Millar (1879-1952), Gabrielle Ray (1883-1973), the sisters Zena (1887-1975) and Phyllis Dare (1890-1975), and Gladys Cooper (1888-1971). American actresses include Julia Marlowe (1865-1950), Maude Adams (1872-1953), and Ethel Barrymore (1879-1959).

6   "A New Picture Every Day in the Year for Lily Elsie," *Chicago Examiner*, May 1, 1910.

7   Some of the well-known theaters he managed were the Gaiety Theatre and the Adelphi Theatre, both on the Strand, and Daly's Theatre near Leicester Square. See Thomas Postlewait, "George Edwardes and Musical Comedy: the Transformation of London Theatre and Society, 1878-1914," in *The Performing Century: Nineteenth-Century Theatre's History*, ed. Tracy Davis and Peter Holland (Basingstoke: Palgrave Macmillan, 2007), 82-87.

8   Lily Elsie has a large fan base today attested by the demand for postcards of the actress and a website devoted entirely to her. See http://lily-elsie.com/.

9   See Lenard R. Berlanstein, *Daughters of Eve: A Cultural History of French Theater Women from*

the *Old Regime to the Fin de Siècle* (Cambridge MA: Harvard University Press, 2001), ch. 1, 5, and 6; Benjamin McArthur, *Actors and American Culture, 1880-1920* (Philadelphia: Temple University Press, 1984), 123-25, 128-30; and Tracy Davis, *Actresses as Working Women: Their Social Identity in Victorian Culture* (London: Routledge, 1991), ch. 5.

10 A number of scholars have explored this cultural shift during the period. The texts that were most helpful and relevant to our study include: Berlanstein, *Daughters of Eve*, see ch. 7 and 9; Marlis Schweitzer, *When Broadway Was the Runway: Theater, Fashion, and American Culture* (Philadelphia: University of Pennsylvania Press, 2009), see ch. 3 and 4; McArthur, *Actors and American Culture*, see ch. 5 and 6; Davis, *Actresses as Working Women*, see ch. 3; and Anne Martin-Fugier, *Comédiennes: Les actrices en France au XIXe siècle* (Paris: Éditions du Seuil, 2001), ch. 8 and conclusion.

11 It was also the case that actresses were sometimes perceived differently when they performed outside their individual countries. See Susan A. Glenn, "The Bernhardt Effect: Self-Advertising and the Age of Spectacle," in Glenn, *Female Spectacle: The Theatrical Roots of Modern Feminism* (Cambridge MA: Harvard University Press, 2000), 9-39. The author examines Sarah Bernhardt as an important cultural figure in the United States, especially for women, and suggests that the actress's Jewish background did not provoke the same kind of harsh anti-Semitism that she was subject to in France; ibid., 10, 31-34. See also Gail Marshall, "Cultural Formations: The Nineteenth-Century Touring Actress and her International Audiences," in *The Cambridge Companion to the Actress*, ed. Maggie B. Gale and John Stokes (Cambridge: Cambridge University Press, 2007), 52-73.

12 On the growth of the theater in France, Britain, and the United States during this period, see F. W. J. Hemmings, *The Theatre Industry in Nineteenth-Century France* (Cambridge: Cambridge University Press, 1993), 1-4; Christopher Breward, "The Actress: Covent Garden and the Strand, 1880-1914," in *Fashion: Critical and Primary Sources*, vol. 3: *The Nineteenth Century*, ed. Peter McNeil (Oxford: Berg, 2009), 96; and McArthur, *Actors and American Culture*, 126-28. On the regendering of the theater, see Berlanstein, *Daughters of Eve*, 167-69; and Schweitzer, *When Broadway Was the Runway*, 35-39, 56-58, 84-88. In *Female Spectacle*, Glenn addresses both these developments, see 12-15.

13 Glenn, *Female Spectacle*, 14.

14 In-depth studies of this type of play and the issues it raised include: Joel H. Kaplan and Sheila Stowell, *Theatre and Fashion: Oscar Wilde to the Suffragettes* (Cambridge: Cambridge University Press, 1994), see ch. 1, 3, and 4; Nancy J. Troy, *Couture Culture: A Study in Modern Art and Fashion* (Cambridge MA: MIT Press, 2003), ch. 2.

15 Peter Bailey, "'Naughty but Nice': musical comedy and the rhetoric of the girl, 1892-1914," in *The Edwardian Theatre: Essays on Performance and the Stage*, eds. Michael R. Booth and Joel H. Kaplan (Cambridge: Cambridge University Press, 1996): 38-39. Also see Troy, *Couture Culture*, ch. 2.

16 Kaplan and Stowell, *Theatre and Fashion*, 10.

17 A.E.W. Mason, *Sir George Alexander and the St. James's Theatre* (London: Macmillan, 1935), cited in Kaplan and Stowell, *Theatre and Fashion*, 9.

18 Diana de Marly, *Worth: Father of Haute Couture*, 2nd ed. (London and New York: Holmes & Meier, 1990), see ch. 11.

19 "Comme public il y avait un curieux public, et tout d'abord Worth et sa femme, sans l'inspection desquels Mme Plessy ne joue jamais, et avec eux tout le monde des modistes et des tailleuses célèbres..." Edmond and Jules de Goncourt, *Journal, Mémoires de la vie littéraire*, vol. 2 (1862-65; Paris: Ernest Flammarion and Fasquelle, 1935), 255.

20 Regarding the theatrical work of Jeanne Paquin and Paul Poiret, see Troy, *Couture Culture*, ch. 2. Regarding Lucile and other British dressmakers from this period, see Kaplan and Stowell, *Theatre and Fashion*, ch. 1 and 4.

21 Pierre Véron, *Le Monde illustré* (July 30, 1881), cited in Berlanstein, *Daughters of Eve*, 112. Elisabeth Rachel Félix (1821-1858) was a famous French tragedienne, particularly known for her roles from the classical theater.

22 "Costly Dressing on the Stage," *Theatre Magazine* (December 1906), cited in Schweitzer, *When Broadway Was the Runway*, 65.

23 Schweitzer, *When Broadway Was the Runway*, 117.

24 Berlanstein, *Daughters of Eve*, 111-12. Berlanstein relates that, in the 18th and 19th centuries, actresses often wore fabulous gowns and jewels on stage that were gifts from their wealthy admirers and that served to make public their liaison; see ibid., 46, 144. Regarding French

actresses' expenditures on their costumes and the custom of having a protector, see also Martin-Fugier, *Comédiennes*, 73-76, and Hemmings, *The Theatre Industry in Nineteenth-Century France*, 199-201. In England actresses generally supplied their own costumes but were subsequently reimbursed by the theater company. See Aileen Ribeiro, "Costuming the Part: A Discourse of Fashion and Fiction in the Image of the Actress in England, 1776-1812," in *Notorious Muse: The Actress in British Art and Culture, 1776-1812*, ed. Robyn Asleson (New Haven and London: Yale University Press, 2003), 106; and Diana de Marly, *Costume on the Stage, 1600-1940* (Totowa, NJ: Barnes and Noble, 1982), ch. 2.

25 Schweitzer, *When Broadway Was the Runway*, 106-7. The author cites Ethel Barrymore, who noted the irony that a "star's" clothes were provided by the management while struggling actresses had to pay for theirs; ibid.

26 Martin-Fugier, *Comédiennes*, 74. Perrin was clearly more worried about actresses than actors, as he issued a *Règlement sur les costumes et toilettes de ville des Dames artistes*, which indicated maximum prices for four types of garments: ball gowns (1,000 to 1,200 francs), "costumes de grande toilette de ville" (800 to 1,000 francs), "costumes de demi-toilette" (500 to 700 francs) and "costumes ordinaires" (300 to 500 francs); ibid. Perrin's initiative, however, was not consistently adopted; Jane Hading's one-year contract with the Comédie-Française from 1892 to 1893 stipulated that she was obliged to furnish "à ses frais tous les habits nécessaires et convenables à ses rôles et emplois, tant pour la tragédie que pour la comédie et le drame." "Comédie-Française Mme Jane Hading Engagement d'Act Pensionnaire Année 1892-1893" in Jane Hading file, Bibliothèque de la Comédie-Française, Paris. The management did, however, pay for *costumes extraordinaires*, presumably like those she would have worn in *Plus que Reine* and *La Pompadour*.

27 Schweitzer, *When Broadway Was the Runway*, 65.

28 Martin-Fugier, *Comédiennes*, 76. For example, a "robe de ville" (formal day dress) was 300 francs, whereas a "robe du soir" (evening gown) was 500 francs. Compared to the range of prices stipulated by Perrin some twenty years earlier for similar pieces, these are clearly moderate.

29 Breward, "The Actress," 101.

30 *Dictionnaire international de la mode*, ed. Bruno Remaury and Lydia Kamitsis (Paris: Éditions du Regard, 2004), 497. Regarding Redfern's involvement with the London stage in the 1890s, see Kaplan and Stowell, *Theatre and Fashion*, 9. Jane Hading was by no means the only French actress who wore Redfern; the pages of *Les Modes* and *Le Théatre* are full of photographs of actresses dressed by this top couturier.

31 *Les Modes*, *Vogue*, and *Harper's Bazar* regularly illustrated and discussed the work of leading designers and also included photographs of actresses in ensembles by these same designers. See also Berlanstein, *Daughters of Eve*, 235-36. The House of Worth was extensively patronized by American society women at the turn of the 20th century. The Costume Institute in the Metropolitan Museum of Art, for example, has in its collection Worth gowns that belonged to Mrs. William Astor, Mrs. Caroline Schermerhorn Astor Wilson, Mrs. John Pierpont Morgan Jr., Mrs. Andrew Carnegie, and Sarah Cooper Hewitt. The Museum of Fine Arts, Boston, has Worth gowns that belonged to Mrs. Stanford White, Mrs. Cornelius Vanderbilt, and Mrs. David Lyon Gardiner, as well as gowns by Redfern and Paquin, also worn by American clients.

32 Schweitzer, *When Broadway Was the Runway*, 162.

33 Ibid., 163. Schweitzer discusses the different meanings of these "copy acts" as they related to issues such as age, class, and ethnicity as well as who it was that women "copied ... what they copied, how they copied it, and where they staged their performances"; ibid., 163-77. For specific examples of society women who wore copies of stage costumes at social gatherings, see ibid., 164-66. In Britain actresses acted as fashion advisors to elite women as early as the 18th century; see Ribeiro, "Costuming the Part," 107. In mid-19th-century France, Empress Eugénie ordered a copy of a gown worn on stage by the actress Marie Delaporte; see de Marly, *Worth*, 174. Even ready-made copies of actresses' couture dresses were available at this time; a gown that Worth designed for the actress Sylvie Arnould-Plessy in 1867 was adapted by French department stores; see Berlanstein, *Daughters of Eve*, 234.

34 Roger Hargreaves, "Putting Faces to the Names: Social and Celebrity Portrait Photography," in Peter Hamilton and Roger Hargreaves, *The Beautiful and the Damned: The Creation of Identity in Nineteenth-Century Photography* (Aldershot, Hampshire: Lund Humphries, 2001), 37.

35 For an overview of the development of mid-19th-century photography in France, see Elizabeth

Anne McCauley, *Industrial Madness: Commercial Photography in Paris, 1848-1871* (New Haven: Yale University Press, 1994). Other sources that discuss the significance of the *carte de visite* include Hargreaves, "Putting Faces to the Names," 17-55; Jean Sagne, "All Kinds of Portraits" in *A New History of Photography*, ed. Michel Frizot (Cologne: Könemann, 1998), 103-22; and Laurence Senelick, "Eroticism in Early Theatrical Photography" in *Theatre History Studies* 9 (1991): 1-49.

36   See Schweitzer, *When Broadway Was the Runway*, 110-11, 113-17.

37   David Mayer, "The Actress as Photographic Icon: From Early Photography to Early Film," in *The Cambridge Companion to the Actress*, ed. Maggie B. Gale and John Stokes (Cambridge: Cambridge University Press, 2007), 83. The New York photographer Napoleon Sarony reportedly paid Sarah Bernhardt $10,000 for a sitting; see Hargreaves, "Putting Faces to the Names," 40. Mayer also makes the important point that until the 1890s and even later in some circumstances, "theatrical photographs were made in a photographer's studio" rather than on stage as theatrical lighting was not suitable to producing acceptable photographs; Mayer, "The Actress as Photographic Icon," 80.

38   Margaret Illington Banes, "The Mad Search for Beauty: And the Slight Chance that the Average Actress Can Guide the Average Woman," *Green Book Magazine* (May 1912), cited in Schweitzer, *When Broadway Was the Runway*, 122.

39   See for example, Hargreaves, "Putting Faces to the Names," 51-52, and Kelly, "Beauty and the Market," 105-6, 109-16.

40   Hargreaves, "Putting Faces to the Names," 19.

41   Regarding this perception, see, for example, Mayer, "The Actress as Photographic Icon," 74-93; Hargreaves, "Putting Faces to the Names"; Kelly, "Beauty and the Market"; and Senelick, "Eroticism in Early Theatrical Photography," 1-49.

42   Mayer, "The Actress as Photographic Icon," 83.

43   Hargreaves, "Putting Faces to the Names," 47.

44   Ibid., 43, 46-47.

45   Senelick, "Eroticism in Early Theatrical Photography," 2.

46   Regarding the importance of comportment and ideal body type for actresses, see Stowell and Kaplan, *Theatre and Fashion*, 117; Bailey, "'Naughty but Nice,'" 38-39; and Schweitzer, *When Broadway Was the Runway*, 107, 109-10.

47   At this date, there were publications in France and Britain while American periodicals usually excerpted fashion information from British magazines. The first American fashion periodical of significance was *Godey's Lady's Book*, which was published in Philadelphia and first appeared in 1830. For information on the fashion press in France, Britain and the U.S., see Alice Mackrell, *An Illustrated History of Fashion: 500 Years of Fashion Illustration* (New York: Costume & Fashion Press, 1997); Raymond Gaudriault, *La Gravure de mode féminine en France* (Paris: Editions de l'Amateur, 1983); and Phyllis G. Tortora, "The Evolution of the American Fashion Magazine as Exemplified in Selected Fashion Journals, 1830-1969," PhD diss., New York University, 1973.

48   Hargreaves, "Putting Faces to the Names," 50.

49   Mayer, "The Actress as Photographic Icon," 86, 88-89.

50   Ibid., 86, 89. Byron's method involved the use of magnesium flash powder, electric lights, and reduced shutter speeds.

51   Some of these include *The Theatre* (1901) and the *Play-goer* (1902) in New York, *The Play Pictorial* (1902) and the *Playgoer and Society Illustrated* (1909) in London, and *Le Théatre* (1898) and *Comœdia Illustré* (1908) in Paris. Cecil Beaton wrote that as an adolescent, he became obsessed with "the world of musical comedy" and that his "passion was nurtured on the photographs [he] found in the weekly magazines and in *The Play Pictorial*." Cecil Beaton, "Lovely Lily Elsie," in *The Rise and Fall of the Matinée Idol: Past deities of stage and screen, their roles, their magic, and their worshippers*, ed. Anthony Curtis (New York: St. Martin's Press, 1974), 13.

52   Other theater magazines also advertised earlier issues. The inside back cover of *The Play Pictorial* 18, no. 108 (1911) lists many earlier issues available for purchase, as well as a "Gaiety Souvenir" volume for 9/- and a "Daly's Special Souvenir" volume for 12/6-.

53   The well-known French actress Réjane, for example, appeared on the cover of an early issue of *Les Modes* in 1902, and in 1904, *Les Modes* covers featured Mademoiselle Marville in February, Mademoiselle Eve Lavallière in July, and Madame Marthe Régnier in November.

54 Schweitzer, *When Broadway Was the Runway*, 8.

55 *Les Modes* (1901-1937) was published by Boussod, Manzi, Joyant & Cie. From its inception in 1898, the title of *Le Théatre* was spelled without a circumflex on the "a," although the spelling *théâtre* does appear in articles and columns within the pages of the magazine. Most of the photographs from the early decades were taken by the Reutlinger Studio.

56 See for example, Rita Detmold, "Frocks & Frills," *The Play Pictorial* 18, no. 108 (1911). The issue is devoted to *The Count of Luxembourg*, starring Lily Elsie, which opened at Daly's Theatre on May 20, 1911. Also see, for example, Mrs. Robert E. Noble, "Fascinating Fashions behind the Footlights at Daly's," *The Play Pictorial* 15, no. 88 (1909): 22-23.

57 For "Furs, Frocks and Footwear," see *The Theatre* (November 1908): xvi, xviii, xx, xxii. For "Footlight Fashions at a Certain Matinee," see *The Theatre* (September 1916): 156-57.

58 See, for example, *Le Théatre*, no. 6 (June 1898); no. 11 (November 1898); no. 14 (February 1899); no. 29 (March 1900). There are no page numbers for these articles, which appear on the last page of each issue.

59 Schweitzer, *When Broadway Was the Runway*, 93.

60 Ibid., 92.

61 It should be noted that the aggressive "New Journalism" that emerged during this period published sensationalist stories about actors and actresses. Actresses themselves also engaged in outlandish stunts in order to get publicity. See Glenn, "The Bernhardt Effect," 34-35; McArthur, *Actors and American Culture*, 145-46; and Marlis Schweitzer, "Surviving the City: Press Agents, Publicity Stunts, and the Spectacle of the Urban Female Body," in *Performance and the City*, ed. D. J. Hopkins, Shelley Orr and Kim Solga (Houndsmills and New York: Palgrave Macmillan, 2009), 133-51.

62 For Jane Hading, see *Le Théatre* (November 1900), and Gaston Bonnefont, *Nos Grandes Artistes, Les Parisiennes chez elles* (Paris: Ernest Flammarion, 1897); for Lily Elsie, see Alan Dale, "The Girl Who Made Good," *Cosmpolitan* (December 1911): 85; and for Billie Burke, see Billie Burke, "Under My Own Vine and Fig Tree," in *Harper's Bazar* (August 1913): 19, 45, and Ada Patterson, "The Lady of Burkeleigh Crest," *The Theatre* 17, no. 143 (1913): 28-30.

63 See also Berlanstein, *Daughters of Eve*, 166.

64 Martin-Fugier, *Comédiennes*, 359.

65 Abigail Solomon-Godeau, "The Other Side of Venus: The Visual Economy of Feminine Display," in *The Sex of Things: Gender and Consumption in Historical Perspective*, ed. Victoria de Grazia and Ellen Furlough (Berkley: University of California Press, 1996), 113.

66 Schweitzer, *When Broadway Was the Runway*, 138-39, 141-42; Berlanstein, *Daughters of Eve*, 231-33.

67 Berlanstein, *Daughters of Eve*, 233.

68 Regarding the notion of "personality," see Schweitzer, *When Broadway Was the Runway*, 103-5, and McArthur, *Actors and American Culture*, 166-67.

69 Schweitzer, *When Broadway Was the Runway*, 8-9.

70 Ibid., 135.

71 *The Theatre* 15, no. 140 (1912): xxv.

72 Schweitzer, *When Broadway Was the Runway*, 132. See also Kathy Peiss, *Hope in a Jar: The Making of America's Beauty Culture* (New York: Metropolitan Books, Henry Holt and Company, 1998), ch. 3 and 4, and Lois W. Banner, *American Beauty* (Chicago: University of Chicago Press, 1983), ch. 10.

73 Marlis Schweitzer discusses Billie Burke and Créme Nerol in her essay in this volume. See also Schweitzer, *When Broadway Was the Runway*, 133, and Leslie Midkiff DeBauche, "Testimonial Advertising Using Movie Stars in the 1910s: How Billie Burke Came to Sell Pond's Vanishing Cream in 1917," *Charm* (2007): 146-56.

1
Dangerous and Influential Women:
Actresses in Nineteenth-Century French Culture
Lenard R. Berlanstein

In 1867 the society columnist for the widely read newspaper *Le Monde illustré* described audience reaction to a play starring two attractive performers, Blanche Pierson and Céline Montaland, in this way: "Women in the audience look at [Pierson] and say: 'That dress is evidently from Madame Laferrière [a noted dressmaker]. No one else could make such a skirt. And the hat! It is ravishing!' Men look through their glasses and murmur under their breath [to avoid offending their wives], 'I don't know. The blond is softer, but the brunette is more spirited. But maybe.... Well the blond has a stunning mouth. And the curls on her neck. Wow!'"[1]

The journalist, far from preparing to denounce the superficial response to art, was illustrating what was so worldly and intoxicating about French theater. Candid about men's sexualized appreciation of Pierson and Montaland, the columnist evoked only the best-case scenario for the female spectators—that they would learn nothing more from the actresses than what was fashionable to wear. The journalist must have been censoring himself, because he surely knew that actresses had far more subversive lessons to impart. The performers could easily teach women about empowerment and individuality, lessons that were thought to be unwomanly at the time and anathema to most men (and women, too). Jean-Jacques Rousseau, one of the thinkers most responsible for providing modern France with its governing ideology, had posited in the mid-eighteenth century that when women were strong, men were weak, and the specter of strong women and weak men haunted France, as it dazzled the rest of the world by experimenting with self-government, national sovereignty, the rule of the common man, and secularism.[2]

Actresses served as prime examples in French culture of strong women who bent men to their wills. As such, they were in absolute violation of the gender principles on which modern France was founded. Those principles broke with the pre-1789 society founded on monarchy and hierarchy and instead constructed an individualistic, competitive social order in which men might govern themselves and pursue their self-interest. The new masculine code of competitive individualism insisted on women being "the opposite sex"—not individualistic at all; in fact, they were to be self-abnegating, chaste, and dependent on the men in their lives. As the new gender order developed, a powerful domestic ideology would direct women to consider wifehood and motherhood the only worthy achievements in their lives. It would instruct them to find happiness by making others happy.[3] Actresses, however, would stand outside the sanctioned gender order.

How did actresses come to represent the powerful women who reversed gender norms that were supposedly "natural"? Almost from the moment that women were allowed to perform on stage in the mid-seventeenth century, actresses became central to elite sociability, which did not fail to influence the bourgeoisie long thereafter. French men of exceptional wealth and power competed to keep actresses as their mistresses. In theory, aristocratic males were using the actresses to bolster their reputations for conquest and potency, but especially desirable actresses very quickly reversed the power relationship and made lords compete for them. In fact, instances in which men threw away fortunes and committed follies of all sorts for their lovers became commonplace.[4] Nearly a century before the term "celebrity" was coined in the 1830s, actresses assumed that status. Eighteenth-century newsletters and reports on elite gossip showed that the emerging public was intensely curious about actresses—their debuts and their performances, but also their lovers and sexual escapades.[5] Stage women received more mention than any other women, including the queen and ladies of the French court. As much as actresses were denounced for their depravity—the French church excommunicated them and denied them Christian burial as long as they practiced their trade—even aristocratic women were under the spell of the fashions that they set.[6]

In the mix of reformers' critiques of absolutist France on the eve of the Revolution was the growing fear of women's independence, deepening the quest for basic moral and political change.[7] With the Revolution of 1789, leaders aimed to create a purified nation in which strong, rational, individualistic men and self-abnegating women would contribute to a well-governed France. The Revolution, seconded by the Napoleonic law codes, did indeed lay down the framework for a France governed by male citizens.[8] However, the pre-revolutionary, aristocratic quality of elite sociability would persist until the last third of the nineteenth century by adapting to new conditions rather than yielding to them. Thus actresses retained their position as the most visible example of strong women who made men weak and irrational even as a democratizing France was seen to require competent men and submissive women.

For the first two-thirds of the nineteenth century, the theatrical experience entailed a combination of art and eroticism. It was understood that male spectators would lust over actresses and that female spectators were in a morally hazardous environment.[9] Actresses' dressing rooms and backstage lounges reeked of sexual disorder. When an intermission lasted longer than expected, audiences readily assumed that the star and her lover were enjoying a tryst (fig. 1.A). Sexual intrigue, necessarily public in order to have its desirable impact on reputations, prevented performers from constructing the "fourth wall" between themselves and the audience. Actresses on stage addressed their lines to lovers seated in the theater or signaled that they had changed lovers by showering attention on the new ones. Mistress-keepers in the audience ostentatiously acknowledged amorous signals from the stage or sent visual messages that the affair was over and that a new mistress was currently in favor.[10] "The theater is a circle of debauchery," the Goncourt brothers wrote with good reason in their journal of literary life. "From the stage to the audience, from the wings to the stage. From the audience to the stage. Dancers' legs, actresses' smiles. . . . It is like a night market in women!"[11] The most fashionable locale in all of France was probably the dancers' lounge at the Opéra de Paris, where important men made their liaisons with the young ballerinas. This moment of flirtation and sexual entanglement doubled as an instance of state-sponsored prostitution, because the Ministry of the Interior controlled access to the lounge and doled it out as a political favor.[12]

Actresses appeared frequently as characters in popular fiction during the first two-thirds of the century, because they allowed novelists and playwrights to explore the contradiction between a moral order insisting on women's domestic virtues and the reality of the celebrated outcasts being so integral to elite values. The question that writers found most pressing was whether actresses retained even a vestige of virtuous womanhood within their souls. Their answer depended on the general climate of political opinion—how confident they were that men were really in control. Before the Revolution of 1848, the parliamentary form of government and ascendancy of the bourgeoisie in politics promoted confidence. Hence, actresses as protagonists were mainly fallen heroines. They expiated their sins by accepting the love of one man, subjugating themselves, and withdrawing into domesticity.[13] With the violence of the Revolution of 1848 and the establishment of the Second

LA LOGE DE NANA.

« Je bois à Son Altesse ! dit royalement le vieux Bosc. — A Vénus ! cria Fontan » — (Page 430.)

NANA.   LIV. 17

FIG. 1.A The fictional actress Nana, based on the eponymous novel by Émile Zola, holds court in her dressing room while changing. This illustration reaffirmed the image of actresses as models of depravity and of control over men. Georges Clairin, *La Loge de Nana*, 1882. Bibliothèque nationale de France, Paris.

Empire between 1852 and 1870, France returned to an authoritarian regime that supported a self-indulgent aristocratic life, and confidence in rational men being in control of themselves or their society plummeted. The cultural response was a furious attack on actresses as dangerous harlots, the vehemence of which surpassed even the reform offensive before the Revolution of 1789.[14] Authors between 1850 and 1880 consistently portrayed actresses as predators at war with respectable society.[15] The novel in this category that is still read today is Émile Zola's *Nana* (1879), which is based loosely on the singer and actress Blanche d'Antigny. Through the seductiveness of her body, Nana causes a distinguished officer of the Second Empire to abandon a lifetime of Catholic morality, to humiliate himself in a hundred ways, and to ruin himself financially for her benefit—"a gust of gutter sex sweeping away . . . a hundred years of honor and Christian belief," according to Zola.[16] So completely did cultural authorities assimilate actresses into the category of harlot that the government removed them from the governing committee of the Comédie-Française, which became an all-male board for the first time in its centuries-old history.[17] With France's shocking defeat in the Franco-Prussian War of 1870, followed by the anarchic Commune of 1871, the public had little trouble understanding that actresses had contributed to the nation's degradation. Crowds on the streets taunted the real-life d'Antigny.[18]

Frenchwomen, told incessantly that they were naturally weak, chaste, self-sacrificing, and dependent on men, found actresses to be revealing counter-examples. For all their immorality, actresses enjoyed indisputable prestige. The average woman could not have helped admiring their personal freedom and the male attention that actresses elicited—which normative womanly virtue did not bestow to the same degree. Looking past the sexual excesses, Frenchwomen took the power of actresses over men as a metaphor for a life in which women had more scope and in which there was a more favorable balance of sexual power. The female public was apt to appropriate performers' fashions, hairstyles, and gestures to emulate this balance in both the public and private spheres.

Basic political change after the disastrous Franco-Prussian War of 1870–71 led to new and more proper, though still challenging, cultural roles for actresses. The erotic culture of the stage had been courtly in inspiration, and when the French people definitively chose a republic as their form of government in the late 1870s, public discourse had to shift toward a republican vision of the social order, in which respectability and didacticism had a much greater part. After all, the political base of the new democratic regime was the provincial middle classes and the peasantry.[19] Although erotic practices hardly disappeared (the Republic never even suppressed the state-sponsored prostitution at the Opéra), theatrical observers soon accepted that representing the stage as a worldly mix of eroticism and art was inappropriate. Reversing the outrage over actresses/harlots of mid-century, the observers reimagined French theater as a chaste milieu in which professionalized actresses did their jobs and did not create scandal.[20] Thus the editors of the bourgeois newspaper *Le temps* assumed the authority to challenge the venerable playwright Alexandre Dumas fils, when he insisted on the inevitable immorality of actresses in 1895. "Haven't we seen the fantastic qualities of our actresses fade since they had become good bourgeois women and excellent citizens?" countered the newspaper.[21] The editor was evidently eager to have "fantastic" qualities fade even though actresses were still not good bourgeois women in the strict sense. Jane Hading, who had recently been the subject of scandalous reporting in the American press during her tour there, even dared to publish a letter to the editor rebuking the senior playwright for his outmoded views.[22] Novelists between 1880 and 1914 supported the moralized representations. Gone were the threatening "Nanas" of the fictional world. Instead, authors endowed their theatrical protagonists with an unprecedented level of complexity. In the post-1880 actress novel, she regularly had much to teach the male protagonist about getting along in life.[23] The novelists were effectively upending Rousseau's fateful formula, because they foresaw men and women being strong at the same time.

French culture had long been unique in the West for placing actresses so near the levers of power and influence as it so resolutely withheld respectability. Foreign governments had bestowed honors on French actresses, whereas their own government still treated them as celebrated outcasts. Fears of disrupting the conventional systems of representing the public good had been too strong to do otherwise.[24] Yet the ancient French taboo withered at the turn of the century. For the first time in the 1890s, town councils dared to raise statues to their native daughters who had gained fame on the stage.[25] Paris, the world capital of theater, had yet to name a street in honor of an actress, as was customary with other well-known figures, but in 1899 finally did so, if timidly, by choosing to christen an out-of-the way thoroughfare after the great mid-century actress Elisabeth Rachel Félix. One alderman joked that when the day came to name a street after the notorious Sarah Bernhardt, she would settle for nothing less than the most

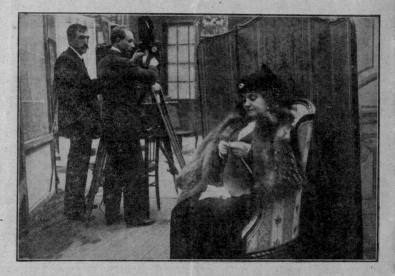

Mme RÉJANE

Pendant les répétitions d'

" ALSACE "

Profitant des moindres loisirs que lui laissent les répétitions et les changements de décors.

Mme RÉJANE

Tricote pour nos poilus

Photo prise aux ateliers
de la « Société Générale de Cinématographie »

14, Rue Chauveau　　　　　　　　　**NEUILLY-SUR-SEINE**

FIG. 1.B The image of French actresses shifted from perverse to respectable during the final third of the 19th century. This illustration portrays Réjane as a model of patriotic womanhood as she knitted for World War I soldiers during a break in the rehearsal. "Mme Réjane pendant les répétitions d'Alsace . . . Tricote pour nos poilus," *Ciné-journal* (October 22, 1915): back cover. Bibliothèque nationale de France, Paris.

central site in the city.[26] All observers agreed that the acknowledgment of actresses as contributors to French culture would triumph only when the national government found the courage to admit them to the Légion d'Honneur, whose membership defined national distinction since Napoléon founded it in 1802. Courage was lacking until 1904, when national leaders finally consecrated Julia Bartet of the Comédie-Française.[27] France had finally caught up with its neighbors in treating leading actresses as national treasures (fig. 1.B). The shift in public opinion was deep enough to convince many more bourgeois parents than ever to allow their daughters to attend the Acting Conservatory (Le Conservatoire national de musique et de déclamation) in Paris, which not long before had been one more fashionable forum for wealthy men to find young mistresses.[28]

As the erotic ties between the actress and her male fans finally became less imposing than the rapport between the actress and her female fans, the makers of popular and elite culture had a powerful new representation of the actress with which to work. The expansion of the press, rapid urbanism, and deepening commercialization provided a fruitful environment for elaboration. So did new ideas about women advanced by feminism.[29] The female rapport could be openly acknowledged, too, since it was no longer about seduction. Advertisers quickly recognized the possibilities and used actresses to recommend products to their fans. Fashion experts, who used to have to insist that actresses' corruption made them detestable fashion influences, acknowledged their role in promoting the latest fashions. Indeed, dressmakers contracted with actresses to launch their lines.[30]

Presumed celebrity respectability opened the way for actresses to challenge gender orthodoxy in new ways. One magazine, *Femina*, with a large subscription base of over 100,000 and quite a bit of influence upon the feminine press, led the way when it began publication in 1901. *Femina* appropriated the actress to illustrate its idea of "modern femininity," which called for worldly accomplishment accompanied by the conventional feminine attributes.[31] The seductive actress had once threatened the gender order at its very core. However, the image of the respectable actress, who resembled her female fans except for being famous, had the capacity to operate within the established gender order and simply make it more malleable. Sarah Bernhardt's hold on the public from the 1880s on rendered her the embodiment of the individual in a fluid, success-oriented social order. Her sway was unique, unnerving many French in that it publicized a thoroughgoing and gender-neutral individuality for which France was not yet ready.[32] *Femina* and other women's magazines, sometimes inspired by an expanding feminist outlook, took a more measured but still aggressive lead in offering a new kind of copy about actresses, the up-close-and-personal interview in which the star displayed her everyday life to the public.[33] Inevitably, a glamorous version of ordinariness was revealed. The new representation of actress was the distinguished and accomplished woman. Above scandal, Bernhardt maintained the highest standards of femininity although she had a life outside the home, indeed, a flourishing career. The 1893 interview with Jane Hading in *La revue illustrée* portrayed her as admirably serious and reclusive.[34] The suppression of the nasty rumors that had surrounded her in the recent past illustrated that the press was inclined to promote actresses as plausible New Women. Clearly, actresses were leading French women back into the public sphere from which they had been excluded a century earlier.

Being fully feminine yet having a non-domestic identity and personal preoccupations that took a woman's thoughts away from the family—these were not widely accepted attributes of womanhood prior to World War I. That commercially successful women's magazines presented the images to their readers so innocently and relentlessly, however, showed that they were under consideration.[35] It was in this way that the actress-celebrity of the turn of the century rendered a cloistering domesticity into a choice rather than a destiny for women.[36]

By the eve of the Great War, the press was setting up one actress after another as a national treasure. The decorated actress Julia Bartet became a national hero when she ostentatiously turned down the invitation of the German emperor Wilhelm II to perform in Berlin as he was threatening war. Patriots were thrilled with Bartet for showing the fortitude that all France needed if its daunting international challenges were to be met.[37] When war finally came, in 1914, and proved so taxing for France, actresses were active in serving the nation as dutiful women citizens.[38] Although their respectability had recent roots, they had long been mentors for the individuality and the professional achievement to which Frenchwomen would eventually lay claim.

1   Charles Monselet, "Compte rendue, " *Le Monde illustré* (December 14, 1867): 362.

2   Victor Wexler, "Made for Man's Delight: Rousseau as Antifeminist," *American Historical Review* 81 (April 1979): 266-91; Joan Landes, *Women in the Public Sphere in the Age of the French Revolution* (Ithaca NY: Cornell University Press, 1980); Michelle Perrot, "Women, Power, and History: The Case of Nineteenth-Century France," in *Women, State and Revolution: Essays on Power and Gender in Europe since 1789*, ed. Sian Reynolds (Brighton, UK: Wheatsheaf Books, 1986), 44-59.

3   Liselotte Steinbrügge, *The Moral Sex: Women's Nature in the French Enlightenment*, trans. Pamela Selwyn (New York: Oxford University Press, 1995); Anne Martin-Fugier, *La bourgeoise: Femme au temps de Paul Bourget* (Paris: B. Grasset, 1983).

4   The most important sources on the role of actresses in aristocratic libertinism are the police reports in the Bibliothèque de l'Arsenal, Archives de la Bastille, nos. 10235-10237. Useful published accounts include Jean Hervez, *Les femmes et la galanterie au XVIIe siècle* (Paris: H. Daragon, 1907); Léopold Lacour, *Les premières actrices françaises* (Paris: Librarie française, 1921); Lorédon Larchy, ed., *Documents inédits sur le règne de Louis XV, ou anecdotes galantes sur les actrices, demoiselles entretenues, grisettes, etc. formant le journal de Monsieur le lieutenant de police de Sartine* (Brussels: Parent, 1863); and Gaston Capon and Robert Yve-Plessis, *Paris galant au dix-huitième siècle: La vie privée du Prince de Conty* (Paris: J. Schemit, 1907). I have treated this subject in *Daughters of Eve: A Cultural History of French Theater Women from the Old Regime to the Fin-de-Siècle* (Cambridge MA: Harvard University Press, 2001), ch. 2.

5   Pamela Cheek, "The *Mémoires secrets* and the Actress: Tribadism, Performance, and Property," in *The Mémoires secrets and the Culture of Publicity in Eighteenth-Century France*, ed. Jeremy Popkin and Bernadette Fort (Oxford: Voltaire Foundation, 1998), 107-28.

6   John McManners, *Abbés and Actresses: The Church and the Theatrical Profession in the Eighteenth Century* (Oxford: Clarendon Press, 1984).

7   Virginia Scott, "The Actress and Utopian Theatre Reform in Eighteenth-Century France: Riccoboni, Rousseau, and Restif," *Theatre Research International* 27 (March 2002): 18-28; Berlanstein, *Daughters of Eve*, 59-73. On the broader effort to purify France by removing women from the public sphere, see Landes, *Women in the Public Sphere*, and Madelyn Gutwirth, *The Twilight of the Goddesses: Women and Representation in the French Revolutionary Era* (New Brunswick NJ: Rutgers University Press, 1992).

8   Robert A. Nye, *Masculinity and Male Codes of Honor in Modern France* (New York: Oxford University Press, 1993), ch. 4.

9   Berlanstein, *Daughters of Eve*, ch. 5.

10   The tumultuous affair carried on between the great mid-century star Virginie Déjazet and her lover Arthur Bertand during her performances illustrates very well the erotic culture of the French stage. See L.-Henry Lecomte, ed., *Un amour de Déjazet. Histoire et correspondance inédite, 1834-1844* (Paris: H. Daragon, 1908), 122-45.

11   Edmond and Jules de Goncourt, *Journal, Mémoires de la vie littéraire*, ed. Robert Ricatte, vol. 1 (Paris: R. Laffont, 1989), 1,075.

12   "Les rats de l'Opéra, " *La Vie parisienne* (September 19, 1891): 528-29. On the "official" aspects of access to the dancers' lounge, see Archives nationals, AJ 13 787-98.

13   Berlanstein, *Daughters of Eve*, 95-98.

14   A classic evocation of the libertine social life under the Second Empire is Siegfried Kracauer, *Orpheus in Paris: Offenbach and the Paris of his Time*, trans. Gwenda David and Eric Mosbacher (New York: A. Knopf, 1938).

15   Berlanstein, *Daughters of Eve*, 135-42.

16   Émile Zola, *Nana*, trans. Douglas Parmée (New York: Penguin, 1992), 353.

17   F. W. J. Hemmings, "Play-writers and Play-actors: the controversy over the *comités de lecture* in France, 1757-1910," *French Studies* (October 1989), 416-20. The findings in this article should be supplemented with the documents in Archives nationals, F21 4648.

18   Guy Vauzat, *Blanche d'Antigny, actrice et demi-mondaine* (Paris: Lahure, 1933), 23-54.

19   For the gender implications of republican ideology in France, see Judith F. Stone, "The Republican Brotherhood: Gender and Ideology," in *Gender and the Politics of Social Reform in France, 1870-1914*, ed. Elinor A. Accampo, Rachel G. Fuchs, and Mary Lynn Stewart (Baltimore: Johns Hopkins University Press, 1995), 28-58.

20   The essential work on the professional lives of actresses (with coverage of cultural issues, too) is Anne Martin-Fugier, *Comédiennes. Les actrices en France au XIXe siècle* (Paris: Seuil, 2001).

21 "Monsieur Dumas et les Comédiennes," *Le temps*, no. 12,352, March 24, 1895, 3. Dumas made the argument, which had passed as self-evident at mid-century, that actresses had to be the kind of woman who had affairs and broke moral conventions; otherwise, they would not be able to feign love and other powerful emotions on stage.

22 *Le temps*, no. 12,356, March 28, 1895, 3. On Hading's misbehavior, see Albert Carré, *Souvenirs de théâtre* (Paris: Plon, 1976), 145. The married actress had deserted her husband and run away with the actor Benoît-Constant Coquelin to tour in America.

23 Berlanstein, *Daughters of Eve*, 175-81.

24 The distinctive power of actresses to represent women who were beyond the limits of respectability is shown by the fact that eccentric women who were not actresses, such as the painter Rosa Bonheur, did receive state honors without much controversy. On Bonheur's unconventionality, see Albert Boime, "The Case of Rosa Bonheur: Why Should a Woman Want to Be More like a Man?" *Art History* 4 (December 1981): 384-409.

25 "Mademoiselle Duchesnois au Nord," *Le temps*, no. 12,788, June 4, 1896, 4.

26 Conseil municipal de Paris, *Procès-verbaux. Année 1899* (Paris: Imprimerie nationale, 1899), I : 1,309, 1,683; II : 179-80. Bernhardt did not get a street in Paris named after her until 1936.

27 Robert Dieudonné, "En honneur de Madame Bartet," *Femina* (September 1, 1905): 396; Joseph Galtier, "Les grandes artistes modernes: Bartet," *Je sais tout*, April 15, 1910, 370-72; Albert Dubeux, *Julia Bartet* (Paris: E. Sansot, 1938), 44. On the public reception of the honor and on speculation about the politics of giving it to Bartet in particular, see Jacques Porel, *Fils de Réjane: Souvenirs 1895-1920*, vol. 1 (Paris: Plon, 1951), 165-70.

28 Lenard R. Berlanstein, "Cultural Change and the Acting Conservatory in Late-Nineteenth-Century France," *The Historical Journal* 46 (2003): 583-97.

29 Diana Holmes and Carrie Tarr, eds., *A 'Belle Epoque'? Women in French Society and Culture, 1890-1914* (New York: Berghahn Books, 2006).

30 Madame Catulle Mendès, "La mode au théâtre," *Femina* (November 15, 1906): 57-58; Madame Catulle Mendès, "Robes de théâtre," *Femina* (October 15, 1908): 474-76; Robert Isébor, "Le théâtre du grand couturier," *Femina* (December 15, 1911): 679; Martin-Fugier, *Comédiennes*, 196-97.

31 See my analysis, "Selling Modern Femininity: *Femina*, a Forgotten Feminist Publishing Success in Belle Epoque France," *French Historical Studies* 30 (Fall 2007): 623-50.

32 Kenneth E. Silver, "Celebrity, Patriotism, and Sarah Bernhardt," in *Constructing Charisma: Celebrity, Fame, and Power in Nineteenth-Century Europe*, ed. Edward Berenson and Eva Giloi (New York: Berghahn Books, 2010), 145-54; Heather McPherson, "Sarah Bernhardt: Portrait of the Actress as Spectacle," *Nineteenth-Century Contexts* 20 (March 1999): 409-54; Mary-Louise Roberts, *Disruptive Acts: The New Woman in Fin-de-Siècle France* (Chicago: University of Chicago Press, 2002), ch. 6. The biographical literature on Bernhardt is vast but does not adequately explore her celebrity innovations.

33 Lenard R. Berlanstein, "Historicizing and Gendering Celebrity Culture: Famous Women in Nineteenth-Century France," *Journal of Women's History* 16 (Autumn 2004): 65-91; Mary-Louise Roberts, "Rethinking Female Celebrity: The Eccentric Stars of Nineteenth-Century France," in Berenson and Giloi, *Constructing Charisma*, 103-18. Roberts's essay brings out the large extent to which the behavior of actresses remained scandalous despite the changes of representation and perception, which are my focus.

34 Charles de Nérode, "Une heure chez Madame Jane Hading," *La revue illustrée* (May 1, 1893): 347-53.

35 On the limited progress of feminist ideas, see Susan K. Foley, *Women in France since 1789* (New York: Palgrave Macmillan, 2004), 103-52; Lenard R. Berlanstein, "Ready for Progress? Opinion Surveys on Women's Roles and Opportunities in Belle Epoque France," *French Politics, Society, and Culture* 27 (Spring 2009): 1-22; Florence Rochefort, "The French Feminist Movement and Republicanism, 1868-1914," in *Women's Emancipation Movements in Nineteenth-Century Europe: A European Perspective*, eds. Sylvia Paletshek and Bianca Pietrow-Ennker (Stanford CA: Stanford University Press, 2004), 77-101.

36 Roberts, *Disruptive Acts*, ch. 1. Roberts argues that during the Belle Epoque, the well-publicized lives of women in the theater and in the press disrupted gender orthodoxies by exposing their artificiality. For a case in point, see Robert's essay on the one-time actress and feminist journalist Marguerite Durand, "Acting Up: The Feminist Theatrics of Marguerite Durand,"

French Historical Studies 19 (Fall 1996): 1,103-38. It should be noted that most actresses avoided explicitly siding themselves with feminism but did allow the feminist-leaning press to appropriate their lives.

37 Dubeux, *Bartet*, 220-22. Venita Datta shows that the French public had become somewhat accustomed to women being portrayed as heroes in the press and theater of the fin-de-siècle in *Heroes and Legends of Fin-de-Siècle France: Gender, Politics, and National Identity* (Cambridge: Cambridge University Press, 2011), ch. 1, 4.

38 In this respect, see the memoirs of Lola Noyr, an actress who volunteered as a nurse, in Camille Clermont, *Souvenirs des parisennes en temps de guerre* (Paris: Berger-Levrault, 1918), 189-213. The most memorable intervention of actresses in the war effort was Sarah Bernhardt's acclaimed performance of the dramatic poem *Les Cathédrales* on November 6, 1915. For the significance, see Leonard V. Smith, Stéphanie Audoin-Rouzeau, and Annette Becker, *France and the Great War* (Cambridge: Cambridge University Press, 2003), 1-3.

2
Lucile and the
Theatricalization of Fashion
Sheila Stowell

During the 1890s, "Lucile" (1863-1935)—then known as Mrs. James Wallace—was one of a group of young English dressmakers determined to use the theater for marketing purposes.[1] Along with Mary Elizabeth Humble, Madame Eroom, and Mesdames Savage and Purdue, Lucile helped to transform the fashionable playhouses of London's West End into second showrooms, with leading ladies serving as living mannequins. Yet as her rivals, one by one, abandoned the stage after receiving the Drawing Room commissions that enabled them to call themselves "Court Dressmakers," Lucile, throughout her career, embraced both the theater and the notion of theatricality.[2] Indeed, her very first commission was based on a gown she had seen paraded on stage by actress Letty Lind, and her first "real opportunity," she tells us in her autobiography, came about as a result of gowns she designed for an amateur production of Victorien Sardou's *Diplomacy* in 1895. "I shocked a great many people, who brought against me the terrible indictment (in those days) of making 'stagey' clothes. I took it as a compliment."[3] Within a few years Lucile had become London's most notorious couturiere. Through the preceding half decade, she had championed an exuberant collection of "personality gowns," provocative creations in light fabric meant to harmonize with the characteristics of her clients. Lavishly trimmed and worked in a bold palette of scarlet, jade, viridian, and tyrian purple, they anticipated by two decades Léon Bakst's designs for the Ballets Russes. Introduced at court by the intrepid Mrs. Willy James, they formed the outer limit of what was permissible to wear in good society. By 1895 Lucile had taken commercial premises on Old Burlington Street, where she compounded her reputation for the risqué by providing a much-talked-of "Rose Room" for the marketing of scanty undergarments. Shown "by appointment only," Lucile's transparent nighties, lace undies, and chiffon petticoats were intended, in her words, to replace "the ugly nun's veiling or linen-cum-Swiss embroidery which was all that the really virtuous woman of those days permitted herself." Lucile notes both the initial shock and eventual acquiescence

FIG. 2.A Miss Irene Vanbrugh's dress in shades of yellow in *The Liars*,
Act I. Illustration from *The Sketch* (October 13, 1897). General Research
Division, The New York Public Library, Astor, Lenox and Tilden Foundations.

of her society patrons: "Those cunning little lace motifs let in just over
the heart, those saucy velvet bows on the shoulder might surely be the
weapons of the woman who was 'not quite nice'? They all wanted to
wear them, but they were not certain of their ground. They had to fly in
the face of the conventional idea as to how a good woman went to bed
at night—and it took a little coaxing for them to do it."[4]

In the summer of 1897, Lucile was engaged by actor manager
Charles Wyndham to design the principal gowns for Henry Arthur
Jones's society comedy *The Liars*. The commission included personal

FIG. 2.B Miss Mary Moore's dress of pink and silver tissue in *The Liars*, Act I. Illustration from *The Sketch* (October 13, 1897). General Research Division, The New York Public Library, Astor, Lenox and Tilden Foundations.

responsibility for the wardrobes of Mary Moore and Irene Vanbrugh. Lucile had been brought to Wyndham's attention by Moore, who had been impressed by Lucile's dramatic instinct and her willingness to subordinate her craft to larger concerns of text and production. She was, Moore tells us, "the first costumier to ask us to let her read the play, so that she might the better understand how to garb the different characters."[5] For Wyndham, at the Criterion (Piccadilly Circus), the collaboration had an additional advantage. Lucile's earlier stage work had been informed by the same flamboyant eroticism that had characterized her offstage garments. Indeed, her designs for *Diplomacy* had noticeably shocked her society audiences in both London and Edinburgh. In *The*

FIG. 2.C "Paraders of Dream Dresses Before the Four Hundred: Lady Duff-Gordon's Beautiful Mannequins," from *The Sketch* (March 30, 1910). General Research Division, The New York Public Library, Astor, Lenox and Tilden Foundations.

Liars such smart wickedness would be used to argue, through the language of clothes, the moral bankruptcy of the play's gilded society. Not only did Lucile dress all five of the play's women in revealing combinations of lace, net, and chiffon, but she also capitalized on her reputation for chic impropriety by stripping bodices of their linings, an unheard-of move that enabled playgoers to see clear through her costumes to their flesh-colored corset covers. Irene Vanbrugh refused outright to wear one especially clinging gown of buttercup yellow until Lucile convinced her that her own fine figure might itself be a marketable asset (fig. 2.A). Mary Moore's Act I outfit, worn while Lady Jessica carries on a potentially adulterous flirtation, consisted of little more than an appliqué of lace and sequins on an undergarment of flesh-colored chiffon. The device was clearly meant to look "naughty" from the stalls and gallery (fig. 2.B). The critic for *Modern Society* noted the manner in which light played upon the sequins of Moore's overgown and seemed to pick out what he slyly calls "a tracery of deeper pink."[6] It was a strategy calculated to attract the more adventurous members of society, which it did, helping to create a vogue that would itself become the fashion to be followed in the last years of Queen Victoria's reign (1837-1901).

Having drawn on the power of the stage to display clothes, Lucile went on to employ specifically theatrical devices to market them in her showroom. However, her broadest claim, which was to have invented the mannequin, or live fashion model, is a blatant piece of self-puffery. Madame Worth (Marie Vernet), usually cited as the first professional model, regularly launched her husband's designs and then seasonal lines in Paris beginning in the mid-1850s.[7] Yet Lucile's point is well taken. In an age when many fashion houses still displayed gowns draped over wooden figures or propped up on chairs and stuffed with tissue paper, Lucile had aligned herself with a group of designers, including Jeanne Paquin and Paul Poiret, who insisted on the persuasiveness of fabric in motion. Indeed, Lucile drew on her stage experience and took the concept one step further, harping on the erotic possibilities of such exhibits. Her mannequins abjured the undergarments of "rigid black satin, reaching from chin to feet" conventionally worn by couture house models, nor were they shod in "unappetizing laced boots." Such devices merely perpetuated a Victorian reticence at odds with Lucile's determination to harness the trade aspects of sexual temptation. In fact, Lucile recruited and trained her own corps of "glorious goddess-like girls" drawn largely from the working-class suburbs of East and South London. Selected for the kind of full-breasted, long-limbed figures Lucile would help to make popular, each was drilled in carriage and deportment before being given a sonorous stage name like Hebe, Gamela, or Dolores (fig. 2.c). Although one detractor likened Lucile's amazons "mincing about in their turbans and trailing trains" to "impertinent lobsters," they were widely admired by the Edwardian fashion press, which used them to proclaim the arrival of a new English glamour. By the decade's close, many would be celebrities in their own right, the first supermodels of an emerging couture house industry.

In or about 1900, Lucile's drive to theatricalize fashion marketing was made literal with the building of a ramp and curtained recess at one end of her showroom in Hanover Square. Here, picked out by limelight and accompanied by soft music, the most accomplished of her mannequins introduced gowns to small groups of invited clients (fig. 2.D). The resulting mannequin parades, forerunners of the contemporary fashion show, were innovations of which Lucile could justifiably boast. Rival houses advertised similar events, but as often as not these were attempts to replicate on a showroom floor the ambience of a society gathering. Lucile's displays, in sharp contrast, used the paraphernalia of stage representation—ramp, curtains, wings, limelight, and music—to establish a voyeuristic bond between mannequin and

FIG. 2.D A private showing at Lucile Ltd.'s Paris store, after 1911. © Victoria & Albert Museum, London.

spectator. The process was intended to draw a mixed audience of male and female viewers, the former lured to Lucile's premises by the prospect of inspecting flesh as well as fabric. This in itself was unusual. As late as 1908 public displays of women's clothing, such as the *Earl's Court Dress Exhibition* of that year, specifically excluded men from their more intimate tableaux. Lucile, however, encouraged male attendance, using such terms as "model" and "gown" to refer simultaneously to her mannequins and their garments. The complex eroticism of her spectacles—working-class women dressed as society ladies promenading silently before audiences of middle- and upper-class men—was further augmented by Lucile's decision to replace the numbers by which gowns had hitherto been identified with suggestive titles like "Passion's Thrall" and "A Frenzied Song of Amorous Things" (fig. 2.E).

Beginning with a series of simple walk-abouts called collectively "Gowns of Emotion," such displays soon took the form of thematic pageants. The most elaborate had texts prepared by Lucile's sister, the society novelist Elinor Glyn. The series culminated in 1909, after Lucile's return from North America, with the ambitious *Seven Ages of Woman*, a stage piece in seven acts tracing from birth to death the

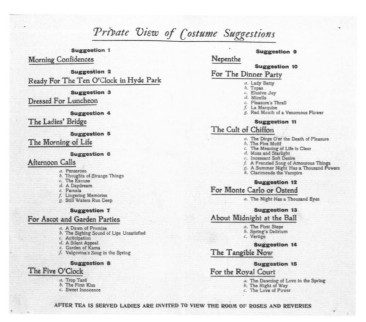

FIG. 2.E Lucile Ltd. Program of "Private View of Costume Suggestions" (April 28, 1904). © Victoria & Albert Museum, London.

dress-cycle of a society dame. Playing to an audience that included Queen Marie of Romania, the Queen of Spain, and Princess Patricia of Connaught, Lucile began with "The Schoolgirl" and progressed, in turn, through "The Debutante," "The Fiancée," "The Bride," "The Wife," "The Hostess," and "The Dowager." The most developed episode, which reflected Lucile's business sense as well as her calculated sensuality, was "The Hostess," a succession of four scenes and three tableaux whose subtext was unmistakable: "The Desire of the Eyes" led to "Persuasive Delight," which was in turn followed by "A Frenzied Hour," "Salut d'Amour," "Afterwards," and "Contentment."

The full hothouse effect of Lucile's mannequin parades—at least as they appeared to unsympathetic eyes—is preserved in Marie Corelli's *Bystander* column of July 27, 1904. Although neither Lucile nor Elinor Glyn is mentioned by name, Corelli's sub-acid account of a "fashion symposium" held under the joint auspices of "Madame la Modiste" and her novelist sister left few readers in the dark:

> A stage was erected at one end of a long room, and on that stage, with effective lashes of limelight played from the "wings" at intervals and the accompaniment of a Hungarian band, young

FIG. 2.F Lucile Ltd. Sketch number 28, labeled both "Red Mouth of a Venomous Flower" (below) and "In Pleasures Thrall." © Victoria & Albert Museum, London.

ladies wearing "creations" in costume, stood, sat, turned, twisted and twirled, and finally walked down the room between rows of spectators to show themselves, and the gowns they carried, to the best possible advantage. The whole thing was much better than a stage comedy. Nothing could surpass the quaint peacock-like vanity of the girl mannequins who strutted up and down, moving their hips to accentuate the fall and flow of flounces and draperies.[8]

Among gowns catalogued in Glyn's program we find "Elusive Joy,"
"Incessant Soft Desire," and the sensationally titled "Red Mouth of
a Venomous Flower"—the last, as it turned out, "a harmless-looking
girl in a bright scarlet toilette" (fig. 2.F). Corelli's most telling comments, however, were reserved for the show's reception. Surprised at
both the number and type of male viewers who had elbowed their way
into Lucile's salon for the occasion, she transcribed a range of responses
that made clear what, in fact, was being sold:

> Curious to relate, there were quite a large number of "gentlemen"
> at this remarkable exhibition of feminine clothes, many of them
> well-known and easily recognisable. Certain flaneurs of Bond
> Street, various loafers familiar to the Carlton lounge, and cele-
> brated Piccadilly-trotters, formed nearly one half of the audience,
> and stared with easy insolence at the "Red Mouth of a Venomous
> Flower" or smiled suggestively at "Incessant Soft Desire." They
> were invited to stare and smile, and they did. But there was some-
> thing remarkably offensive in their way of doing it.[9]

Corelli's parting suggestion, that such voyeurs might profitably have
the "smoothness" kicked out of them by "a few thick boots worn on the
feet of rough but honest workmen," hints none too subtly, at the class
and gender antagonisms upon which such showmanship had been built.
   Lucile's marriage in May 1900 to Sir Cosmo Duff Gordon, who
had been a principal backer of her fashion business since 1895, affected
the fortunes of both London's West End theater and its dressmaking
trade. As Lady Duff Gordon, England's first titled *modiste*, Lucile could
approach society patrons on equal footing. At the same time, her mint-
new status encouraged a special relationship with the era's "Dollar
Princesses," American heiresses fast marrying into Mayfair's power
elite.[10] It was for this market that Lucile championed the S-bend corset
with its mono-bosom silhouette, and, after 1908, following the lead of
Parisian counterpart Paul Poiret, a Directoire revival—sheath dresses,
cutaway jackets, and outsized hats—whose re-inscription of the female
form is best summed up by Poiret's boast to have "freed the bust but ...
shackled the legs."[11] On stage Lucile exploited both looks in a string
of commissions executed for the most opulent of Edwardian pleasure
palaces, the Vaudeville and the refurbished Gaiety Theatre. Using the
homes of Britain's musical comedy much as she had used Charles
Wyndham's Criterion in the 1890s, Lucile completed her construction
of turn-of-the-century womanhood by dressing a succession of show-

Private View

FRIDAY SEPTEMBER **2**ND AT **5** P.M.

AT

LA SALLE LUCILE

23 Hanover Square London W.

OF

Costumes

All Designed Personally By Lucile
And Made In London By Lucile Ltd.
To Be Worn In

"The Catch of the Season"

A New Musical Play

By SEYMOUR HICKS and COSMO HAMILTON

Lyrics by CHARLES TAYLOR

Music by H. E. HAINES and EVELYN BAKER

Under the Management of

A. and S. GATTI and CHARLES FROHMAN

First production Wednesday Evening Sept. 7th
at the
VAUDEVILLE THEATRE

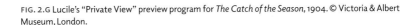

FIG. 2.G Lucile's "Private View" preview program for *The Catch of the Season*, 1904. © Victoria & Albert Museum, London.

Photo. Foulsham and Banfield

MISS LILY ELSIE as Sonia (The Merry Widow)

88

FIG. 2.H Lily Elsie from Act I of *The Merry Widow*, photograph by Foulsham & Banfield (English, 1906–20), published in *The Play Pictorial* 61 (August 1907): 88. Private collection.

girls for impresarios Seymour Hicks and George Edwardes. In 1904 *The Catch of the Season* (Vaudeville)—a Cinderella piece about a young lady who marries well on the strength of her wardrobe and figure—took London by storm. Lucile had been asked to design the dresses and managed to turn the commission into an advertising coup. A few days before the play opened, its "emotional gowns" were previewed in a private fashion parade at her show room in Hanover Square.[12] Invitations were sent out and advance copies of the play's program featuring Lucile's distinctive trademark distributed to prospective clients (fig. 2.G). Throughout her career, Lucile proclaimed and celebrated such links with actresses and the stage and the enhanced sales opportunities they afforded her. Although it is possible that some more conservative members of society may have withheld patronage, it is obvious that for Lucile such marketing advantages far outweighed any potential losses. In fact, in attendance at the *Catch of the Season* fashion show was the Countess of Somers, for whose great niece Lucile would produce a copy of the "demure little dress" she had designed for Zena Dare, the ingénue of the musical. When the countess first balked at the price, Lucile assured her—in a confidant assertion of Wilde's quip about life in the end imitating art—that the gown would catch a rich husband. Which, she goes on to assure us, it did.

The pinnacle of Lucile's Edwardian career was reached with George Edwardes's production of *The Merry Widow* in 1907. The title role was to be taken by the then relatively unknown Lily Elsie, whom Edwardes felt had the potential to "astonish" audiences, but who needed to be given "coaching" and "a personality." Elsie was entrusted to Lucile for both. Taken back to Hanover Square, Elsie, like the mannequins before her, was stripped to her undergarments and effectively rebuilt. Lucile carefully studied her posture, the manner in which she held her head, and her ability to stand absolutely still. Before her costumes were fitted, she was given a new complexion and coiffure and trained to walk with an elegant Gibson Girl glide. "There was not a movement across the stage," Lucile later recalled, "not a single gesture of her part . . . that we did not go through together."[13] In performance such comportment was complemented by a stunning wardrobe that included an Act I gown of silver and gold embroidery over oyster white satin that one critic likened to "woven sunshine" (fig. 2.H). In Act III Elsie appeared in a clinging white chiffon Empire gown worn over the palest pink satin. The outfit included a rose satin coat trimmed with black and gold and was topped with what would become the production's iconic, and best-selling, "Merry Widow hat"—black

DANILO, HEARING THAT A SECOND MARRIAGE WILL LOSE SONIA HER FORTUNE, WHISPERS
WHAT HE HAS VOWED NOT TO SAY, AND IS ACCEPTED

Photo: Foulsham and Banfield

MR. JOSEPH COYNE (Prince Danilo)   MISS LILY ELSIE (Sonia)

Sonia explains that *she* loses her fortune and her husband gets it!

FIG. 2.1 Lily Elsie and Joseph Coyne from Act III of *The Merry Widow*, photograph by Foulsham & Banfield published in *The Play Pictorial* 61 (August 1907): 108. Private collection.

FIG. 2.J *Fleurette's Dream*, 1917. © Victoria & Albert Museum, London.

with an immense brim and sporting bird-of-paradise plumes (fig. 2.I).
After the sensational reception of *The Merry Widow*, Lucile's position
as London's first dressmaker of international stature was assured.
And Elsie became, in effect, the most formidable of her advertisements.
"From that day," Lucile wrote, "I designed all her clothes for her *both*
for the stage and in private life, and some of my most successful
models were created for her, for once she had 'found herself' she wore
her clothes so charmingly that every woman who saw them wanted
to have them copied."[14]

Indeed, in many ways Lucile's collaborations with Lily Elsie and
George Edwardes form the high-water mark of her attempts to fuse
theater, fashion, and merchandising. She continued to design for the
stage, but as her "brand" became international, with houses established
in Paris and New York, her relationship to the theater shifted. During
World War I, when she was residing in the United States, Lucile produced *Fleurette's Dream*, a *tableau vivant* designed to raise money for
the war effort (fig. 2.J). Originally envisioned for a single performance,
it showed the wretched Fleurette, represented by mannequin Phyllis
Francatelli amid the ruins of a French market town. With a breath-

FIG. 2.K Rose gown from Ziegfeld's *Flower Pageant* of 1917. © Victoria & Albert Museum, London.

taking lack of irony, Lucile has her protagonist, in reveries of happier times, selecting frocks for a variety of society occasions—attending a dance, hosting a party, going to the couturieres. The final scene returns Fleurette to the cellar in which she has been hiding, with enemy shells falling overhead. Although this was seemingly a perfect format to showcase her designs, Lucile determined, somewhat surprisingly, "not [to] try to sell my models" but to devise "a production to please myself."[15] Picked up for a vaudeville tour of North America, it succeeded in functioning as "an entertainment" in its own right, "in no sense a fashion show [but] . . . a series of exquisite pictures and imaginative conceptions."[16] Florenz Ziegfeld, then married to actress (and Lucile customer) Billie Burke, saw the show at New York's Little

Theatre. He was so taken by the experience that he decided to employ some of its mannequins in his current review. What followed was the engagement of Lucile herself as principal designer for six successive Ziegfeld Follies, and, according to Lucile's biographer, Meredith Etherington-Smith, the emergence of the Showgirl—the non-singing, non-dancing, non-talking clotheshorse. The journey that had started with the progressive drama of the late Victorians, and then moved to the musical comedies of the Edwardians, reached its climax in the silent spectacles of the war and postwar years. Neither the fantastical flower gowns of Ziegfeld's *Flower Pageant* of 1917—mannequins appearing as outsized lilies, marguerites, and roses (fig. 2.K)—nor the exotic Egyptian, Chinese, or pseudo-classical ensembles Lucile designed for his other entertainments, had direct commercial possibilities. It was rather the spectacle itself that was to be consumed. A career that had begun by using the stage for both inspiration and advertisement concluded, appropriately enough, with the theatricalized fashion show becoming its own raison d'être.

1 This essay draws upon material that first appeared in *Theatre and Fashion: Oscar Wilde to the Suffragettes* (Cambridge: Cambridge University Press, 1994), which I co-authored with Joel Kaplan.

2 Lucile (Mrs. James Wallace) received her first commission for a gown to be worn at a Drawing Room presentation to the queen in 1894. This is indicated by a marginal cross in that year's edition of Kelly's annual *Trades and Court Directories*. For further information about "Lucile" and her influence, see her (often unreliable) autobiography, Lady Duff Gordon, *Discretions and Indiscretions* (New York, Frederick A. Stokes, 1932); Meredith Etherington-Smith and Jeremy Pilchard, *The It Girls* (London, Hamish Hamilton, 1986); and Valerie D. Mendes and Amy de la Haye, *Lucile Ltd.* (London: V & A Publishing, 2009). I would like to thank Gill Disley and the staff of the Lucile Archive at the Victoria and Albert Museum for their assistance in the preparation of this essay.

3 Duff Gordon, *Discretions and Indiscretions*, 65.

4 Ibid., 41-43.

5 Mary Moore, *Charles Wyndham and Mary Moore* (Edinburgh: Privately printed, 1925), 242.

6 *Modern Society* (October 16, 1897): 1558-59.

7 Charles Frederick Worth, often called the father of haute couture, dominated the international fashion world through for the last half of the 19th century. From his Parisian House of Worth, Europe's first "man-milliner" reshaped the look as well as the methods of luxury dressmaking; see Diana de Marly, *Worth: Father of Haute Couture* (London: Elm Tree, 1980), and Edith Saunders, *The Age of Worth* (London: Longmans, 1954).

8 *The Bystander* (July 27, 1904):437-38.

9 Ibid.

10 Indeed, Lucile's title seems to have especially impressed Americans, initially in the United Kingdom, but eventually and more particularly after the establishment of her New York outlet.

11 Paul Poiret, *My First Fifty Years*, trans. Stephen Haden Guest (London: Victor Gollancz, 1931), 73.

12 *The Daily Mail*, September 10, 1904.

13 Duff Gordon, 109.

14 Ibid., 103.

15 Ibid., 234.

16 Ibid., 244.

Stylish Effervescence:
Billie Burke and the Rise of the Fashionable Broadway Star
Marlis Schweitzer

In her 1959 memoirs, *With Powder on My Nose,* Billie Burke admitted that she owed her early success on Broadway to factors other than talent.[1] "I was amusing onstage," she wrote, "because I had delightful costumes, because I had witty lines to say, written by the wittiest authors, and because I worked."[2] Better known today for her portrayal of Glinda the Good Witch in *The Wizard of Oz* (1939) and her marriage to legendary *Ziegfeld Follies* producer Florenz Ziegfeld, Burke was a Broadway star long before her 1914 wedding, celebrated for her "saucy and piquantly sophisticated youth and prettiness."[3]

Although few of Burke's stage hits were praised for their aesthetic merit, they were ideal vehicles for displaying her bubbly personality and elegant stage costumes. "She has comeliness, girlishness and sprightliness, but perhaps the chief trait of her personal charm is wholesomeness," one critic rhapsodized in January 1908.[4] Even the sardonic critic Alan Dale could not resist her perky cuteness. Playfully noting that "there are fashions in actresses just as marked as the styles of the clothes they wear," he credited Burke with setting the fashion for 1908, that of "the saucy little ingénue, whose apparent mission in stage life is to be 'cute.'" Unlike Olga Nethersole and other stars who played dark, brooding women with complicated sexual histories, Burke's girlish charm made "stage girlhood possible." Dale anticipated that with Burke as inspiration, Broadway managers would soon turn away from psycho-sexual dramas to cater more directly to a "young and frolicsome public."[5] He was right. Burke's youthful effervescence, expressed onstage through her characters and offstage in interviews, public appearances, and advertisements, drew thousands of matinee girls to her plays. Many of these fans modeled their own performances of modern American "girlishness" on her costumes, hairstyle, and beautifying practices. In what follows, I describe the role of fashion in Burke's rise to celebrity status, emphasizing the work involved in the creation of her appealing public image.

FIG. 3.A Billie Burke, ca. 1904, after scoring her first major success in *The School Girl*. Her photos were incredibly popular and appeared in studio display windows alongside those of the queen. "Transatlantic Girls in a Musical Comedy—Miss Billie" Scrapbook clipping. Billy Rose Theatre Division, The New York Public Library for the Performing Arts, Astor, Lenox and Tilden Foundations.

A STAR IS BORN

As the daughter of a clown, Billie Burke spent her teen years "trouping" throughout Europe with her parents, yet she claims that she "was never stage-struck."[6] Her mother had other ideas, however, and enrolled her daughter in singing, elocution, and ballet classes, determined to make her a star. After a less than successful music hall debut at age fourteen, Burke made her foray into the world of musical comedy and drama. Her first major success came in 1903 in George Edwardes's and Charles Frohman's London production of *The School Girl* (fig. 3.A). Although her part was small, her performance of "Mamie, I Have a Little Canoe," sung while she and three other chorus girls paddled a canoe, stole the show and made her a celebrity. Nicknamed "The American Flapper," a name she attributes to the way her "red hair flapped" when she performed, she soon became a favorite subject for theatrical photographers, who displayed her pictures in show windows alongside Lady Randolph Churchill and Queen Alexandra of Denmark, the stylish wife of Edward VII.[7]

Burke crossed over from musical comedy into "legitimate" drama in the 1906 production of *Mr. George*, as leading lady to Charles Hawtrey. Hawtrey had recognized her potential for comedy and devoted many hours instructing her in the finer points of delivery, gesture, and comportment.[8] Burke's success in *Mr. George* caught the attention of the American impresario Charles Frohman, one of the world's most influential theater managers. Always on the lookout for new talent, he offered Burke a role in the upcoming New York production of *My Wife*, a star vehicle for John Drew. Burke agreed and thus began the professional relationship that would transform her from an ingenue into a Broadway headliner.[9]

Charles Frohman's biographers note that his particular talent as a manager was the ability to amplify his performers' most appealing characteristics by selecting plays that best revealed their personalities.[10] A businessman first and foremost, Frohman used the latest developments in commercial advertising—from newspapers and magazines to electric lighting—to transform his actors and actresses into desirable commodities. Although critics railed against the emergence of a standardized star system that rewarded those with attractive personalities over those with talent, Frohman insisted that his primary concern was meeting the public's desire for fun and lively role models.[11] "I was a new kind of actress, carefree and red-headed, and I had beautiful clothes," Burke explained matter-of-factly in her memoirs, and Frohman found plays that allowed her to be herself onstage, only magnified.[12] After her success in *My Wife*, Frohman promoted her to full-fledged stardom the following season with *Love Watches*, a contemporary comedy about a couple's first year of marriage.[13] Burke would remain a Frohman star for seven more seasons until her marriage to Ziegfeld and Frohman's untimely demise aboard the *Lusitania* brought their partnership to an end.

PERFECTING THE LOOK

Like many of her contemporaries, Billie Burke knew that acquiring a fashionable wardrobe was one of the most significant barriers to entry for young actresses hoping to make their way onto the Broadway stage. "Clothes impress the managers," she observed in a 1909 article, "and for this reason most actresses wear their best bib and tucker when they go to the manager to talk about an engagement."[14] Prior to the 1919 Actor's Equity Strike, which resulted in the formalization of managerial responsibilities for costuming, among other things, most actresses were expected to purchase their own contemporary costumes with little if any managerial support; as a result, getting the gowns for a particular role was often more challenging than landing the role itself.[15] And with so many eager young women vying for very few jobs, managers often privileged those who demonstrated that they had style and the money to purchase elegant stage gowns.[16]

Billie Burke was one of the fortunate ones. As an actress in Charles Frohman's employ, she enjoyed both the financial support and the aesthetic freedom to select her stage wardrobe. In the mid-1890s Frohman had decided to forego the standard practice of paying *only* for actresses' historical costumes and to pay for contemporary costumes as well. Free to purchase "handsomer dresses than [they] could otherwise afford" from leading couturiers in New York, London, and Paris, Frohman's actresses transformed his productions into sparkling fashion spectacles that attracted the social elite and a cadre of dressmakers.[17] By 1901 Frohman could boast that "society is about five months behind the stage in the correctness of its apparel."[18]

As a Frohman star, Burke recognized the importance of perfecting a fashionable appearance, and she spent numerous hours consulting with dressmakers and milliners over all aspects of costuming. Like fellow Frohman star Ethel Barrymore, she enlisted the services of Madame Hayward, a London dressmaker with a talent for predicting the latest Parisian trends. After visiting the Paris salons each season, Hayward "would return to London and design new frocks for me," Burke recalled. "I would appear in New York with all my things at least a season ahead of the style in America."[19] As these comments suggest, the time lag between the introduction of new fashions in Paris and their eventual arrival in the United States heightened the importance of actresses as fashion arbiters, turning Broadway into a "school of fashion," where women learned how, where, and when to wear the latest styles.[20]

Well aware that she owed her popularity to her stylish appearance, Burke updated her gowns, gloves, and hats on a regular basis, even when the originals were still in serviceable condition.[21] For her performance in *My Wife*, she purchased dozens of pairs of white kid gloves, insisting that "they have to be pure white or I don't feel fresh."[22] In 1910 she infuriated Frohman's business manager, Alf Hayman, by ordering a completely new stage wardrobe from the New York department store Lord & Taylor and the Lichtenstein Millinery Company "without consultation" partway through the run of *Mrs. Dot*.[23] The original estimate for the gowns was $800, but when the final invoices arrived, the total exceeded $1,200, much to Hayman's horror. When he wrote to his boss to complain about the exorbitant cost of the gowns, accusing Lichtenstein of being "the biggest robbers in the world," Frohman calmly responded that he should pay the bills.[24]

Burke's unrelenting quest for a fashionable appearance extended beyond stores such as Lord & Taylor and the Lichtenstein Millinery Company to her own body. Attentive to new developments in physical culture and the growing emphasis on maintaining a thin, lean figure, Burke embraced a regular exercise regime.[25] In addition to undertaking long walks and working out with "Indian clubs" and a barbell, she adopted some rather unconventional practices, including a wake-up routine involving somersaults and standing on her head.[26] In contrast to many of the fuller-figured actresses who had dominated Broadway in the 1890s and early 1900s, Burke's lithe, slim form represented a distinctly modern ideal.

BILLIE BURKE'S PERSONAL STYLE AND FASHION PHILOSOPHY

Simplicity and elegance, combined with youthfulness and a certain insouciant playfulness, defined Billie Burke's style for much of her career. Commenting on her costumes in *My Wife*, a fashion writer for the *Harrisburg Telegraph* waxed enthusiastic over the way her gray crepe-de-chine gown, with a "simple long, circular skirt . . . outline[d] the curves of her graceful young figure (fig. 3.B)."[27] This gown, which anticipated Paris designer Paul Poiret's radical reintroduction of the lean Directoire silhouette by several months,[28] distinguished Burke from her theatrical rivals and quickly made her a favorite among New York dressmakers and matinee girls. "I always like to see Billie Burke's gowns as I get such good ideas for debutante frocks," one dressmaker commented in 1909.[29] In fact, many society women sent their dressmakers to the theater for the express purpose of copying Burke's gowns. By 1909 fashion columnist for *Woman Beautiful* observed that "copies of [Burke's] stage gowns are constantly appearing at exclusive functions." Some matinee girls went so far as to imitate every detail of her "second act" gown for *Love Watches*, "even to the ermine stole, shape of muff and style and coloring of the hat."[30] More than seeing Burke as a

MISS BILLIE BURKE
JOHN DREW'S LEADING LADY THIS SEASON IN "MY WIFE"
PHOTOGRAPH BY OTTO SARONY CO. N.Y.

COLOR SUPPLEMENT
FROM THE MAY 1908 ISSUE OF
THE BLUE BOOK MAGAZINE

FIG. 3.B A portrait of Billie Burke wearing the much-discussed *My Wife* gown designed by Madame Hayward. While on tour, Burke and her mother visited department stores where knock-off versions of the gown were sold. The photograph appeared in *The Blue Book Magazine* (May 1908). Scrapbook clipping. Billy Rose Theatre Division, The New York Public Library for the Performing Arts, Astor, Lenox and Tilden Foundations.

FIG. 3.C Some matinee girls copied every detail of this attractive ensemble from *Love Watches*, including the stole, muff, and hat. Scrapbook clipping. Billy Rose Theatre Division, The New York Public Library for the Performing Arts, Astor, Lenox and Tilden Foundations.

model for their own self-creations, these girls reproduced themselves in her image, furthering her fame, popularity, and influence through devoted mimicry (fig. 3.c).

Fashion-obsessed matinee girls also inundated Burke with questions about style and beauty in letters sent to her dressing room. "Tell me how I can have as fine a back as yours?" one girl asked, referring to the elegant fall of her gowns. "See that the back of your gown fits and trim it, but don't over trim it," Burke advised, stressing the need for simplicity. "The most beautiful line in a woman's figure is that from shoulder to waist. I am always careful of that line in my gowns. It should be long, flat, and unbroken."[31] Self-aware and attentive to detail, Burke perfected a style that suited her body and personality, and she encouraged others to do likewise.

In an effort to capitalize on her loyal fan following, department stores and consumer goods manufacturers sold Billie Burke-inspired clothing, accessories, and beauty products. "Have you a 'Billie Burke'?" the *New York Telegraph* quizzed readers in November 1907, referencing the "stunning sartorial creations" worn by the actress in *My Wife*. "If not your wardrobe is neither complete nor classy.... There is such a craze for them that the proprietors of all the swell gown emporiums say it is impossible to supply the popular demand."[32] Burke recalled that, while she was on tour later that season, many of the department stores she visited with her mother sold Billie Burke curls and dresses with "flat lace collars and lace," a variation on the actress's "artistic last-act gown."[33] Billie Burke was suddenly everywhere—onstage, in department stores, in newspapers, and in magazines.[34]

In addition to setting trends in fashion, actresses like Burke encouraged women to adopt new beautifying habits. Indeed, as I have argued elsewhere, early twentieth-century actresses played an instrumental role in the expansion of the American cosmetics industry by demonstrating how women might use products such as cold cream to enhance their "natural" beauty without transforming it in an artificial way.[35] Although most early twentieth-century actresses refused to admit to using "artificial" beauty products for anything but their stage appearance—wary of lingering associations with prostitutes and other "painted women"—cold cream was something different.[36] In a June 1911 article in *The Delineator*, a leading women's magazine, Burke offered readers suggestions for how to select and apply cold cream as part of their regular beauty regimen. Four months later, she joined nine other prominent actresses and opera divas in an advertisement for *Créme Nerol* (the incorrect accent appears in the original), a new cold cream, published in *Vogue* magazine.[37] "I have used your CREME NEROL and appreciate its rare qualities," Burke claimed in a testimonial statement printed beside her photograph and signature, proof that Forrest D. Pullen, maker of *Créme Nerol*, had secured her official endorsement.[38]

With her reputation as one of the "most fashionable women on Fifth Avenue" firmly established, Burke was called upon by fashion editors to share fashion tips and her personal "philosophy of dress" with their readers. In 1913 she was one of a select group of celebrated actresses chosen as a guest "Fashion Editor" for an issue of *Ladies' Home Journal*. Articles illustrated by ample photographs of Burke in her stage gowns also appeared in *The Delineator*, *Vogue*, and *Harper's Bazar*, as well as in dozens of newspapers across North America. Like many of her peers, Burke used these articles to encourage women to find a personal style that accentuated their best features and challenge accepted fashion truisms. For example, while stressing that "suitability or appropriateness should be the first word in selecting a costume," she also promoted the more radical view that, in matters of color, women should make decisions based on eye color rather than hair color. "My London dressmaker [Madame Hayward] taught me that," she explained to the readers of *Human Life*, lending an air of authority and privilege to her statement. "A red-haired girl can wear almost any color except a dull shade of brown."[39]

Burke offered convincing evidence of her color theory in the costumes she selected (presumably with Madame Hayward's assistance) for *Love Watches* in 1909 (fig. 3.D). Rejecting conventional wisdom, she appeared in "a stunning pink satin gown" in the last act, accented by two "brilliant red roses," one in her corsage, the other in her hair. *The Theatre's* fashion columnist applauded this "bit of audacity" and urged other "Titian-haired women" to avoid the "poor overworked blue" that many believed was the only suitable color they could wear and to experiment more freely with other shades.[40] "[A] beautiful woman can look lovely in any combination of colors," the *New York Star* concurred, "if she knows how to artistically combine them."[41]

In addition to urging women to play with a more varied color palate, Burke emphasized the relationship between color and emotion, joining many of her contemporaries in exploring fashion's communicative potential. "One of the fine arts in stage dressing is to adapt your costume, or rather the color of it, to the character or emotion that you are called upon to interpret," she instructed the readers of *The Saturday Evening Post* in 1909. "Black is always the color of suffering. It is the appeal of the waif, the wronged wife, or the persecuted person gener-

FIG. 3.D In *Love Watches*, Billie Burke defied conventional wisdom about the kinds of colors that were appropriate for red-haired women by wearing a pink satin gown accented by two prominently placed red roses. From *Vogue* (December 1908). Scrapbook clipping. Billy Rose Theatre Division, The New York Public Library for the Performing Arts, Astor, Lenox and Tilden Foundations.

ally. Red denotes animation; brown, reserve."[42] Incorporating aspects of modern color theory, which attributed different emotional responses to variations in color wavelength, Burke presented herself as a distinctly modern actress, well versed in the psychological aspects of clothing.[43]

One of Burke's most memorable and *colorful* costumes was the pair of pink pajamas she wore for the third act of *Jerry*, a lively 1914 comedy tailor-made to suit her bubbly personality with ample opportunity for costume changes (fig. 3.E).[44] Although she received mixed reviews for her performance of the "spoiled" and tomboyish

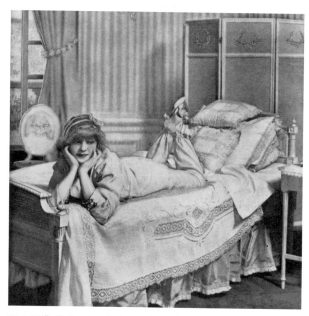

FIG. 3.E Billie Burke as Jerry in the naughty pink pajamas. Although Burke was hardly the first actress to appear onstage in pajamas, she still raised many eyebrows with the carefree way she flounced about the stage in the provocative nightwear. Scrapbook clipping. Billy Rose Theatre Division, The New York Public Library for the Performing Arts, Astor, Lenox and Tilden Foundations.

Philadelphia society girl, few could deny the pleasure of seeing the actress bound about the stage on, over, and into a large bed dressed in pajamas and a pair of heeled slippers. "She flounced into bed and out of bed with that wriggling agility that none can mistake to be characteristically billy-burkian," joked the *New York World*.[45] Burke was not the first actress to appear onstage in pajamas—that honor apparently belongs to fellow Frohman protégée Pauline Chase, who scandalized American audiences when she appeared in a clinging pair of pink pajamas in *The Liberty Belles* (1901)[46]—yet her trendsetter status cast a new light on the playfully risqué apparel and further extended her celebrity; photographs of the actress in her pajamas appeared in newspapers as far away as Tacoma, Washington, and Paris, Kentucky (fig. 3.F).[47]

But breaking news of Burke's surprise marriage to Florenz Ziegfeld on April 11, 1914, quickly usurped stories about flashy pink pajamas. Fully embracing Jerry's rebellious spirit, Burke had defied Frohman's pleas to put off marriage to a man he viewed as a hopeless womanizer and married Ziegfeld in secret between her matinee and evening performances. Although she fulfilled her contract and led a

FIG. 3.F A publicity photograph of Burke in her scandalous *Jerry* pajamas. Note the design detailing on the sleeve cuffs and gathered pajama bottoms. The date on the back of the photograph is April 16, 1914, five days after Burke's secret marriage to Florenz Ziegfeld. Photograph copyrighted by Charles Frohman. Private collection. Cat. 125.

successful road tour of *Jerry*, she had now become Ziegfeld's girl. Indeed, it is no surprise that the actress who epitomized American girlhood should choose for her husband the man celebrated for "Glorifying the American Girl."[48] She never saw Frohman again.

Billie Burke maintained her stylish reputation long after her marriage to Ziegfeld, benefiting from her husband's unique promotional talents and the creative designs of Lucile, Lady Duff Gordon, the controversial British dressmaker who relocated to New York in the 1910s.[49] But Burke's new responsibilities as wife and mother and her interest in a motion-picture career soon took her away from Broadway and the matinee girls who had made her their fashion idol. Something of her early sparkle nonetheless remains in the hundreds, if not thousands, of postcards, photographs, and advertisements that circulate today on eBay and fan sites. In these images she is forever young, forever stylish, forever "bill[ie]-burkian."

1   I owe special thanks to my research assistant, Rebecca Halliday, for helping to track down sources on Burke's early career, and to Michele Majer for inviting me to write this essay.

2   Billie Burke (with Cameron Shipp), *With Powder on My Nose* (New York: Coward-McCann, Inc., 1959), 18.

3   Walter Prichard Eaton, "Personality and the Player: The Matter of Individual Charm and Technical Efficiency," *Collier's* (October 22, 1910): 17, 34.

4   "Billy [*sic*] Burke a Real Star," Image ID: V86_047, Billie Burke Scrapbooks, Part V, Robinson Locke Collection, The New York Public Library for the Performing Arts/Billy Rose Theatre Division [hereafter RLC], http://digitalgallery.nypl.org/nypldigital/dgkeysearchresult. cfm?trg=1&parent_id=668001&word=&s=&notword=&d=&c=&f=&k=0&sScope=&sLevel=& sLabel=&lword=&lfield=&num=40&imgs=20&snum=&pNum= accessed May 24, 2011.

5   "The Actress Who Is Cute Will Be the Season's Style," *Los Angeles Sunday Examiner*, September 27, 1908, Image ID: V86_080, RLC, http://digitalgallery.nypl.org/nypldigital/dgkeysearchresult.cfm?num=60&parent_id=668001&word=&snum=&s=&notword=&d=&c=&f=&k= 0&sScope=&sLevel=&sLabel=&imgs=20&pNum= accessed May 24, 2011.

6   Billie Burke (with Cameron Shipp), *With a Feather on My Nose* (New York: Appleton-Century-Crofts, 1949), 2-11, 16.

7   Ibid., 28-29.

8   Ibid., 41.

9   Ibid., 44-47.

10 On Frohman as a "star-maker," see Isaac F. Marcosson and Daniel Frohman, *Charles Frohman: Manager and Man* (New York and London: Harper & Brothers, 1916); Kim Marra, "Elsie de Wolfe *Circa* 1901: The Dynamics of Prescriptive Feminine Performance in American Theatre and Society," *Theatre Survey* 35, no. 1 (1994): 100-120; and Kim Marra, *Strange Duets: Impresarios and Actresses in the American Theatre, 1865-1914* (Iowa City: University of Iowa Press), esp. chs. 3 and 4.

11 Marcosson and Frohman, *Charles Frohman*, 139. For more on critics responses to the star system, see Schweitzer, *When Broadway Was the Runway: Theater, Fashion, and American Culture* (Philadelphia: University of Pennsylvania Press, 2009), 26-29.

12 Burke, *With a Feather on My Nose*, 79.

13 Ibid., 83-85.

14 Billie Burke, "The Actress and Her Clothes," *Saturday Evening Post* (February 20, 1909): 8. Billie Burke Scrapbooks, Part IV, Image ID: V87_008, RLC, http://digitalgallery.nypl.org/ nypldigital/dgkeysearchdetail.cfm?trg=1&strucID=672566&imageID=V87_008&parent_id=6 68000&word=&snum=&s=&notword=&d=&c=&f=&k=0&sScope=&sLevel=&sLabel=&total= 108&num=0&imgs=20&pNum=&pos=8, accessed May 24, 2011.

15 On the Actor's Equity Strike, see Sean P. Holmes, "Weavers of Dreams, Unite: Constructing an Occupational Identity in the Actor's Equity Association, 1913-1934," PhD diss., New York University, 1994; Burke, "The Actress and Her Clothes," 8.

16 Frohman's contemporary David Belasco estimated that he saw 4,000 stagestruck girls every year. David Belasco, "Seeing Four Thousand Stage-Struck Women Every Year," *New York Times*, September 5, 1909, 3; Albert Auster, *Actresses and Suffragists: Women in the American Theatre, 1890-1920* (New York: Praeger, 1984), ch. 1. On the professionalization of acting in the late 19th and early 20th centuries, see Benjamin McArthur, *Actors and American Culture: 1880-1920* (1983; Iowa City: University of Iowa Press, 2000).

17 Vanderheyden Fyles, "Clothes and the Actress," *Green Book Album* (June 1911): 1181.

18 Quoted in Marra, "Elsie de Wolfe *Circa* 1901," 107.

19 Burke, *With a Feather on My Nose*, 79-80; Janet Loring, "Costuming on the New York Stage from 1895 to 1915 with Particular Emphasis on Charles Frohman's Companies," PhD diss., State University of Iowa, 1961, 176.

20 Gustav Kobbé, "The Stage as a School of Costume," *The Delineator* (January 1905): 63.

21 Less-than-ideal conditions backstage (e.g., uncovered floorboards, narrow hallways, and steep stairways to dressing rooms) combined with physical business onstage often necessitated costume updates in the middle of a run. Schweitzer, *When Broadway Was the Runway*, 107. Theater managers also recognized the financial benefits of updating stage wardrobes. Since the 1870s, managers such as Augustin Daly had "redressed" productions partway through the run as a promotional scheme to encourage repeat visits. Genevieve Richardson, "Costuming on the American Stage, 1751-1901: A Study of the Major Developments in Wardrobe Practice and Costume Style," PhD diss., University of Illinois, 1953, 82, 111-12.

22 Burke, *With a Feather on My Nose*, 80.

23 Alf Hayman letter to Charles Frohman, Box 3, Hayman, Alf. Letterpress copies. March 12, 1908-May 31, 1910. 54M107. March 23, 1910, p. 372, Frohman (Charles) Letterpress copybooks, New York Public Library [hereafter NYPL].

24 Charles Frohman letter to Alf Hayman. Box 3, Hayman, Alf. Letterpress copies. March 12, 1908-May 31, 1910. 54M107. April 26, 1909, p. 136 and March 14, 1910[2], p. 355, Frohman (Charles) Letterpress copybooks, NYPL. See also Loring, "Costuming on the New York Stage," 47-51. "I appreciate that she is a big card and [so] let many a thing go through charged to the company that I wouldn't for anybody else," Hayman wrote the following year, hoping that Frohman would remember this fact when reviewing the weekly receipts. Alf Hayman letter to Charles Frohman. Box 4, Hayman, Alf. Letterpress copies, May 31, 1910-June 20, 1913, 54M107, May 17, 1911, p. 224, Frohman (Charles) Letterpress copybooks, NYPL.

25 On early 20th-century attitudes toward the body, see Mike Featherstone, "The Body in Consumer Culture," in *The American Body in Context: An Anthology*, ed. Jessica R. Johnston (Wilmington: Scholarly Resources Inc., 2001), 83; Joan Jacobs Blumberg, *The Body Project: An Intimate History of American Girls* (New York: Random House, 1997); Margaret Lowe, *Looking Good: College Women and Body Image* (Baltimore: Johns Hopkins University Press, 2003); and Marie Griffith, *Born Again Bodies: Flesh and Spirit in American Christianity* (Berkeley: University of California Press, 2004).

26 Burke, *With a Feather on My Nose*, 82.

27 "Popular Plays and Their Costuming—Individuality is Not General—Simplicity the Keynote—House Gowns of One Well-Known Emotional Star," *Harrisburg Telegraph* 28 (January 1908), Image ID: V86_046, Billie Burke Scrapbooks, Part V, RLC, http://digitalgallery.nypl.org/nypldigital/dgkeysearchdetail.cfm?trg=1&strucID=672497&imageID=V86_046&parent_id=668001&word=&snum=&s=&notword=&d=&c=&f=&k=0&sScope=&sLevel=&sLabel=&total=107&num=40&imgs=20&pNum=&pos=46, accessed May 24, 2011.

28 For a lengthier discussion of the "sheath style" and actresses' appearances in it onstage and off, see Schweitzer, *When Broadway Was the Runway*, 143-54.

29 Untitled, *The Theatre* (December 1908), Billie Burke Scrapbooks, Part V, Image ID: V86_102, RLC, http://digitalgallery.nypl.org/nypldigital/dgkeysearchdetail.cfm?trg=1&strucID=672552&imageID=V86_102&parent_id=668001&word=&snum=&s=&notword=&d=&c=&f=&k=0&sScope=&sLevel=&sLabel=&total=107&num=100&imgs=20&pNum=&pos=101, accessed May 24, 2011.

30 Untitled, *Woman Beautiful* (January 1909), Billie Burke Scrapbooks, Part IV, Image ID: V87_004, RLC, http://digitalgallery.nypl.org/nypldigital/dgkeysearchdetail.cfm?trg=1&strucID=672562&imageID=V87_004&parent_id=668000&word=&snum=&s=&notword=&d=&c=&f=&k=0&sScope=&sLevel=&sLabel=&total=108&num=0&imgs=20&pNum=&pos=4, accessed May 24, 2011.

31 Untitled, *New York Mirror*, October 24, 1908, Billie Burke Scrapbooks, Part V, Image ID: V86_085, RLC, http://digitalgallery.nypl.org/nypldigital/dgkeysearchdetail.cfm?trg=1&strucID=672536&imageID=V86_085&total=107&num=80&parent_id=668001&word=&s=&notword=&d=&c=&f=&k=0&sScope=&sLevel=&sLabel=&lword=&lfield=&imgs=20&pos=85&snum=&e=w, accessed May 24, 2001.

32 "All About Billie Burke," *New York Telegraph*, November 9, 1907, Billie Burke Scrapbooks, Part V, Image ID: V86_042, RLC, http://digitalgallery.nypl.org/nypldigital/dgkeysearchdetail.cfm?trg=1&strucID=672493&imageID=V86_042&parent_id=668001&word=&snum=&s=&notword=&d=&c=&f=&k=0&sScope=&sLevel=&sLabel=&total=107&num=40&imgs=20&pNum=&pos=42, accessed May 24, 2011.

33 Burke, *With a Feather on My Nose*, 77.

34 In 1909 a patent medicine company used Burke's photograph in a series of subway train advertisements without her permission, a not infrequent practice that outraged many performers. "It isn't so long since [actress] Gertrude Quinlan recovered a large sum from a manufacturer of another sort of proprietary medicine for using her photograph," the *New York Telegraph's* Mlle. Manhattan observed, "and if Miss Burke is the spirited young woman she looks (in her pill picture) I expect she will go and do likewise." Mlle. Manhattan, untitled, Billie Burke Scrapbooks, Part V, Image ID: V86_045, RLC, http://digitalgallery.nypl.org/nypldigital/dgkeysearchdetail.cfm?trg=1&strucID=672496&imageID=V86_045&total=107&num=40&parent_id=668001&word=&s=&notword=&d=&c=&f=&k=0&sScope=&sLevel=&sLabel=&lword=&lfield=&imgs=20&pos=45&snum=&e=w, accessed May 24, 2011.

35   Schweitzer, "'The Mad Search for Beauty: Actresses' Testimonials and the 'Democratization' of Beauty," *Journal of the Gilded Age and Progressive Era* 4, no. 3 (2005): 255-92; and *When Broadway Was the Runway*, 131-37.

36   Burke herself claims that she avoided wearing rouge offstage until her 1914 marriage to Florenz Ziegfeld and only used "enough to look right with stage lighting" onstage. Burke, *With Powder on My Nose*, 36.

37   For more on Billie Burke and the Pond's campaign, see Leslie Midkiff DeBauche, "Testimonial Advertising Using Movie Stars in the 1910s: How Billie Burke Came to Sell Pond's Vanishing Cream in 1917," *Charm* (2007): 146-56. On the Pond's campaign, see also Kathy Peiss, *Hope in a Jar*, 121-22, 126, 137-40; Jennifer Scanlon, *Inarticulate Longings: The Ladies' Home Journal, Gender, and the Promises of Consumer Culture* (New York: Routledge, 1995), 169-98; and Schweitzer, *When Broadway Was the Runway*, 134-37.

38   Forrest D. Pullen's *Créme Nerol*, advertisement, *Vogue* (October 15, 1911), 69. Several years later, as her stage career expanded into the cinema, Burke appeared in full-page color advertisements for Pond's Vanishing Cream, advising women that the secret to beauty success lay in the successful application of not one but *two* creams. Her involvement in this landmark campaign—considered by historians to be a turning point in the history of beauty culture and advertising—signaled her enduring appeal among American women a decade after her Broadway debut.

39   "Actresses of Today," *Human Life* (December 1908), Billie Burke Scrapbooks, Part V, Image ID: V86_106, RLC, http://digitalgallery.nypl.org/nypldigital/dgkeysearchdetail.cfm?trg=1&strucI D=672556&imageID=V86_106&parent_id=668001&word=&snum=&s=&notword=&d=&c= &f=&k=0&sScope=&sLevel=&sLabel=&total=107&num=100&imgs=20&pNum=&pos=105, accessed May 24, 2011.

40   *The Theatre* (Dec. 1908) Image ID: V86_102, RLC.

41   "Billie Burke's Curls," *New York Star*, October 31, 1908, Billie Burke Scrapbooks, Part V, Image ID: V86_086, RLC, http://digitalgallery.nypl.org/nypldigital/dgkeysearchdetail.cfm?trg =1&strucID=672537&imageID=V86_086&parent_id=668001&word=&snum=&s=&notword =&d=&c=&f=&k=0&sScope=&sLevel=&sLabel=&total=107&num=80&imgs=20&pNum=&p os=86, accessed May 24, 2011.

42   Burke, "The Actress and Her Clothes," 12.

43   On early 20th-century color theory and its application in commercial theater, see Lillian L. Bentley, "Does Red Make Us Nervous?" *Ladies' Home Journal* (March 1908); 20; Howard Kenneth Greer, "The Psychology of Color," *Theatre Magazine* (December 1917): 374-76; and Arnold Aronson, "Architect of Dreams," in *Looking Into the Abyss: Essays on Scenography* (Ann Arbor: University of Michigan Press, 2005), 148-49.

44   "Billie Burke Shows Some Pink Pajama Art," *New York World*, March 30, 1914, Billie Burke Scrapbooks, Part I, Image ID: V89_004, RLC, http://digitalgallery.nypl.org/nypldigital/dgkey-searchdetail.cfm?trg=1&strucID=672776&imageID=V89_004&parent_id=667985&word= &snum=&s=&notword=&d=&c=&f=&k=0&sScope=&sLevel=&sLabel=&total=108&num=0 &imgs=20&pNum=&pos=4. Some of the reviews refer to blue pajamas, which suggests that Burke either switched costumes early in the run or alternated between wearing pink and blue from performance to performance. See St. Claire Street, *Toledo Blade*, April 2, 1914, Billie Burke Scrapbooks, Part I, Image ID: V89_005, http://digitalgallery.nypl.org/nypldigital/dgkeysearch-detail.cfm?trg=1&strucID=672777&imageID=V89_005&parent_id=667985&word=&snum=& s=&notword=&d=&c=&f=&k=0&sScope=&sLevel=&sLabel=&total=108&num=0&imgs=20& pNum=&pos=5, accessed May 24, 2011.

45   "Billie Burke Shows Some Pink Pajama Art," Billie Burke Scrapbooks, Part I, Image ID: V89_005 .

46   See St. Claire Street, *Toledo Blade*, April 2, 1914, Billie Burke Scrapbooks, Part I, Image ID: V89_005.

47   "Billie Burke in Pajamas," *The Tacoma Times*, May 6, 1916, 5; http://chroniclingamerica.loc. gov/lccn/sn88085187/1914-05-06/ed-1/seq-5/;words=Billie+PAJAMAS+Burke+BURKE+BILL IE; "Coming Attractions to the Ben Ali," *The Bourbon News*, November 24, 1914, http://chroni-clingamerica.loc.gov/lccn/sn86069873/1914-11-24/ed-1/seq-4/.

48   On the "American Girl" see DeBauche, "Testimonial Advertising Using Movie Stars in the 1910s"; Martha Banta, *Imaging American Women: Ideas and Ideals in Cultural History* (New York: Columbia University Press, 1987); Jane H. Hunter, *How Young Ladies Became Girls:*

The Victorian Origins of American Girlhood (New Haven and London: Yale University Press, 2002); and The Modern Girl Around the World Research Group, *The Modern Girl Around the World: Consumption, Modernity, and Globalization* (Durham: Duke University Press, 2008). On Ziegfeld, see Randolph Carter, et al., *Ziegfeld Follies* (New York: G.P. Putnam's Sons, 1956); Randolph Carter, *The World of Flo Ziegfeld* (New York: Praeger Publishers, 1974); Richard and Paulette Ziegfeld, *The Life and Times of Florenz Ziegfeld, Jr.* (New York: Harry N. Abrams, 1993); Linda Mizejewski, *Ziegfeld Girl: Image and Icon in American Culture and Cinema* (Durham: Duke University Press, 1999); and Ethan Mordden, *Ziegfeld: The Man Who Invented Show Business* (New York: St. Martin's Press, 2008).

49 Billie Burke played a central role in introducing Ziegfeld to Lucile's work. Ziegfeld biographers Marjorie Farnsworth and Randolph Carter both claim that Ziegfeld met Lucile in 1915, when he visited her salon on 57th Street with his new wife, Billie Burke. Neither gives a date for this meeting, but they argue that it was here that Ziegfeld first witnessed one of Lucile's fashion parades and became captivated with her mannequin, Dolores, whom he later hired to appear in the *Follies*. Lucile worked for Ziegfeld from 1915 to 1921, creating many memorable costumes for the *Ziegfeld Follies* and *Frolics*; Carter, *The World of Flo Ziegfeld*, 5; Farnsworth, *Ziegfeld Follies*, 96. On Lucile's work for the *Follies*, see Lady Duff Gordon (Lucile), *Discretions and Indiscretions* (New York: Frederick A. Stokes Co., 1932); Meredith Etherington-Smith and Jeremy Pilcher, *The "It" Girls: Lucy, Lady Duff Gordon, Couturière "Lucile," and Elinor Glyn, Romantic Novelist* (London: Hamish Hamilton, 1986); Mizejewski, *Ziegfeld Girl*, 89-108; Schweitzer, *When Broadway Was the Runway*, 194-202. See also Sheila Stowell's essay in this volume.

I
Jane Hading
(1859–1941)

"And you want my biography—my adventures?
Well, so many people ask for them I am ashamed
to think how prosaic my life has been and what a
stupid interviewée I make. There is so little to tell."
—Jane Hading, *The World*, 1888

UNLIKE THAT OF HER CONTEMPORARY SARAH BERNHARDT, Jane Hading's life has remained unstudied by scholars of theatrical history. In this exhibition, we come to know her in the same way that a nineteenth-century fan would have, via the biased and sometimes mawkish celebrity press of the day. Beginning as an "enfant de la balle," or the child of a performer, she rose through the ranks of provincial opéra-bouffe troupes, eventually becoming a respected dramatic actress known for her passion and beauty and a rival to the formidable Bernhardt, to whom she was compared throughout her professional life.[1]

Obituaries indicate that Jane Hading, née Jeanne Alfredine Trefouret, was born in Marseilles, probably on November 25, 1859.[2] At some point, according to the actress, her father, named Jean-Louis, a successful actor in Marseilles theaters, changed his name to "Hadingue" and Jane later anglicized the name further to Hading.[3] She had at least one sibling, a brother named Maxime, whom she lovingly referred to as "l'enfant," and possibly others, though apparently only young Jeanne followed in her father's footsteps.[4] Her debut at age three or four was in a production of Le Bossu in which her father was performing, and it was from him that young Jeanne learned to play "la comédie," that "terrible and delicious art" (fig. 1.1).[5] At about age thirteen, she traveled to the then French colony of Algiers, where she played ingénue parts at her father's behest.[6] She returned briefly to Marseilles to study voice and piano at the Conservatoire—she was talented enough to win the prix de Solfège in piano there—and then made her operetta debut at the Khédive Theater in Cairo in about 1873.[7] Back in France by the following year, she again acted with her father in such mixed fare as Ruy Blas, Le Roman d'un jeune homme pauvre, Henri III et sa cour, and La Jeunesse des Mousquetaires from about 1874 to 1876.[8] By sixteen, according to Hading, she was making "oceans of money in comic opera" and caught the eye of the director of the Théâtre du Palais-Royal in Paris.[9] In 1877 she debuted there in the vaude-

FIG. 1.1 Camus (French?, active 19th century). Jane Hading at age three and her father in Le Bossu, ca. 1862. From Le Théâtre (November 1900): 11. Private collection.

ville production La Chaste Suzanne by Paul Ferrier and was soon also engaged at the Théâtre de la Renaissance, where she replaced the ailing popular actress Jeanne Granier in several productions, including Héloïse et Abélard (1879), L'Œil crevé (1881), and Belle Lurette (1880), Jacques Offenbach's last work, which he created especially for Hading (fig. 1.2 and see fig. A.2).[10] The theater critic Françisque Sarcey later noted that, at the time, the leaders of society "were amused with her as with a pretty toy; her name was on every tongue; she became the fashion."[11]

On December 15, 1883, Hading debuted at the Théâtre du Gymnase in her first major theatrical

FIG. 1.2 Paul Nadar (French, 1856–1939). Jane Hading in *L'Œil crevé*, ca. 1881. From *Le Théatre* (November 1900): 14. Private collection.

FIG. 1.3 Jane Hading and Jacques Damala in *Le Maître de Forges*, 1884. Cabinet photograph. Courtesy of the Victoria & Albert Museum, London, bequeathed by Guy Little, S.137:286-2007.

success as Claire de Beaulieu in Georges Ohnet's *Le Maître de Forges* (fig. 1.3).[12] Victor Koning (1842–1894), the director who had engaged Hading for *Belle Lurette*, cast her in Ohnet's play. He married her the following year and went on to play a decisive role in her early renown. "If a director ever created an artist," noted one publication, "Koning created Jane Hading."[13] *The Illustrated American* put the motivation behind their marriage matter-of-factly, stating: "He was very rich and she was very poor," a sentiment that would be repeated many times in the sensationalistic reports on their subsequent divorce.[14] The pair were apparently mismatched from the start;

writer Léon Daudet described Koning as "curly, greasy as a little sausage, anxiously eyeing his shirt-front and trousers," whereas Hading appeared "as lovely as the dawn," and seeing them together was like watching "a gargoyle gibbering at a Titian Venus."[15] According to Hading, Koning took "every sou" she earned, and by 1887 she had begun the proceedings to file for divorce, an almost unheard-of act at the time, coming only three years after the law prohibiting divorce in France was struck down in 1884.[16] Hading's was one of the first high-profile celebrity divorces to be widely reported on (and sensationalized) in the press (fig. 1.4). In May 1887, one foreign cor-

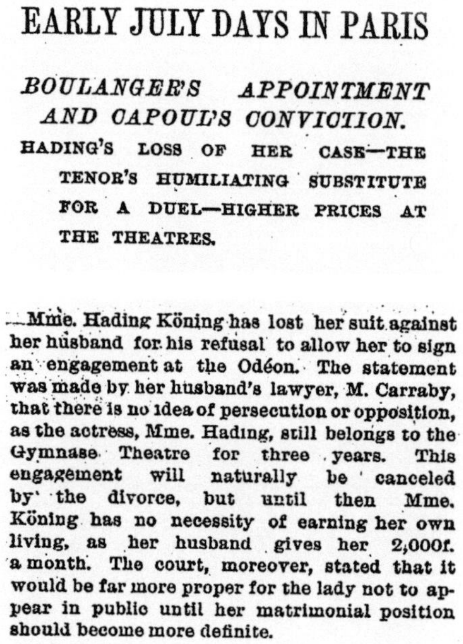

EARLY JULY DAYS IN PARIS

BOULANGER'S APPOINTMENT AND CAPOUL'S CONVICTION.

HADING'S LOSS OF HER CASE—THE TENOR'S HUMILIATING SUBSTITUTE FOR A DUEL—HIGHER PRICES AT THE THEATRES.

Mme. Hading Köning has lost her suit against her husband for his refusal to allow her to sign an engagement at the Odéon. The statement was made by her husband's lawyer, M. Carraby, that there is no idea of persecution or opposition, as the actress, Mme. Hading, still belongs to the Gymnase Theatre for three years. This engagement will naturally be canceled by the divorce, but until then Mme. Köning has no necessity of earning her own living, as her husband gives her 2,000f. a month. The court, moreover, stated that it would be far more proper for the lady not to appear in public until her matrimonial position should become more definite.

FIG. 1.4 "Early July Days in Paris." From the *New York Times*, July 3, 1887.

respondent reported that "Mlle. de Rothschild is no longer the chief topic for gossip in clubs and salons. Already is she replaced by Mme. Jane Hading, the brilliant actress, who has, with M. Damala, the husband of Sarah Bernhardt, made a success of 'Le Maitre des Forges' [sic] and 'La Comtesse Sarah' by Georges Ohnet."[17] During the divorce proceedings, which lasted for a year, Koning prevented Hading from working at any of the Parisian theaters, forcing the actress to make her first trip to America to tour with the famous actor Benoît-Constant Coquelin, an enormous success that propelled her to international stardom.[18]

After *Le Maître de Forges* and her divorce, Hading was constantly compared with Sarah Ber-

nhardt. At one point, it was even rumored, perhaps facetiously, that the two actresses would star in an adaptation of *Romeo and Juliet* at the Porte-Saint-Martin with Bernhardt in the male role.[19] Sarcey, editor of the magazine *Le Théatre*, agreed with the laudatory public that Hading was wonderful in *Le Maître de Forges* but tempered his enthusiasm by noting that "she had, above all, studied Sarah Bernhardt's style and appropriated some of her mannerisms. It was imitation, but an imitation so free that only connoisseurs could recognize it."[20] Throughout the 1880s and into the 1890s, Hading and Bernhardt performed many of the same roles in such plays as *Frou-Frou* and Alphonse Daudet's *Sapho*. Many thought that the two women also shared Jacques Damala, Bernhardt's husband and Hading's costar in *Le Maître de Forges*, and that he had been the cause of Hading's divorce from Koning.[21] By the time of her death in 1941, Hading's supposed affair with Damala had become romantic legend.[22] In addition to their profession, the two actresses were also linked by fashion, as they were both costumed by Maison Laferrière in the late 1880s. In 1888 *The Woman's World* described very similar Laferrière gowns for the two stars, who were each appearing in Alexandre Dumas's *La Dame aux Camélias*, Bernhardt in Paris and Hading ("who in art is the divine Sarah's rival") in America.[23]

Throughout the 1890s, Hading played a series of important dramatic roles at the top Boulevard theaters, such as the Princesse d'Aurec in Henri Lavedan's *Le Prince d'Aurec* at the Vaudeville in 1892 (see Appendix for full performance history) (see fig. A.1). The following year, she appeared at the most prestigious theater in Paris, the Comédie-Française, cementing her status as a dramatic interpreter of the highest level. In many of her mature roles, she played virtuous yet fallen women who were ultimately redeemed by the men who had previously scorned her, including Maud de Rouvre in *Les Demi-Vierges* (1895) and Ely in *Une Idylle tragique* (1896). She also performed in productions set in the historic past, such as *La Jeunesse de Louis XIV* (1897), *Plus que Reine* (1899), and *La Pompadour* (1901). Between 1888 and 1906, Hading toured extensively in the Americas and Europe and appeared in a reprisal of her signature role in *Le Maître de Forges* in 1905 (see Appendix).[24] Her last role was as Madame du Barry in Lavedan's one-act play *La Chienne du Roi*, which had a respectable run—at the Théâtre Sarah-Bernhardt—in 1913.[25]

Hading never remarried, and from about 1889 she lived with her mother in a well-appointed home outside Paris in affluent Neuilly-sur-Seine.[26] In a 1920 interview, she claimed that Paris had lost all of its charms for her and that she preferred to spend her last days "among the sun and the flowers" of Provence.[27] Her retirement from the theater in the second decade of the century led to her being confused with another star of the day, singer Jane Harding. When Harding died in 1934, many newspapers mistakenly printed obituaries for Hading, despite the fact that as early as 1895, *Harper's Bazar* had warned its readers not to mistake one for the other.[28] Hading herself died on February 18, 1941, at the age of eighty-one in Neuilly.[29] The following month, Hading's belongings were sold at auction at the Hôtel Drouot in Paris, an act that at least one French writer found almost sacrilegious. He wrote elegiacally of her "Bonheur-du-jour, on which are arrayed the letters of admirers and lovers" and of "all the décor with which the great actress Jane Hading once lived being dispersed in the frenzy of an auction."[30]

Before her death, one of the last press notices about her also concerned a Drouot auction. In 1920 *The Illustrated London News* reported that Hading, "silent since the war" and now "wiping the dust of Paris off her feet to end her days in the land of Sunshine," had created much "bustle and interest" by showing up at the same auction as Bernhardt, causing a sensation in the crowd.[31] Almost fifty years after Hading had supposedly stolen the heart of Bernhardt's husband, the two stars remained inexorably linked in the public imagination. —WD

"I think that the fashions of the past season or so have been abominable. Truly, are not those tight skirts frightful? . . . Ah, you see I am by no means a worshipper at fashion's shrine. I like styles that are individual, personal, in both hats and gowns."
—Jane Hading, *The Theatre*, 1909

Theatergoers in turn-of-the-century Paris followed the evolution of Jane Hading's fashionable look on stage, as well as in various print media, as she moved from lesser couture houses to image-defining partnerships with the leading houses of Laferrière and Redfern and the millinery establishment of Madame Carlier. Over the course of her career, Hading became well known for a personal style predicated on simplicity and ease, the result of her fruitful collaborations with these designers.

In the early 1880s, Hading patronized some of the minor couture houses for her fashionable stage costumes, although she did not actively promote their work as she would later with prominent couturiers.[32] Her first such collaborative relationship was with the Maison Laferrière, a venerable establishment that rivaled Maison Worth for prestige and an aristocratic clientele.[33] Madame Laferrière created twenty-two gowns for Hading's touring productions in 1888, the first evidence of their affiliation. In 1893, when Hading debuted at the Comédie-Française as the marquise in *Les Effrontés*, *La Vie parisienne* devoted a full page to her Laferrière gowns that included descriptions of all the toilettes, even indicating the fabric and color of each part of the gown so that readers could have their dressmakers copy them accurately (fig. 1.5).[34] By the end of the century, Hading was effectively promoting the house through pseudo-advertisements. In September 1898, the inside front cover of *Le Théatre* carried an article-cum-advertisement that described the actress's latest European tour in terms of her travel trousseau of thirty gowns entirely furnished by Maison Laferrière. "The unprecedented variety of the forms,

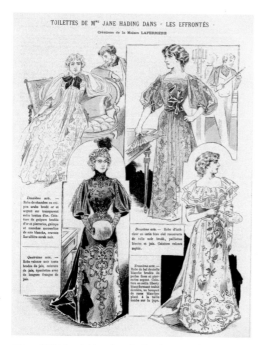

FIG. 1.5 "Toilettes de Mme. Jane Hading dans *Les Effrontés*: Créations de la Maison Laferrière." From *La Vie parisienne*, April 1, 1893, 182. Library, Bard Graduate Center: Decorative Arts, Design History, Material Culture; New York. Cat. 3.

FIG. 1.6 Reutlinger Studio (French, 1850-1937). Postcard of Jane Hading in *La Châtelaine*, ca. 1902. Hand-colored photograph with glitter and metallic gold pigment. Private collection. Cat. 11.

the richness of the fabrics and the trimmings, the intelligent taste of the ensemble," wrote an author named only C. de C., "gives us the most exquisite, the most rare sensation of the imagination and of the feminine art of which one could dream."[35]

The appearance of this "article" in the space normally reserved for advertisements makes it clear that the relationship between Laferrière and Hading was probably one of paid endorsement, or at least complicit cooperation. The text notes that the gowns were available for viewing at the house's headquarters in Paris before Hading embarked on her tour, and both actress and designer certainly benefited from the arrangement—Laferrière

gained publicity and Hading furthered the perception of her artistry and sartorial self-knowledge by claiming some hand in the design process. In 1895 *Harper's Bazar* wrote that Hading "is noted for her beautiful gowns, and while Laferrière makes them, she herself designs them, and half of Laferrière's models come from suggestions they have got from Mlle. Hading."[36] Indeed, Hading had a reputation from her earliest successes for playing a hands-on role in her costuming. "Her toilet in the 'Maitre [sic] de Forges,'" observed the *New York Times* in 1884, "gave all the fashions for last Summer's styles, yet they were entirely made by the lady herself, with the aid of her maid."[37] Hading's personal preference in fashionable dress was for looser silhouettes, which became a signature look for the actress. In a lengthy review of *Une Idylle tragique* (1896), for which Laferrière likely provided the gowns, one critic wrote: "[Hading] can say that it is she who has invented the draping fronts of bodices. But even now there is an originality about her bodices which almost defies imitation. You can hardly ever tell where they are fastened, and although seemingly tight fitting, they look loose and oftentimes baggy."[38] Hading sported these bodices with a softly boned corset worn "very low and very short on the hips," like a dancer's.[39]

The most successful of Hading's couture relationships was with the British House of Redfern,

founded by John Redfern in the late 1840s as a tailor's shop in Cowes on the Isle of Wight and, by the second half of the century, one of the most prestigious and profitable couture houses in the world, patronized by royalty, high society, and such actresses as Lily Langtry.[40] By 1892 Redfern had branches in Cowes, London, Edinburgh, Manchester, Paris, Nice, Aix-les Bains, Cannes, New York, Chicago, and Newport, Rhode Island.[41] In 1900 the house contributed pieces to the Exposition Universelle in Paris, and that same year Hading chose the house's designer in Paris, Charles Poynter, as her exclusive dressmaker.[42] She named Redfern as her favorite couturier in a 1903 interview in which she also identified her other preferred purveyors,

FIG. 1.7 Leonetto Cappiello (Italian, active in Paris, 1875–1942). "Jane Hading ou la 'Demi-Vierge' Rêvée." From *Le Rire* (November 3, 1900). Private collection. Cat. 5.

FIG. 1.8 "Mme Jane Hading, Toilette créée par Redfern, Pour les représentations de Serge Panine au Théâtre de la Gaîté." From *Les Modes* (February 1906): n.p. General Research Division, The New York Public Library for the Performing Arts, Astor, Lenox and Tilden Foundations.

FIG. 1.9 Charles Poynter (English, 1853–1929) for the House of Redfern (English, 1881–1929). Evening gown, ca. 1904. Silk taffeta, silk satin, silk chiffon, lace, iridescent sequins, and beads. Museum of the City of New York, Gift of Mrs. Ruth Fahnestock and Mrs. Faith Fahnestock Paine, 41.339.15. Cat. 2.

FIG. 1.10 Detail of fig. 1.9.

including Madame Carlier for millinery.[43]

Redfern's loose and blousy silhouettes for Hading were in keeping with the general "pouter-pigeon" mode of the early 1900s, but they came to be strongly identified with the star and were seen as complementary to her modest yet stately persona. Redfern's dresses of beige lace with short jacket-like bodices and balloon undersleeves remained a particularly characteristic style for Hading—she first wore them in *L'Enchantement* in 1900, and they were featured in the fashion magazine *La Nouvelle Mode* that year. Hading wore similar dresses by Redfern in *La Châtelaine* in 1902 and other subsequent productions (fig. 1.6).[44] The

Italian caricaturist Leonetto Cappiello captured Hading's typical loosely corseted dress style and preference for lace sleeves in a drawing that appeared on the back cover of the humor magazine *Le Rire* in 1900 (fig. 1.7). Already a highly regarded actress by 1900, Hading became a fashion icon as well through her relationship with Redfern and was featured in the top fashion publications of the day, such as *Les Modes*.

The gown shown here is very similar to the type of dress that Hading wore in some of her early twentieth-century productions, such as *Serge Panine* (1906) (figs. 1.8, 1.9, and 1.10). An example of Redfern's elaborate evening wear dating to about

FIG. 1.11 Maurice-Quentin de La Tour (French, 1704–1788). *Portrait of the Marquise de Pompadour*, 1748–55. Pastel on gray-blue paper with gouache highlights. Réunion des musées nationaux / Art Resource, NY, INV27614.

FIG. 1.12 Jane Hading in court costume from *La Pompadour*. From *Le Théâtre* (December 1901): 9. Private collection.

1904, it is made of cream silk taffeta overlaid with lace and is encrusted with wired floral appliqués in the shape of chrysanthemums made from blue-violet sequins. Semi-transparent sequins extend vertically in bands down the length of the dress and graduate in size from small at the bust to large at the hem, which is trimmed with a ruffle of pink, green, and lavender chiffon. Strands of iridescent beads run over the shoulders and along the top of the bodice, turning into elaborately constructed drops that would have swayed as the wearer moved.

Hading's most lavish Redfern ensembles were not, in fact, fashionable dress but rather the period costumes she wore in the 1901 production of Émile Bergerat's *La Pompadour*. Many of the toilettes in the play were clearly inspired by famous portraits of the Marquise.[45] In an interview in the *Pall Mall Gazette* from 1902, Redfern stated that he used Charles André van Loo's half-length portrait of Pompadour (1754–55), known as "La belle jardinière," as well as Maurice-Quentin de La Tour's full-length pastel (1748–55), as sources for the gowns (figs. 1.11 and 1.12).[46] He also probably conflated François-Hubert Drouais's portrait of his wife (1758, Musée du Louvre) with the painter's famous portrait of the Marquise de Pompadour (1764, Musée des beaux arts d'Orléans), in which

FIG. 1.13 Reutlinger Studio. Postcard of Jane Hading in *La Pompadour*, ca. 1901. Hand-colored photograph with signature. Private collection. Cat. 9.

FIG. 1.14 "Modèles de Madame Carlier." From *Millinery Trade Review* (February 1897): pl. 4. Courtesy of the Library of Congress.

the sitters wear similar headwear, to create at least one other costume (fig. 1.13).[47] Early twentieth-century drama critic Henry Fouquier characterized the play as a "portrait gallery which every lady will enjoy to see; the pictures live before one's eyes."[48] Although he took issue with Hading's "stagey" impersonation of Pompadour, he nonetheless praised "the toilettes, [which] are really artistic masterpieces," adding that "when Mme. Hading enters in court dress, covered with embroideries from the waist to the long court train, or in the garb of a Watteau shepherdess, we have applauded enthusiastically, and justly, for we were applauding a work of art, a marvelous restoration of the past."[49]

Hading's costumes were a sensation and were featured in every manner of published media, from postcards to fashion periodicals and society magazines.[50] *The Paris Review* declared Hading's court dress "a masterpiece of the dressmaking art, quite unique in its way, and for ever proclaiming the undeniable supremacy of Redfern."[51] The inside front cover of this periodical features a full-page advertisement for Redfern touting his "marvellous Pompadour Creations" and noting that with these he had "achieved the greatest artistic success of the age in dress."[52] British *Vogue* recalled "the furore created by [Poynter's] costumes for Madame Jane Hading in the role of Madame de

FIG. 1.15 "Coiffures inspirées des Tableaux du Temps créées pour Jane Hading dans Plus que Reine par Mᵉ Carlier." From *L'Art et la Mode* (April 8, 1899): 261–62. General Research Division, New York Public Library, Astor, Lenox and Tilden Foundations.

Pompadour" over twenty years later.[53]

In addition to Laferrière and Redfern, from the late 1890s Hading worked with Madame Carlier, a milliner located on the prestigious rue de la Paix in Paris. By 1897 the actress's patronage of Madame Carlier was already firmly established even across the Atlantic; that year, the *Millinery Trade Review* of New York printed a color plate entitled "Modèles de Madame Carlier," in which Hading is depicted along with hats named after two other Théâtre du Gymnase actresses (fig. 1.14). A pseudo-article devoted to Hading's upcoming European tour appeared on the inside back cover of the September 1898 issue of *Le Théâtre*

and described all of the hats designed expressly by Carlier. Referred to as "la grande modiste parisienne aristocratique," the designer provided Hading with the "quintessence of elegance, beauty, and richness" to match her Laferrière gowns.[54] The following year, Carlier created the hats for *Plus que Reine*, which were featured in both fashion magazines and on postcards (figs. 1.15 and 1.16). A hat by the New York milliner Ruland shown in this exhibition is very similar to one worn by Hading on the cover of *Le Théâtre* in 1900, undoubtedly a Carlier creation, and demonstrates the necessity of American milliners to associate themselves with Parisian style (see frontispiece). The label reads

"Ruland, New York & Paris," although the brand probably did not have a branch in the French city.[55] Carlier's creations for Hading continued to arouse public interest well into the new century, and in 1909 *The Theatre* called her "the milliner par excellence."[56] The same article quoted Hading as saying, "while I may change my couturiere, always it is Carlier who creates my hats."[57]

Hading's millinery was influential well before her association with Carlier began, especially in America, where fashion-conscious women eagerly anticipated news of the latest French styles transmitted by actresses on tour. In 1887 *Cassell's Family Magazine* wrote: "The Jane Hading hat is the fashion of the moment. It has a very large turned-up brim with a good broach piece on the left side, and it has always very prominent tufts of ostrich feathers."[58] In 1891 *The Illustrated American* noted that during Hading's triumph in *Le Maître de Forges*, "Parisian *femmes du monde* wore Hading hats, Hading shoes, Hading veils, and even adopted her favorite perfumes."[59] The Hading veil, in particular, seems to have been quite popular; another magazine noted: "Some years ago, in Paris, Jane Hading appeared in a pretty little comedy and during the action of the play wore a peculiar veil! Well, from that hour to this, that particular veil has been known as the 'Jane Hading veil.'"[60]

Hading's recognizably individual look, which she maintained to the end of her career, was cause

FIG. 1.16 Paul Boyer (French, active late 19th–early 20th century). Postcard of Jane Hading in *Plus que Reine*, ca. 1899. Hand-colored photograph with metallic gold pigment. Private collection. Cat. 8.

FIG. 1.17 Reutlinger Studio. Jane Hading in *L'Alibi*. From *Le Théatre* (June 1908): 5. Private collection.

FIG. 1.18 Van Bosch Studio (French, active 1880s–1890s). Cabinet card of Jane Hading, ca. 1885. Billy Rose Theatre Division, The New York Public Library for the Performing Arts, Astor, Lenox and Tilden Foundations. Cat. 14.

FIG. 1.19 Van Bosch Studio. Cabinet card of Jane Hading, ca. 1885–89. Billy Rose Theatre Division, The New York Public Library for the Performing Arts, Astor, Lenox and Tilden Foundations. Cat. 15.

for praise (fig. 1.17). In 1910 *Les Modes* wrote that the toilettes "of Madame Hading are . . . quintessentially Jane Hading, and we are grateful to the artist for maintaining a trademark look that is so personal to her beauty: long, straight dresses without exaggerated narrowness, allowing the body a great suppleness of movement."[61] Although by this date, the slender Empire-revival silhouette was in vogue, Hading elicited admiration for sustaining a distinctive silhouette and style well-suited to her figure and personality, a quintessential example of French *élégance*. —WD

IN THE PHOTOGRAPHER'S STUDIO

Photographs of Jane Hading were distributed far and wide, and the surviving body of cabinet cards and postcards with her image testify to the actress's extensive and long-lasting appeal. Her career coincides with a time of great change in the technology and art of photography, when the *carte de visite* and the cabinet card were overtaken by the inexpensive and ubiquitous photographic postcard.[62] Thus, many of Hading's earlier plays that were considered her greatest successes, such as *Le Maître de Forges* (1883), *Sapho* (1885), and

FIG. 1.20 Reutlinger Studio. Cabinet card of Jane Hading in *Nos Intimes*, ca. 1891. Billy Rose Theatre Division, The New York Public Library for the Performing Arts, Astor, Lenox and Tilden Foundations. Cat. 18.

FIG. 1.21 Verso of cabinet card in fig. 1.20.

Frou-Frou (1886), did not produce the same pictorial impact as some later lesser hits, including *Plus que Reine* (1899) and *La Pompadour* (1901), a phenomenon explained in part by technological changes but also by the elaborate costumes and the concomitant opportunity for decorating postcards that featured images from these productions.

The earliest photographs of Hading in this exhibition are cabinet cards from the mid-1880s. The studio of Otto van Bosch, a German photographer whose Parisian branch was run by Paul Boyer, produced cards of Hading in the tightly corseted style of the 1880s, in plays such as *Sapho*

(see fig. v). One pair of cards functions like a nineteenth-century fashion plate, showing front and back views of the actress in a daringly low-cut crystal-studded evening gown of dark velvet and silk with a prominent bustle and sporting a fur foulard scarf around her neck (figs. 1.18 and 1.19). Her distinctive, alluring stare is present even in these early cards, and her bearing is more poised than the playful images of her early opéra-bouffe performances (see fig. 1.2), as befitted her new status as a serious dramatic actress (and her elaborate gown). Unlike Lily Elsie and Billie Burke, Hading had a smile that was never purely candid or open-mouthed but instead remained enigmatically demure. One writer described her smile "as if it were veiled by a shadow of sadness that stops it from fully blooming."[63] The style of dress dates these cards to the middle of the 1880s, but we can also date them based on their elaborately decorated versos, which feature the photography studios' logos and a list of awards won at various expositions.[64]

By the late 1890s, the family-run Reutlinger Studio, listed as her favorite photographers in a 1903 interview, supplied most of Hading's photographs (see fig. II).[65] Seen in tandem with Van Bosch's earlier shots, Reutlinger's cabinet cards of Hading display her changing style and public persona. From the bare-armed and tight-laced ingénue who, in some photographs, coyly smiles

and in others meets the viewer's gaze with a brazen stare, Hading transformed in the 1890s into a mature and somewhat aloof dramatic *artiste*. Two Reutlinger cabinet cards show Hading as Cécile, the wife of a much-older wealthy Parisian who falls in love with her husband's young friend, in *Nos Intimes* (fig. 1.20 and see fig. A.3).[66] The *New York Times* described her in this role as "charming, frail, and terrible as an equinoxial sky in a part which once reaches the height of the very dramatic," and some of this variable character is certainly displayed in these cards, which depict the actress as alternatively pensive and defiant.[67] In offering an array of poses, Reutlinger appealed both to discerning consumers who may have passed up one shot in favor of another and inveterate collectors who wanted to have them all. In these two cards, Hading shows off a white silk and lace day ensemble supplied by Maison Laferrière, a more relaxed style than she had sported in the previous decade. The backs of these cards also tell us where these cards were sold, as they often include stickers or stamps for the stationers or booksellers

FIG. 1.22 Reutlinger Studio. Bookmark postcard of Jane Hading in a Laferrière dress, ca. 1898. Photograph. Private collection. Cat. 21.

FIG. 1.23 Reutlinger Studio. Postcard of Jane Hading in a Laferrière dress, ca. 1898–1904. Photograph. Private collection. Cat. 22.

FIG. 1.24 Reutlinger Studio. Postcard of Jane Hading in *Plus que Reine*, ca. 1899. Photograph. Private collection. Cat. 23.

FIG. 1.25 Reutlinger Studio. Postcard of Jane Hading in *La Pompadour*, ca. 1901. Hand-colored photograph with glitter. Private collection. Cat. 27.

where they were purchased (fig. 1.21).[68] The photograph that shows Hading leaning on a chair was presumably sold in America, as it is stamped "Meyer Bros. & Co." with a New York City address; the one with her left hand on her hip (see fig. A.3) was sold in Paris, as it includes a stamp on the reverse for the "Ingénieur-Opticien" Hazebroucq located on the rue de la Paix. Reutlinger also licensed photos of Hading in her white Laferrière gown to postcard publishers (figs. 1.22 and 1.23). The "book post card" is inscribed on the front "Your image when 20," and signed affectionately "From one you know, Ta Ra Ra." Sent within the city of Nairn, Scotland, it testifies to Hading's

international appeal and her youthful image (she was about forty when the photograph was shot). Both this example and the card printed with "Lundi," the French word for Monday, were sent in 1904, six years after these images were first taken, a lapse revealing their enduring legacy and appeal.

Postcards, cheaper and even more portable than cabinet cards, were the most widespread medium for the diffusion of actress photographs by the 1890s. Most surviving postcards present Hading in two of her most iconic roles, Empress Joséphine in Émile Bergerat's *Plus que Reine* (1899) and as the Marquise de Pompadour in Bergerat's *La Pompadour* (1901) (figs. 1.24, 1.25, and see figs.

A.4 and A.5). Both plays were highly publicized in the press, although that did not result in favorable reviews or long runs. Commentators, in fact, spent most of their time focusing on Hading's costumes, many of which were re-creations of gowns worn in famous paintings.[69] All of the photographs used on these postcards were taken by the Reutlinger Studio, and most have the characteristic, undivided back that was standard in France until 1903.[70] Some cards, like the 1899 postcard of Hading in *Plus que Reine*, left a space for the sender to include a note on the front of the card; others simply wrote directly on the image. The existence of *Plus que Reine* cards with divided backs suggests the continued popularity of images of Hading in this seminal role into the twentieth century.

Many postcards were available with hand-coloring that was applied by professional colorists employed by various publishers in France.[71] Additionally, women (and men) sometimes personalized their cards with hand-coloring and embellishments, such as glitter and metallic paints. Another 1899 postcard of Jane Hading in *Plus que Reine* is ornamented with watercolor washes, and gold paint picks out details of embroidery and jewelry or freely invents these details (see fig. A.4). Many postcards in this exhibition feature identical photographs treated in various ways to appeal to the collector—enriched with color and glitter, cropped and retouched, or surrounded by decorative graphic elements.[72] One card, shown here (fig. 1.26), was certainly enhanced at home rather than by a professional. Its decorator added a glitter crown, necklace, and earrings to the image; now

FIG. 1.26 Reutlinger Studio. Postcard of Jane Hading, ca. 1902. Hand-colored photograph with glitter and applied ornaments (now missing). Private collection. Cat. 34.

missing are the small stones or beads that once adorned these fantasy *bijoux*.

In addition to the application of color to enhance black-and-white images, the photograph itself was sometimes retouched to create an image of ideal beauty. Hading's mole periodically disappears and reappears on postcards, especially in close-up shots as in figure 1.26. (The original photograph on this card appears on many postcards of differing formats, sometimes with Hading's mole obscured.) Such retouching was clearly not a new phenomenon, as Hading's early cabinet cards show evidence of photo-manipulation. For example, the color of the background in the areas around her waist in figure 1.18 is clearly a different shade than the rest, indicating that the photographer painted out the sides of her torso to make her appear slimmer, and her fur scarf does not continue under her right arm as it should.

In 1901 Reutlinger also provided all of the photos for an even greater sartorial success, *La Pompadour*. As with *Plus que Reine*, the historical veracity of the play was questioned, but the costumes were praised.[73] The play seems to have provided the perfect template for colorists' fantasies, as the colors of Hading's costumes vary greatly from image to image. On the cover of *Le Théatre*, Hading appears in a *bergère* ensemble of a pink bodice with green velvet bows and a flower-trimmed straw hat modeled after a portrait of the Marquise de Pompadour by Charles André Van Loo (1754–55, Château de Versailles; see fig. 1.29). Postcard colorists often took liberties with theatrical "reality," freely changing the color of costumes or covering them over with fanciful swirls of glitter. Once again, Hading's mole vanishes and reappears on these cards, more evidence of the retoucher's brush. Another image of Hading in a different costume from the play, probably signed by Hading during her 1903 tour of England, shows the continued appeal of this imagery, as she did not perform the role of Pompadour on that tour (see fig. 1.13).

Finally, it is important to mention Reutlinger's photographs of Hading that were published in the fascicules or bound photographic albums, which were very popular at the turn of the century. In 1895 Léopold Reutlinger and the art publisher Ludovic Baschet produced *Le Panorama*, which was made up of individual sections, such as "Nos Jolies Actrices" featuring well-known actresses including Hading (fig. 1.27). One critic wrote that *Le Panorama* "publishes a gallery of portraits of our prettiest actresses photographed by the famous artist Reutlinger. It is pleasant to be able to conserve the fugitive images of these charmers who smile at the crowd from behind the luminous footlights, because all these beauties, all these smiles and all these graces are destined to disappear one day or another. . . . The book is born, the portrait is made and the charming ones become immortal. That is why *Le Panorama* represents each actress in their most famous roles."[74] As this passage makes clear, photography was a means of possession that was irresistible to a turn-of-the-century audience increasingly concerned with fame and celebrity. Through the accumulation of cabinet cards, postcards, and bound photographic volumes, the French public preserved actresses in their most famous roles and most grandiose costumes, fixing an image of them at the peak of their beauty and spectacle. —WD

THE PRESS

The relationship between Jane Hading and the French press between the years 1880 and 1915 reflects the press's increasingly promiscuous relationship with theater and, more specifically, theater actresses. The years between 1830 and 1900 saw significant developments in the press as an instrument of modernity in France: technological advances, changes in the laws governing the publication and distribution of printed materials, and a burgeoning literacy rate made possible the emergence of the mass press in the early years of the July Monarchy (1830–48).[75] Sales of commercial dailies increased exponentially throughout the mid- to late nineteenth century, reaching two

JANE HADING

FIG. 1.27 Jane Hading. From the photograph album *Le Panorama: Nos Jolies Actrices Photographiées par Reutlinger*, ca. 1895. Library, Bard Graduate Center: Decorative Arts, Design History, Material Culture; New York.

1899   MAI   N° 17

LE THÉATRE

DIRECTION, RÉDACTION, PUBLICITÉ :   CONDITIONS DE L'ABONNEMENT :   ABONNEMENT ET VENTE :
24, Boulevard des Capucines.   PARIS : 1 an . . . . . 22 fr | DÉPARTEMENTS : 1 an . . . 24 fr   Librairie du FIGARO, 26, rue Drouot.
                ÉTRANGER (Union postale) : 1 an . . . . 28 fr

Mᵐᵉ JANE HADING (Rôle de Joséphine)

ÉDITEURS : Jean Boussod, Manzi, Joyant & Cⁱᵉ, 24, Boulevard des Capucines, Paris. — PRIX : 2 fr.

FIG. 1.28 Paul Boyer. Jane Hading in *Plus que Reine*.
Cover of *Le Théatre* (May 1899). Private collection. Cat. 36.

FIG. 1.29 Reutlinger Studio. Jane Hading in *La Pompadour*. Cover of *Le Théatre* (December 1901). Library, Bard Graduate Center: Decorative Arts, Design History, Material Culture; New York. Cat. 39.

FIG. 1.30 Reutlinger Studio. Jane Hading in *L'Alibi*. Cover of *Le Théatre* (June 1908). Private collection. Cat. 40.

million in 1880 and tripling in circulation between 1880 and 1914.[76] As the press developed and expanded throughout the nineteenth century, so too did the forms by which it conveyed news of and marketed Parisian theater and actresses such as Jane Hading. From the traditional reviews and summaries found in Boulevard magazines such as *Le Théatre* to the more intimate portraits of Hading's home in *Nos Grandes Artistes*, to hybrid forms of advertisement such as the Reutlinger *Le Panorama* volumes, to newspaper gossip columns, Hading used the press to market her name and conversely, the press used her fame to draw attention to the rising genre of celebrity media.

The close relationship between the press and the theater also paralleled the growing importance of the stage to French cultural life. Parisians, wrote the journalist Pierre Giffard in 1889, "lived with theater, by theater, and for theater."[77] The press played a significant role in promoting plays, developing careers, and building the theater's fashionable image. By intertwining images and accounts of the theater with those of the Grands Boulevards—the boulevard des Italiens and its extension along the boulevards Montmartre and Bonnes Nouvelles—the French press commercialized the fashionable sociability represented by both of these public spaces (see fig. A.1).[78] Boulevard publications such as *Le Figaro, Le Gaulois, L'Echo de Paris, L'Illustration*, and *La Vie parisienne* all had substantial theater coverage.[79] The high-priced *Le Figaro* and *L'Echo de Paris* had circulations of over 100,000 copies and, like expensive subscription magazines such as *Le Théatre*, catered to the large population of the propertied and educated French rather than mass readership.[80] Prestigious critics such as Françisque Sarcey wrote for the Boulevard press rather than the dailies and eventually helped found the theater-specialized subscription press that began to appear in the late nineteenth century. Sarcey was one of the founding editors of *Le Théatre*, first published in January 1898 by the firm Boussod, Manzi, Joyant & Cie.

Le Théatre blended the old style of theater journalism—summaries, reviews, and critiques of plays—with the new celebrity-focused coverage. The magazine's mission was to provide readers with an "instantaneous" snapshot of the gestures, poses, costumes, and mise-en-scène of the leading Parisian, provincial, and international plays of the day.[81] Thanks to technological innovations that made it possible to reproduce affordable high-quality images, *Le Théatre* proudly used photography and colored typogravures "to refresh the memory of those who saw the original, to reveal [the play] to those who were not able to attend, and to be, for the curious of the centuries to come, a source of joy and a lesson."[82] Although each copy sold for two francs, making *Le Théatre* twice as expensive as most illustrated magazines, it was a success: by 1900, the magazine increased its publication from once to twice a month, a rhythm it maintained until the onset of the war in 1914.[83]

The May 1899 issue marked Jane Hading's debut in the pages of *Le Théatre*: not only did she grace the cover of the magazine as Empress Joséphine in the play *Plus que Reine*, but the entire issue was devoted to narrating and reviewing the play (fig. 1.28). Although Hading had already achieved theatrical success, married, divorced, and toured America with renowned actor Benoît-Constant Coquelin before *Le Théatre's* first issue

was even published, she was nevertheless a frequent subject in the periodical: between May 1899 and November 1911, she appeared six times on the cover and eight times inside the magazine. The richly colored covers of Hading in costume underlined her most popular roles: Joséphine in *Plus que Reine* (1899), Maud in *Les Demi-Vierges* (1900), Andrée de Roville in *Le Vertige* (1901), Madame de Pompadour in *La Pompadour* (1901), Thérèse de Rives in *La Châtelaine* (1903), and Madeleine Laroche in *L'Alibi* (1908) (figs. 1.29, 1.30, and see frontispiece and figs. A.6 and A.7).

In these issues, full black-and-white photographs of Hading in costume—on stage or in a studio—were interspersed with posed images of the ensemble cast on the set. At the same time, photographs of Hading at home gave readers a glimpse into her private life (fig. 1.31). Articles on Hading's career and personal interviews, as well as praise from the directors themselves, allowed readers to "know" the woman behind the actress. Often cast in the role of a virtuous but fallen woman, redeemed in the end by the man who initially scorned her but subsequently recognized her inherent goodness, critics commended Hading for her "nuanced," "sincere," "touching," "delicate," and "noble" interpretations, as well as her "beautiful" and "elegant" looks.[84]

Hading, like her peers in the worlds of music hall, opera, and dance who also graced the pages of *Le Théatre*, relied on the magazine to promote her plays and reach out to a public eager for information on her private life and her fashion choices. As powerful marketing tools, actresses were often used by designers to set the tone onstage for the fashion season to come. The designers Redfern and Laferrière purchased full-page ads in *Le Théatre* and other magazines, such as *The Paris Review*, describing the dresses created for Hading's plays and theatrical tours: both designers understood the link between dressing actresses and selling dresses to fashionable theatergoers (see fig. 1.40). Indeed, *Le Théatre* embraced the role of fashion within theater by making "La Mode au Théâtre,"

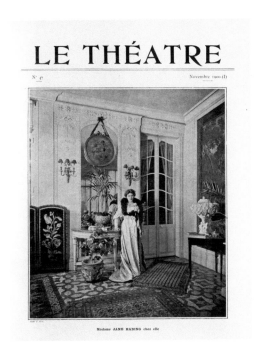

LE THÉATRE

N° 1°   Novembre 1900 (I)

Madame JANE HADING chez elle

FIG. 1.31 Eugène Pirou (French, 1841–1909). "Madame Jane Hading chez elle." Inside cover of *Le Théatre* (November 1900). Private collection.

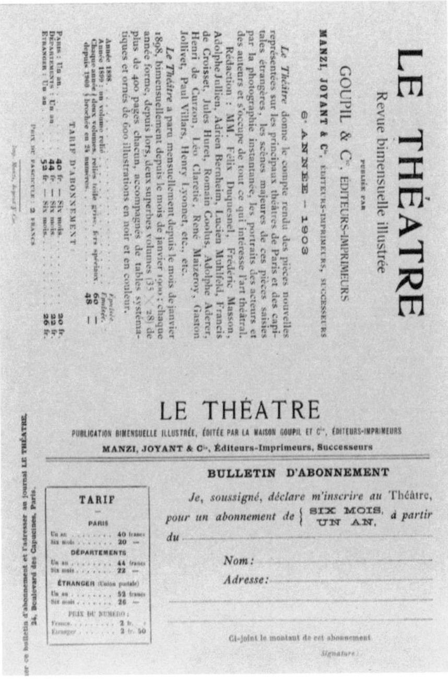

FIG. 1.32 *Le Théatre* subscription card. From *Les Modes* (November 1902). Courtesy of Bibliothèque nationale de France, Paris.

a regular column in the pages of the magazine. Since it was owned by the same publisher as the popular fashion magazine *Les Modes*, subscription cards to *Le Théatre* within *Les Modes* attest to the importance of the stage—the actresses and the theater magazines that promoted them—for the creation and dissemination of new fashions in turn-of-the-century France (fig. 1.32).

If *Le Théatre* tried to balance serious theater reviews with popular articles such as "Madame Jane Hading chez elle," other organs of the press openly stoked the public's hunger for such information. Flammarion published a series of illustrated books called *Les Parisiennes chez elles* featuring

photographs and descriptions of actresses such as Jane Hading in their homes. Hading's home is described in detail—down to water-green velvet wall-coverings in the hall—and her psychology is deconstructed: does her smile betray a veil of sadness, the author wonders?[85] A similar album, *Nos Actrices chez Elles*, published by the photography studio Eugène Pirou in 1890 included three photographs of Hading in her home, one of which was republished in *Le Théatre* ten years later.[86] Some bound photographic albums, such as *Le Panorama*, united portraits and descriptions of actresses (Hading included) with photographs of Parisian street and life scenes and titillating

FIG. 1.33 Henri Manuel (1874–1947) and Larcher. Jane Hading in *La Femme X.* Cover of *Comœdia illustré* (January 1, 1909). Private collection. Cat. 41.

semi-pornographic shots, effectively blurring the division between the theater and the Grands Boulevards as social spaces and the line between public and private behavior represented within (see fig. 1.27).[87]

Although high-end theater magazines and bound photographic volumes excluded gossip, the domain of the newspapers, regional and local papers across Europe and the United States featured articles on such tantalizing topics as Jane Hading's divorce, her physical beauty, her life as an actress, and her rivalry with other actresses such as Sarah Bernhardt. For instance, a full-page article from *The Atlanta Journal* published on February

22, 1903, speculated—based on the Parisian rumor mill—that, as an adolescent, Hading had undergone "a surgery procedure common" in Turkey to make her eyes almond-shaped. Now, the author of the article states, Parisian doctors were being inundated with requests from women to "obtain the Jane Hading eye," despite the "pain and discomfort" caused by such an operation. "Mme Hading," the author concludes, "is the heroine of the hour." The article includes two photographs of Hading along with a close-up illustration of her eyes incorporated into the title, which read "Jane Hading's Wonderful [Eyes] and how they were made."[88] Such gossip kept Hading's name in the press and confirmed her status not only as a celebrity actress but also as a fashion icon whose body, like her home and her clothing, was an attribute to be emulated and commercialized.

Although Hading appeared on the cover of *Comœdia illustré* for its second issue in January 1909, her career was on the wane (fig. 1.33).[89] Hading's last appearance in *Le Théatre* was a full-page black-and-white portrait on the inside cover of the November 1911 issue. Unrelated to the promotion of a play, the picture served as an homage to Hading's beauty, longevity, and status in the world of Paris theater. The image of Hading, now fifty-two years old, had finally begun to fade from the French and international press; although her name was still marketed through her perfume advertisements, the power of her name had now eclipsed the power of her image. —MBK

ADVERTISING

Advertisements featuring actresses such as Jane Hading blended the newsworthy with the commodity: perfume ads, cigarette and biscuit cards, and fashion endorsements capitalized on Hading's reputation as a working actress to sell products, as they allowed Hading herself either to advertise explicitly a role in a play or implicitly advertise her name as an attraction unto itself. Although the variety of such advertisements allowed Hading

FIG. 1.34 Trade card for Duke's Cigarettes with illustration of Jane Hading in Russian costume, ca. 1888–89. Chromolithograph. New York. Private collection. Cat. 42.

FIG. 1.35 Chocolat Guérin-Boutron trade card with photograph of Jane Hading in *L'Aventurière*, ca. 1900. Halftone with hand-applied metallic gold pigment. Private collection. Cat. 47.

FIG. 1.36 Lefèvre-Utile biscuit trade card with illustration of Jane Hading in *Plus que Reine*, ca. 1899. Chromolithograph with embossing and applied halftone. Private collection. Cat. 48.

to amplify and control her image, the possibility of unendorsed advertisements was a constant threat to her authority. In contrast to the detached serialized nature of the cigarette, chocolate, and Lefèvre-Utile trade cards, whereby consumers collected Hading's image alongside those of other actresses or celebrities, the intimate relationship Hading forged between herself and the fashion and beauty products she advertised demonstrated her self-commodification as an elegant and age-less beauty.

Serialized trade cards flourished with the rise of photography and lithography in the 1860s as businesses and manufacturers embraced the new media and the overwhelming response from a consuming public.[90] The small cards were included in the purchase of the object—either a pack of cigarettes, a box of chocolates or biscuits, or a store purchase—and used the lure of serialized collecting to encourage repeat purchases. The back of a Duke's cigarette card with Hading's image specifies that she was one of a collection of fifty, whereas a Chocolat Guérin-Boutron series comprised five hundred "celebrities," Hading included (figs. 1.34 and 1.35). Trade cards could be kept in special books sold for the purpose of displaying a collector's series; some companies such as Chocolat Guérin-Boutron and Lefèvre-

CIGARETTES MELIA. ALGER

FIG. 1.37 Cigarettes Melia trade card with a photograph of Jane Hading in *La Mégère Apprivoisée*, ca. 1900. Hand-colored photograph. Private collection. Cat. 43.

Utile sold their own albums with special slots for the printed cards.[91] The quality of cards ranged from simple photography to complex multistep lithography: the luxurious cards distributed by Lefèvre-Utile, a biscuit company known today by the initials LU, were chromolithographs that were subsequently embossed and painted gold with the halftone photographs pasted on last. The value of these cards as true collectors' items was augmented by the publication of a beautiful art nouveau *Album Lefèvre-Utile*, which included illustrated portraits, autographs, and bibliographical notices of the actresses portrayed on the biscuit cards. Collectors would aim for a complete set of cards but could also purchase the album in order to complement their knowledge of the actresses. Jane Hading was featured in such an album alongside contemporary celebrities such as Sarah Bernhardt, Réjane, and Anatole France.[92]

Most of the collector cards in the exhibition depict Hading in stage costume. Some explicitly refer to the play, either on the front or the back: *L'Aventurière* for Lefèvre-Utile and *Plus que Reine* for Chocolat Guérin-Boutron (fig. 1.36).[93] The unattributed publicity images, such as that for Cigarettes Melia, are all recognizable images of Hading taken by major studios such as Reutlinger and Van Bosch (fig. 1.37).[94] In the Duke's Cigarettes card, Hading is illustrated wearing traditional Russian dress rather than theatrical costume; the conceit of this series of actors and actresses wearing costumes "of all nations, from 600 B.C. to the present time" explains the anomalous representation.

In contrast to the serial nature of trading cards that used Hading as one actress among many others to market a commodity, her endorsements for fashion houses such as Redfern and Laferrière, as well as for her own elixirs and perfumes, show a more personal connection between the actress and her image. Hading used a personal story to market an anti-aging tonic sold under her name as Eau de Jeunesse Jane Hading. As Hading recalled to a journalist in *Les Modes* in 1909, the year that Eau de Jeunesse was launched, she had received the secret formula from a mysterious woman in England many years before but put it away. At the age of fifty, Hading retrieved the scrap of paper with the formula and had it made for her own purposes; enthralled by the age-defying results, she decided to have the elixir produced commercially as a gift to all women.[95] This story, accompanied by pictures of Hading in the prime of her beauty playing her most famous roles and by ads for Eau de Jeunesse, was reprinted twice in *Les Modes* in 1909.[96] One ad featured a drawing of the actress by the artist Daniel de Losques, which was reminiscent of Cappiello's caricature of Hading's silhouette; de Losques used certain recognizable physical traits such as her commanding profile, pigeon-chested figure, and full, upswept hair to sell the elements that constituted the Hading brand: a tonic, a name, and a persona (fig. 1.38 and see fig. 1.7). Ads for the perfume persisted until at least 1913, as documented by a lithographed advertisement from the expensive fashion magazine *Gazette du Bon Ton* (fig. 1.39). The role of Hading's image in advertising Eau de Jeunesse was varied; although her personal anecdote and physical beauty were instrumental for the *Les Modes* advertisements-cum-articles, Hading's name was the sole attraction for the *Gazette* ads that featured youthful women who bear little resemblance to Hading herself.

As or perhaps more important than her promotion of Eau de Jeunesse, Hading's endorsements for the houses of Laferrière, Redfern, and Carlier showed that fashion was an integral part of the Hading "brand." The fashion advertisements either featured photographs of Hading in different costumes from a play with descriptions or else simply stated the essential: "The dresses so admired on Madame Jane Hading in the Théâtre de l'Athénée's successful play 'Le Vertige' are the creation of Redfern 242, Rue de Rivoli, Paris" (fig. 1.40).[97] A successful marketing scheme for both the fashion house and the actress, such advertisements allowed Redfern to use the stage

FIG. 1.38 Daniel de Losques (French, 1880–1915). Advertisement for Eau de Jeunesse Jane Hading, ca. 1910. Courtesy of Bibliothèque nationale de France, Paris.

FIG. 1.39 Pierre Brissaud (French, 1885–1964). Advertisement for Eau de Jeunesse Jane Hading. From *La Gazette du Bon Ton* (ca. 1913). Private collection. Cat. 51.

to showcase and debut their dresses to the society crowd as they provided Hading with the opportunity to display to her audiences her elegant taste in fashion and her acting skills.

As Hading's celebrity rose through the beginning of the century, so too did her advertising power. An advertisement featuring a black woman wearing oriental harem pants and a blue belt with a beaker of distilled rose petals at her feet proves the point that Hading's name had become so recognized as a symbol of fashion and beauty that neither her image nor her likeness was needed any longer: above the woman's upturned head appears the name of the perfume—Parfum Jane Hading

aux Roses d'Orient (fig. 1.41). [98] Hading's name, abstracted from her own image and placed on that of a foreign body, had become merely a whiff of an exotic perfume, an alias for fashionable elegance that had no need for the image of Hading herself to succeed. —MBK

FIG. 1.40 Advertisement for Maison Redfern. Inside cover of *Le Théâtre* (June 1901). Private collection.

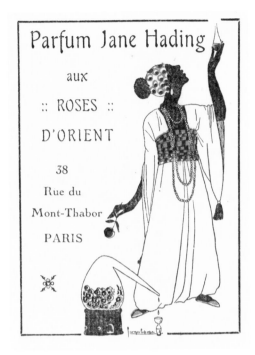

FIG. 1.41 Georges Lepape (French, 1887–1971). Advertisement for Parfum Jane Hading aux Roses d'Orient. From *La Gazette du Bon Ton* (June 1913). Private collection. Cat. 52.

1   "Beautiful Madame Hading: She Chats Gayly About Her Life and Aspirations," *The World*, October 10, 1888; Jane Hading clipping file, New York Public Library for the Performing Arts. This article lays out a standard biography that Hading would recount well into the 20th century.

2   For her full name, see "Jane Hading: Former Favorite of Comedie Francaise Dies at 81," *New York Times*, February 18, 1941. Her actual birthdate is not clearly established and is listed variously as March or November 25, sometimes 26; for the March 25 date, see Roy Day, "Curtain Falls for Jane Hading; A Career Rivaling Bernhardt's," *New York Herald Tribune*, February 3, 1934; for the November 25 date, see *Encyclopedia Britannica*, vol. 12 (Cambridge: Cambridge University Press, 1910), 798. One article ("Portraits of Celebrities at Different Times of Their Lives: Jane Hading," *The Strand* 5 [1893]: 280) gives her date of birth as 1863. Various other clippings give the erroneous birthdate of 1861, although the earliest articles on Hading list the date as November 25, 1859.

3   For her father's full name, see a notice of his death in the Jane Hading scrapbook II, Bibliothèque nationale de France, Paris, Rt 8095, p. 93, dated 1912. Another clipping in the same scrapbook indicates that her father's first name was Paul. See "Les Jolies Actrices de Paris," Rt 8095, p. 8.

4   Amy Leslie, *Some Players: Personal Sketches* (Chicago and New York: Herbert S. Stone & Company, 1899), 524. She may have had a total of three brothers and one sister, according to an article that mentions these siblings as a cause for friction in her subsequent marriage. See "Our Gallery of Players: XXIV. Jane Hading," *The Illustrated American* (December 12, 1891): 179.

5   "Jouer la comédie! ce rêve de mon enfance, a été le roman de toute ma vie. Il n'y a rien au monde que je préfère à cet art terrible et délicieux." Romain Coolus, "Jane Hading: Notes d'Interview," *Le Théâtre* (November 1900): 16.

6   "Our Gallery of Players," *The Illustrated American* (December 12, 1891): 179; Hading notes that she was thirteen in Coolus, "Jane Hading," 16.

7   Félix Jahyer, "Jane Hading de la Renaissance," *Camées Artistiques* (November 27, 1880): n.p.; included in Jane Hading scrapbook II, Bibliothèque nationale de France, Paris, Rt 8095.
8   Coolus, "Jane Hading," 16.
9   "Beautiful Madame Hading," *The World.*
10 Coolus, "Jane Hading," 16.
11 Françisque Sarcey, "In the World of Art and Letters: French Artists in America," *The Cosmopolitan* 18 (1894–April 1895): 752.
12 For this date, see "Croquis Indiscrets," an unattributed clipping in Jane Hading scrapbook I, Bibliothèque nationale de France, Paris, Rt 8096, n.p.
13 "Making an Actress Famous," unattributed clipping, Jane Hading clipping file, New York Public Library for the Performing Arts.
14 "Our Gallery of Players," *The Illustrated American*, 179.
15 Léon Daudet, *Memoirs of Léon Daudet*, ed. Arthur Kingsland Griggs (New York: Dial Press, 1925), 98.
16 "French Talk and Gossip," *New York Times*, May 8, 1887. For more on French divorce laws to 1910, see "Divorce," *Encyclopedia Britannica*, vol. 8 (Cambridge: Cambridge University Press, 1910): 343–44. It is interesting to note that even after Hading filed for divorce, Koning fought a duel with M. Lacour, a journalist who had written an article insulting to her reputation. It is possible this insulting article had something to do with her rumored affairs with Damala, Sarah Bernhardt's husband, or Coquelin. See "Current Foreign Topics," *New York Times*, May 20, 1887.
17 Unknown author and publication, "A Late Parisian Sensation: The Why and the Wherefore of Jane Koning's Divorce Case," with a dateline of "Paris, May 7"; Jane Hading clipping file, New York Public Library for the Performing Arts.
18 The *New York Times* reported that in July 1887 Hading lost her suit against Koning, in which she was asked to be let out of her contract at the Gymnase to play at the Odéon. Koning saw no need for her to work, as he was apparently paying her 2,000 francs per month for living expenses. See "Early July Days in Paris," *New York Times*, July 3, 1887.
19 "Some Recent French Gossip," *New York Times*, July 4, 1884.
20 Sarcey, "In the World of Art and Letters," 753. *Harper's Bazar* called Sarcey "a little, fat, round-headed, red-faced, old man who writes old-fashioned theatrical criticisms for the Temps, and considers it his main business in life to serve as caryatid to hold up the traditions of the French Conservatoire." The *Harper's Bazar* article was reprinted in "Jane Hading at Home: A Visit to the French Actress," *Current Literature: A Magazine of Record and Review* (July–December 1895): 396.
21 One reporter attempted to get at the issue by asking Hading, whom he describes as making "swift, cat-like movements in which she much resembles *la Bernhardt—chez elle*," her opinion on the efficacy of marriage in general. She opined that "Art does not agree with marriage," but the reporter pushed further. Hading, incredulous, asks if he would ever raise such questions to Bernhardt or Lily Langtry. "I suggested that perhaps Mme. Bernhardt could give the public some interesting points upon marriage as a success or as a failure," the author wrote. Hading, "who has been termed

Sarah's rival in more ways than one," replied: "Perhaps she has a better opinion of marriage than I have.... That is why I obtained a divorce." See unattributed clipping, referred to internally as "the Herald" (possibly the *New York Herald*), in the Jane Hading clipping file, New York Public Library for the Performing Arts.
22 The writer of one of Hading's mistakenly published obituaries from 1934 noted that when Damala died in 1889, Hading "made no effort to conceal her grief and for a long period there was a profound note of sadness evident in her personal life." See Day, "Curtain Falls for Jane Hading."
23 "Paris," *The Woman's World* (July 1888): 429–30.
24 Many of these productions are recounted by Hading in the article by Coolus but are also more succinctly listed in an unattributed clipping entitled "Madame Jane Hading," conserved in Jane Hading scrapbook II, Bibliothèque nationale de France, Paris, Rt 8095, pp. 35–36.
25 *Comœdia Illustré* 5, no. 10 (1913): 460, 462. This play is the last notice of Hading playing a regular theatrical run in Paris. A notice of Hading performing in *Le Maître de Forges* at the Apollo Théâtre in Bordeaux, dated October 22, 1916, is included in the Jane Hading scrapbook II, Bibliothèque nationale de France, Paris, Rt 8095, p. 28, indicating she may have made special appearances for short runs in the provinces thereafter.
26 Gaston Bonnefont, *Les Parisiennes chez elles: Nos grandes artistes* (Paris: Ernest Flammarion, 1897), n.p. See also Coolus, "Jane Hading," 14, where the author describes the house, located on the boulevard d'Inkermann, as a "grande maison blanche dans un beau jardin spacieux, de tenue impeccable."
27 "Je retourne au pays qui m'a vu naître. N'ayant plus rien à faire à Paris, puisque je ne peux plus m'occuper de mon art, je préfère finir mes jours dans ma Provence, vers le soleil et les fleurs." A. d'Esparbes, "Mme. Jane Hading évoque les souvenirs de sa brillante carrière"; clipping from unknown publication, Jane Hading scrapbook II, Bibliothèque nationale de France, Paris, Rt 8095.
28 "Jane Hading at Home," 396.
29 Clippings reporting her death are dated February 19 in the Jane Hading scrapbook II, Bibliothèque nationale de France, Paris, Rt 8095. Pierre Guiral and Félix Reynaud, *Les Marseillais dans l'historie* (Paris: Ed. Privat, 1988); 140, lists the 19th as her date of death. However, the dateline on the *New York Times*'s obituary is "Vichy: February 18," and it is logical to assume that she died on that date and that her death was reported the following day.
30 "Bonheur-du-jour, où l'on range les letters d'admirateurs ou d'amoureux.... Tout le décor où vécut la grande actrice Jane Hading vient d'être dispersé au feu des enchères." Louis-Charles Royer, "Le décor où vécut Jane Hading disperse au feu des enchères," *Le Matin*, March 2[1?], 1941. This clipping is in the Jane Hading scrapbook II, Bibliothèque nationale de France, Paris, Rt 8095. The name of the newspaper and the date are written in ink on the clipping.
31 This clipping is housed in the Billy Rose Theatre Collection at the Library for the Performing Arts branch of the New York Public Library in the Robinson Locke scrapbook collection, call number NAFR+ Series 2, vol. 222. The attribution to *The

Illustrated London News is handwritten in ink on the clipping, as is the date of April 10, 1920.

32 These included the houses of the now little-known Félix (for *Le Prince Zilah* in 1885), Magnier et Bruck (for a revival of *Frou-Frou* in 1886) and Mme. Lebouvier (for her 1889 London tour). See Félix, "Les Toilettes de Félix," Supplement to *Le Gaulois*, March 1, 1885: 2; Masque de Velours, "La Vie Mondaine," *Revue Illustrée* (June–December 1886): 724; and Violette, "Paris Fashions," *The Woman's World* (July 1889): 472–73.

33 Information on many early couturiers, including Madame Laferrière, is scant. Surviving Laferrière garments known to have been worn by royalty (such as the gown worn by Princess, later Queen, Alexandra of Denmark now in the Victoria & Albert Museum, London, T.282&A-1974) and some contemporary accounts that name Laferrière as the dressmaker to the court of St. James, make it clear that Laferrière's establishment did indeed rival the House of Worth. See Frederic Lees, "The Evolution of Paris Fashions: An Inquiry," *Pall Mall Gazette* 27 (May–August 1902): 118. Although the house was established by Madame Laferrière (1847–1912) in the 1860s, at some point control of the house's designs apparently passed to an unknown male couturier, as indicated by Hading's reference to Laferrière as "he" in a 1909 article; see Mlle Satoris, "Madame Hading's Ideas of Dress Together with Fashions of the Month," *The Theatre* (October 1909): xvi.

34 Note that the pose of one of the drawings on this page (Hading with her right hand on a table) is clearly modeled on a Reutlinger cabinet card, fig. A.3. The other drawings are probably also based on published photographs with the costumes changed, an example of photography's pervasive power to infiltrate other media and of the iconicity these pictures carried.

35 "La variété inouïe des formes, la richesse des étoffes et des ornements, le goût intelligent de l'ensemble nous donnent la plus exquise, la plus rare sensation de l'imagination et de l'art féminin qu'on puisse rêver." C. de C., "Tournées Artistiques de Madame Jane Hading," *Le Théâtre* (September 1898): inside front cover. The author is likely Claire de Chancenay, who wrote the column "La Mode au Théâtre" for *Le Théâtre*.

36 Jane Hading at Home," 396.

37 "Parisian Stage Topics," *New York Times*, November 16, 1884.

38 Unknown author, "Idylle Tragique: Paul Bourget's Dramatization—A Tiresome Play—Jane Hading's Method of Skirts—Peculiar Architecture of Her Costumes," unknown publication dated 1897, in Robinson Locke Collection of Scrapbooks, New York Public Library of the Performing Arts, call number NAFR, Series 2, vol. 222.

39 Ibid.

40 Langtry first wore Redfern on her American tour in 1882. See Susan North, "Redfern Limited, 1892 to 1940," *Costume* 43 (2009): 88.

41 Susan North, "John Redfern and Sons, 1847–1892," *Costume* 42 (2008): 163.

42 North, "Redfern Limited," 91. Laferrière also contributed designs to the Exposition. See Cecil Beaton and Madeleine Ginsburg, *Fashion: An Anthology* (London: Victoria and Albert Museum, 1971): 34. It should be noted that Laferrière

apparently continued to supply Hading with costumes even after her commitment to Redfern; the program for her 1906 European tour includes advertisements for both dressmaking establishments (as well as Madame Carlier) and notes that Redfern created the gowns for Hading to wear in *Retour de Jérusalem* (as well as her personal wardrobe), while Laferrière created the gowns for *Marquis de Priola*, *Demi-Monde*, and *L'Étrangère*. See "Album-Programme officiel des représentations de Madame Jane Hading et Monsieur Le Bargy," in Jane Hading scrapbook II, Bibliothèque nationale de France, Paris, Rt 8095, p. 71.

43 Hading's luxurious taste is emphasized in her choices, which include her favorite champagne (Moët Impérial Brut), jewelry (Cartier), fan maker (Duvelleroy), perfumier (Guerlain), and photography studio (Reutlinger), all of which were the top suppliers in their fields. "Interview de Mme. Jane Hading," from unknown periodical or program (possibly *Figaro-Modes*), Jane Hading scrapbook I, Bibliothèque nationale de France, Paris, Rt 8096, p. 26.

44 See *La Nouvelle Mode* (June 3, 1900): pls. 43 and 44.

45 Since the 1870s, a dizzying array of historical styles (including many iterations of 18th-century modes) had been popularized by couturiers who predicated their status as artists upon a scholarly knowledge of historical dress, made possible by the many recently published books on the subject, and historically inspired styles or accessories were often touted in the pages of fashion magazines. Many of the historical styles had French referents, and these books were primarily published in France; they included Auguste Racinet's *Le costume historique* (1876–88) and Jules Quicherat's *Histoire du costume en France* (1875).

46 Although Poynter was the designer in Paris, most of the press on the house referred to Mr. Redfern, as Poynter at some point adopted the Redfern surname as his own. Frederic Lees, "The Evolution of Paris Fashions: An Inquiry," *Pall Mall Gazette* (May–August 1902): 118. Van Loo's portrait is housed at the Château de Versailles (MV8616) and de La Tour's at the Musée du Louvre (27614).

47 Although her costume resembles neither portrait entirely, her distinctive lace head covering is most reminiscent of the portrait of Pompadour, whereas the ermine-trimmed domino or cloak she wears resembles the one worn by Madame Drouais. The bust-length portrait of Pompadour (a version of the famous full-length portrait in the National Gallery, London) is housed in the Musée des Beaux Arts d'Orléans (385); Drouais's portrait of his wife (ca. 1758) is in the Musée du Louvre (R.F. 1942-19).

48 Henry Fouquier, "Some Recent French Plays," *The Anglo-American Magazine* (January 1902): 32.

49 Ibid., 31–32.

50 For an image of Hading's costumes in *La Pompadour* from *La Mode Artistique* (December 1901), see North, "Redfern Limited," 93.

51 Marcelle de Mirecour, "Les Succès de Redfern au Théâtre / The Theatrical Successes of Redfern," *Paris Review* (April 1902), n.p.

52 Advertisement for Redfern, *Paris Review* (April 1902).

53 British *Vogue* (February 1, 1923): 63, cited in Susan North, "Redfern Limited," 91.

54 "De même que, pour ses toilettes, Madame Jane Hading a voulu avoir la quintessence de l'élégant, du beau et du riche, de même, pour ses chapeaux, elle a tenu à l'irréprochable et à l'artistique vrai." C. de C., "Tournées Artistiques de Madame Jane Hading," *Le Théâtre* (September 1898): inside back cover.

55 I have found no evidence of a Parisian branch for this firm. The fact that the company cites only its New York address on the label (40 West 36th Street) and the fact that the label in a coat made by the same company in the Costume Institute of the Metropolitan Museum of Art (1986.330) does not cite a Paris connection at all, indicate that a Paris location was likely fictitious.

56 Mlle Sartoris, "Madame Hading's Ideas on Dress Together with Fashions of the Month," *The Theatre* (October 1909): xviii.

57 Ibid.

58 Paris correspondent, "What to Wear: Chit-Chat on Dress," *Cassell's Family Magazine* (June [?] 1887); bound edition (London: Cassell & Company, 1887).

59 Unknown author, "Our Gallery of Players," *The Illustrated American* (December 12, 1891): 179.

60 Unknown author and publication, "The Relation of the Stage to Current Styles of Dress," in Jane Hading clipping file, New York Public Library of the Performing Arts, p. 11. One American entrepreneur used Hading's name to sell fabric, boasting in 1889 that he had "'Belle' Jane Hading Veiling by the yard from 65c up"; see the *Pittsburg Dispatch*, March 13, 1889, 5. From Library of Congress website, http://chroniclingamerica.loc.gov/lccn/sn84024546/1889-03-13/ed-1/seq-3, accessed May 25, 2011.

61 "Au théâtre Michel, les protagonistes, Madame Jane Hading et Mademoiselle Desmond, nous exhibent deux toilettes par acte: réjouissons-nous; celles de Madame Hading sont … des toilettes Jane Hading et l'on sait gré à l'artiste de conserver une marque si personnelle à sa beauté: robes droites et allongeantes sans étroitesse exagérée, laissant au corps une grande souplesse de mouvements." Sybil de Lancey, "La Mode et Les Modes," *Les Modes* 10, no. 120 (1910): 28.

62 John Plunkett, "Carte-de-visite," *The Encyclopedia of Nineteenth-Century Photography* vol. 1, ed. John Hannavy (London: Routlege, 2007): 277; and Plunkett, "Postcard," in the same volume: 1162-63.

63 "Le sourire est comme voilé d'une ombre de tristesse qui en arrête l'épanouïssement." Gaston Bonnefont, *Les Parisiennes chez elles: nos grandes artistes* (Paris: Ernest Flammarion, 1897), n.p.

64 On the reverse of the card showing Hading from the back, the list of awards for Van Bosch ends with a gold medal from Madrid in 1885, indicating that this card dates to sometime thereafter. In 1888 Boyer purchased the Van Bosch Studio, and we might assume that it is at this point that his name begins to be printed on the front of these cards rather than simply stamped.

65 After 1871 the studio was located at 21, boulevard de Montmartre. In 1890 Léopold Reutlinger (1863-1937) met and married Jeanne Seure, the younger sister of the actress Cécile Sorel, née Seure, and this probably facilitated his connections to the theatrical world. He was also the artistic

director of a theater magazine called *Les Feux de la Rampe*. See Jean-Pierre Bourgeron, *Les Reutlinger: Photographes à Paris 1850-1937* (Paris: Jean-Pierre Bourgeron, 1979), 27, 31; and "Interview of Mme. Jane Hading"; from unknown periodical or program, Jane Hading scrapbook no. II, Bibliothèque nationale de France, Paris, Rt 8096, p. 26.

66 Jerome Alfred Hart, *Sardou and the Sardou Plays* (Philadelphia: J. B. Lippincott Company, 1913), 30.

67 "Coquelin as Marecat in 'Nos Intimes,'" *New York Times*, January 10, 1894.

68 From the back of a cabinet card of Hading shot by the famous studio of Nadar now in the New York Public Library for the Performing Arts (call number MWEZ + NC 8110 Jane Hading Photographs), we learn that the photographer charged two francs for such *cartes d'album*, as opposed to one franc each for *cartes de visite*. For more on Nadar, see Elizabeth Anne McCauley, *Industrial Madness: Commercial Photography in Paris 1848-1871* (New Haven and London: Yale University Press, 1994): 105-48.

69 *Plus que Reine* ran for only seventy-five performances in the spring of 1899. Many reviewers despised the play, which they saw as historically inaccurate, but they praised Hading's performance and her costumes, designed by the firm of Goupy. "The actress was preferred to the play," wrote one theater chronicler, and *The Author* reported at the time that the play "lacks cohesion, historical accuracy, and dramatic verve," principally taking issue with the inaccuracy of the costumes. See James Thomas Grein, *Dramatic Criticism*, vol. 5 (1903; repr. London: Eveleigh Nash, 1905), 237; and Darracotte Dene, "Paris Notes," *The Author* (May 1, 1899): 280. Hading's costume for Act III of *Plus que Reine*, curiously absent from postcards but published in *Le Théâtre*, was copied from the Pierre-Paul Prud'hon portrait of Joséphine in the Musée du Louvre (1805, RF270), and the photograph is even staged to approximate the sylvan setting of the original painting. See *Le Théâtre* (May 1899): 6-7, for these photographs. For more information on the specific portraits used as inspiration for *La Pompadour*, see the section on Jane Hading and fashion.

70 Ripert and Frère, *La carte postale*, 66. The United Kingdom did not adopt the divided back until 1902, although by 1896, it had begun to relax regulations against including anything but an address on the versos of these cards. See Richard Carline, *Pictures in the Post: The Story of the Picture Postcard and Its Place in the History of Popular Art* (Philadelphia: Deltiologists of America, 1952), 53.

71 One of these publishers was La Société Industrielle de Photographie, whose mark (S.I.P.) appears on most Reutlinger postcards before 1906. After 1906 Reutlinger gave exclusive rights to the company G. Pirot, which then held the monopoly on publishing Reutlinger postcards throughout the world. See Bourgeron, *Les Reutlinger*, 33-34.

72 Unlike those of Lily Elsie and Billie Burke, most of Hading's postcards are unused, indicating that they were purchased as collectibles.

73 The critic for *Le Théâtre* wrote that the play itself was inaccurate and a simple melodrama, but he had "never seen such pretty and exact costumes in the theatre … of such good taste, after portraits of la favorite." Henry Fouquier,

"Théâtre de la Porte-Saint-Martin," *Le Théâtre* (December 11, 1901): 20.

74 "*Le Panorama* hebdomadaire, de Ludovic Baschet éditeur, publie une galerie de portraits de nos plus jolies actrices photographiées par le célèbre artiste Reutlinger. Il est agréable de pouvoir conserver ces fugitives images de charmeresses que sourient à la foule derrière la trainée lumineuse de la rampe, car toutes ces beautés, tous ces sourires et toutes ces grâces sont destinés à disparaître un jour ou l'autre.... Le livre naît, le portrait se dessine et les charmeuses deviennent immortelles. C'est ainsi que le Panorama hebdomadaire représente chaque actrice dans ses créations les plus célèbres." Albert Vallet, *Le Sélect* (January 1896), as quoted in Bourgeron, *Les Reutlinger*, 31.

75 Dean de la Motte and Jeannene M. Przyblyski, "Introduction," in *Making the News: Modernity & the Mass Press in Nineteenth-Century France*, ed. Dean de la Motte and Jeannene Przyblyski (Amherst: University of Massachusetts Press, 1999), 2.

76 Freed from censorship by the July 29, 1881, law on the freedom of the press, the fin de siècle was the "golden age" and "apogee" of the French press. See Mary Louise Roberts, "Subversive Copy: Feminist Journalism in Fin-de-Siècle France," in *Making the News*, 305.

77 Pierre Giffard, *Nos mœurs, La vie au théâtre* (Paris, 1888), quoted in Lenard Berlanstein, *Daughters of Eve: A Cultural History of French Theater Women from the Old Regime to the Fin-de-Siècle* (Cambridge MA: Harvard University Press, 2001), 11.

78 Berlanstein, *Daughters of Eve*, 17.

79 Ibid., 18.

80 Ibid.

81 *Le Théâtre* was published monthly until 1900 and bimonthly after that. The editors Boussod, Manzi, Joyand & Cie were the successors of Goupil & Cie.

82 "Le Théâtre Instantané," *Le Théâtre* (January 1898): 1. *Le Théâtre* was published continuously from January 1898 until September 1914; publication stopped during the war and resumed on a monthly basis in September 1919. In January 1922, *Le Théâtre* merged with the film magazine *Comœdia Illustré* and became *Le Théâtre et Comœdia Illustré*, a bimonthly publication that ended in December 1925.

83 Françisque Sarcey, "Première Année," *Le Théâtre* (December 1898): 1.

84 The adjectives cited were used in the following reviews: Adolphe Aderer, "Théâtre de l'Athénée," *Le Théâtre* (June 1901): 13; ibid.; Maurice Dumoulin, "Théâtre National de l'Odéon," *Le Théâtre* (June 1908): 8; ibid.; Fernand Nozières, "Théâtre de la Porte-Saint-Martin," *Le Théâtre* (February 1909): 18; Paul Souday, "Théâtre Michel," *Le Théâtre* (December 1910): 23; Jules Huret, "Théâtre de la Renaissance," *Le Théâtre* (November 1902): 12.

85 Gaston Bonnefont, "Madame Jane Hading," *Les Parisiennes chez elles: Nos grandes artistes* (2nd ed. Paris: Flammarion, 1897), 8.

86 *Nos Actrices chez Elles, Photographies de Eug. Pirou* (Paris: Fayard Frères, 1890). Photograph republished as "Madame Jane Hading chez elle," *Le Théâtre* (November 1900).

87 *Le Panorama, Nos Jolies Actrices Photographiées par Reutlinger* (Paris: Ludovic Baschet, 1896). Jane Hading was photographed along with Sarah Bernhardt, Réjane, Cécile Sorel, Anna Held, and others.

88 "Jane Hading's Wonderful [eyes] and how they were made," *Atlanta Journal*, February 22, 1903.

89 *Comœdia illustré* was a 50-centime magazine issued by famed fashion publisher Lucien Vogel and edited by Michel de Brunoff, future editor of French *Vogue*.

90 Virginia Westbrook, "Role of Trade Cards in Marketing Chocolate During the late 19th Century," *Chocolate: History, Culture, and Heritage*, ed. Louis Evan Grivetti and Howards-Yana Shapiro (Hoboken: John Wiley, 2009), 184.

91 The back of the Jane Hading Guérin-Bourton chocolate card advertised the sale of an *Album Livre d'Or des Célébrités Contemporaines* published specifically for the company.

92 *Autographes de la collection Lefèvre-Utile, Les Contemporains célèbres, portraits, autographes, notices biographiques illustrées, portraits humoristiques des célébrités contemporaines* (Paris: O. Beauchamp, 1904).

93 A Chocolat Poulain collector card with an illustration of Jane Handing dressed in costume for *L'Œil crevé* was based on a photograph of the actress by Paul Nadar.

94 The unsigned photographs can be traced to cabinet cards and postcards inscribed with the photography studio's signature.

95 Jane de Céran, "L'Art de Rester Jeune," *Les Modes* (December 1909): n.p.

96 Ibid., and "Jane Hading, La Propagandiste de 'L'Eau de Jeunesse,'" *Les Modes* (August 1909): 25.

97 "Les Toilettes si admirées que porte Madame Jane Hading dans le grand succès du Théâtre de L'Athénée 'Le Vertige' sont des créations de Redfern 242 Rue de Rivoli Paris." Advertisement in *Le Théâtre* (June 1901): inside front cover.

98 This advertisement, with variations in the colors, appeared in the upper left corner of the first page (along with other advertisements) in one issue of the *Gazette du Bon Ton* from 1912 and seven issues from 1913.

II
Lily Elsie
(1886–1962)

*"[Lily Elsie's image] was seen on the popular picture
postcards that arrived by almost every post,
it appeared on chocolate and biscuit boxes, and
newspaper and magazine advertisements
proclaimed the sad wistfulness of her smile."*[1]
—Cecil Beaton

Foulsham & Banfield (English, 1906-20). Postcard of Lily Elsie in
The Merry Widow, ca. 1907. Private collection. Cat. 92.

FIG. 2.1 Foulsham & Banfield. Postcard of Lily Elsie in *The Merry Widow*, ca. 1907. Photograph. Private collection. Cat. 89.

FIG. 2.2 Foulsham & Banfield. Postcard of Lily Elsie in *The Dollar Princess*, ca. 1909. Photograph. Private collection.

LILY ELSIE'S LONDON *TIMES* OBITUARY STATED THAT "her principal assets were her beauty, charm, and personality ... her grace never deserted her."[2] Indeed, Elsie was best known for her classical beauty and the qualities of magnetism and poise she conveyed through her characters on the stage, as she was notoriously shy (fig. 2.1). Unlike many other actresses of the period, she was determined to keep her personal life truly private. However, given the intense and widespread public interest in Elsie, the popular press was relentless in exploiting her popularity, often publishing spurious stories about her, and, as Cecil Beaton later recalled, advertisers also used her image—with or without

her permission—to sell their products.

The British actress was born Elsie Cotton on April 8, 1886, in Wortley, near Leeds. Her family was strictly working class: both of her parents worked in the theater business.[3] She first appeared on the stage at the age of ten in the title role of *Little Red Riding Hood* at the Queen's Theatre in Manchester. At this time, she was known as "Little Elsie," which eventually evolved into her adult stage name. According to Elsie, she "really wasn't an actress" until she began to earn two pounds a week for her part in the chorus of *McKenna's Flirtations*, which toured the United Kingdom for almost a full year in 1900.[4] She went on to play

FIG. 2.3 Foulsham & Banfield. Postcard of Lily Elsie and Robert Michaelis in *A Waltz Dream*, ca. 1911. Photograph. Private collection. Cat. 100.

FIG. 2.4 Foulsham & Banfield. Postcard of Lily Elsie in *The Count of Luxembourg*, ca. 1911. Photograph. Private collection. Cat. 111.

the lead role of Princess Soo-Soo in *A Chinese Honeymoon* at the Royal Strand Theatre in 1903, and in 1906 the famed manager George Edwardes engaged her for a supporting role in *The Little Cherub* at the Prince of Wales Theatre. She did not last long in this role, however; Edwardes witnessed her kicking a ball into the audience at a matinee—an antic she was put up to by her costar, Gabrielle Ray—and he promptly fired her.

But Edwardes soon forgave Elsie and asked her to come work for him again, giving her parts in *The New Aladdin* and *See-See* (both 1906). The following year was a crucial one in Elsie's career: Edwardes offered her the starring role of Sonia in *The Merry Widow* (see figs. A.9 and 2.1). His adaptation of the German operetta *Die lustige Witwe* by Franz Lehár, which had premiered in Vienna in 1905, was an instantaneous success and ran for 778 performances at Daly's Theatre in London.[5] Despite the overwhelming popularity of the show, Elsie later confessed in an interview that the rehearsals were "the most horrible time of [her] life."[6] Rumors abounded that Elsie would be replaced at the last minute by an actress with more experience. But, as she put it, "Mr. Edwardes had made up his mind. He had selected me as an absolute novice, for this important role, in a highly advertised production, and I played the part."[7]

Elsie went on to star in several more Edwardes's productions, including *The Dollar Princess*, *A Waltz Dream*, and *The Count of Luxembourg* (figs. 2.2, 2.3, and 2.4).

Even though Elsie suffered from anxiety, was often ill, and had to undergo an operation right before the opening of *A Waltz Dream*, she was determined to continue acting.[8] Ultimately, it was not her poor health that halted her career on the stage, but her marriage to Ian Bullough in November 1911. Bullough was the son of a Scottish baronet and an extremely wealthy landowner. As soon as their engagement was announced, the press began to speculate about how quickly Elsie would leave the stage for her husband's estate in Cork, Ireland, and many reported that Bullough took it upon himself to close all her professional contracts. Despite rumors that she desperately wanted to return to acting, Elsie disappeared from the stage for almost four years, returning for a charity production of *Mavourneen* at His Majesty's Theatre in 1915. After this, her acting career diminished considerably. She appeared in several more one-day charity productions and only a few plays with multiple performances, her last being *The Truth Game* in 1929. In 1930 she divorced Bullough on grounds of adultery and never remarried.[9]

Lily Elsie retired to Sussex, where she spent her later years in relative anonymity. In 1946 she was one of several former "Gaiety Girls" who gathered for a reunion that was filmed by British Pathé for a newsreel. Her mental and physical health continued to deteriorate, and at an advanced age she underwent a frontal lobotomy, which radically altered her personality and all but destroyed her memory.[10] She died at St. Andrew's Hospital in London on December 16, 1962, at the age of seventy-six. —RP

FASHION

Lily Elsie always appeared both on and off the stage wearing the latest styles, and in addition to her widespread presence on picture postcards,

FIG. 2.5 Rita Martin (English, 1875–1958). Lily Elsie (Mrs. Bullough), ca. 1907. Bromide print. © National Portrait Gallery, London. This photograph appeared in American *Vogue* (May 15, 1913): 93.

she was also photographed extensively for such magazines as *The Play Pictorial*, *Harper's Bazar*, and *Vogue* (fig. 2.5). Elsie was unquestionably an arbiter of elegance to her adoring fans. However, she was not solely responsible for her sartorial choices: the couturiere Lucile (Lady Duff Gordon, 1863–1935) played a central role in Elsie's transformation from an anonymous chorus girl to a star whose name was known worldwide, and the actress wore gowns almost exclusively created by the London-based designer.

Lucile began her career in dressmaking after she divorced her first husband, James Wallace, in 1890 in order to support herself and her young

FIG. 2.7 Sheet music for *The Merry Widow*, ca. 1907. Published by Chappell & Co., Ltd., London, New York & Melbourne. Collection of Marlis Schweitzer. Cat. 85.

FIG. 2.6 Foulsham & Banfield. Postcard of Lily Elsie in *The Merry Widow*, ca. 1907. Hand-colored photograph. Private collection. Cat. 88.

daughter, Esmé. From the outset, Lucile designed costumes for the stage. The first play she dressed was an 1895 amateur charity performance that starred her sister, Elinor Glyn.[11] In 1897 Lucile rose to prominence when she became well known within the theater community for the costumes she designed for *The Liars*.[12] She would later recall that typical Victorian-era stage dresses were "heavy, thick affairs," which "gave their wearers a clumsy appearance," but Lucile defied these conventions and utilized lighter materials, such as silk taffeta and chiffon, in order to flatter actresses and allow them to move freely on stage.[13] Her innovative approach to dressmaking both on and

off the stage made her enormously successful, and throughout her career Lucile created fashions for numerous theatrical productions in Europe and America.

Lily Elsie's relationship with Lucile began in 1907, when her manager, George Edwardes, asked that the renowned couturiere make over Elsie for her first starring role in *The Merry Widow*. As Lucile described the event in her autobiography, *Discretions and Indiscretions*, the young actress was "trembling with nervousness" as Edwardes instructed Lucile to "give her a personality, and coach her so that she can keep it up."[14] The designer completely made over Elsie, not just her

FIG. 2.8 Joseph G. Darlington and Co., Philadelphia (American, active early 20th century). Woman's hat, ca. 1908–10. Straw, silk flowers and leaves. Philadelphia Museum of Art, Gift of an anonymous donor, 1964-123-74. Cat. 53.

appearance, but also her deportment and gestures on the stage. According to Lucile, Elsie credited her with a rapid ascent to celebrity; after the first performance of *The Merry Widow* at Daly's Theatre in London, Elsie supposedly declared to Lucile that "it has been the greatest night of my life, and I owe it all to you!" and threw her arms around the designer.[15] Critics showered praise on the gowns that Lucile designed for *The Merry Widow*. As *The Play Pictorial* described one of Elsie's costumes: "in the third act Miss Elsie...wears a clinging white chiffon Empire gown over palest pink satin. There are gleams of silver on the long trailing skirt, which is beautifully embroidered round the hem with

pink and blue chiffon blossoms. The short silver sleeves and the low-cut bodice are also edged with tassels and knots of palest blue (fig. 2.6).[16] Lucile's greatest sartorial success from *The Merry Widow* was an oversized black hat adorned with pink roses, which became commonly known as the "Merry Widow hat." The first incarnation of the hat was designed for Elsie to wear in the third act of *The Merry Widow*. The original "immense black crinoline hat" was trimmed with a silver band around the crown, feathers, and two "huge" pink roses at the side under the large brim (fig. 2.7).[17]

In the late nineteenth and early twentieth centuries, the theater increasingly became a site

FIG. 2.9 James G. Johnson & Co. (American, active early 20th century). Woman's hat, ca. 1910. Black horsehair lace over wire and bird of paradise. Philadelphia Museum of Art, Gift of Susie McClure, 1958-5-1. Cat. 55.

FIG. 2.10 Suzanne Talbot (French, 1917-57). Woman's hat, ca. 1914-18. Straw, silk velvet, and ostrich feathers. Philadelphia Museum of Art, Gift of Mrs. Richard Greenwood, 1956-106-5. Cat. 56.

FIG. 2.11 Lady Duff Gordon, known as Lucile (English, 1863-1935) for the House of Lucile (English, 1894-1920s). Woman's Merry Widow hat, ca. 1915. Silk and cotton velvet, silk velvet, and egret feathers. Collection of Jan Glier Reeder. Cat. 54.

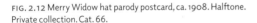

I've all the cash that I can use,
This will of Hubby's fixes that,
There's none to growl next time I choose
To get a MERRY WIDOW HAT.

Copyright 1908
by I. Grollman

FIG. 2.12 Merry Widow hat parody postcard, ca. 1908. Halftone. Private collection. Cat. 66.

He wished to take her arm,
(Now what do you think of that.)
She had to cut a "Man"-hole
In her MERRY WIDOW HAT.

Copyright 1908
by I. Grollman

FIG. 2.13 Merry Widow hat parody postcard, ca. 1908. Halftone. Private collection. Cat. 73.

for women to learn about the latest fashions, not only from their fellow audience members, but also from the actresses on stage. Contemporary plays allowed actresses the opportunity to wear sumptuous gowns by popular designers; this relationship between celebrity and couturier mutually benefitted both parties, as it raised the profile of the designer and enabled the actress to uphold her image as a tastemaker. Even if women could not attend a live performance, they could read vivid descriptions of actresses' costumes in theater periodicals and fashion magazines such as *Harper's Bazar* and *Vogue*. Furthermore, newspaper syndication and developments in the halftone engraving process in the 1890s made it possible for images of stage fashions to be transmitted internationally with relative ease.[18] These advances in technology and the evolving relationship between couturiers and the theater enabled actresses to become "glorious fashion mannequins."[19] Thanks to Lily Elsie's promotion of the Merry Widow hat on the stage and her fans' desire to emulate her, this style of oversized, generously decorated headwear became extremely popular in both Europe and America. Many examples of hats in the Merry Widow style survive, including three from the collection of the Philadelphia Museum of Art (figs. 2.8, 2.9, and 2.10). Although not as extravagant as her theatri-

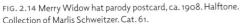

FIG. 2.14 Merry Widow hat parody postcard, ca. 1908. Halftone. Collection of Marlis Schweitzer. Cat. 61.

FIG. 2.15 Marius de Zayas (Mexican, 1880–1961). "Battle of the Hats." From the *New York Evening World*, June 16, 1908. Courtesy of Marlis Schweitzer.

cal confection for Lily Elsie, a black velvet hat by Lucile trimmed with white egret feathers dating to about 1915 shows that the designer continued to create large-proportioned headwear in the years following her earlier millinery triumph (fig. 2.11).

The Merry Widow hat was so prevalent that it commonly appeared in cartoons that greatly exaggerated the size of this fashionable accessory and gently mocked the absurdity and impracticality of the style. In 1908 the American printing company I. Grollman issued a series of postcards featuring humorous photographs of women wearing abnormally large Merry Widow hats. Each postcard also includes a four-line poem on the front describing

the precarious situations these women found themselves in because of their hats (figs. 2.12, 2.13, and 2.14).

An incident at the New Amsterdam Theater in the summer of 1908 revealed the true extent of the Merry Widow hat craze. In celebration of the 275th performance of *The Merry Widow* in New York, the theater promised each woman with a ticket for the show her very own Merry Widow hat. However, when the New Amsterdam Theater came up short by about a hundred hats, a near riot ensued. The June 16, 1908, edition of the *New York Times* included an article outlining the event, entitled "Hot Skirmish Over 'Merry Widow' Hats."

FIG. 2.16 Postcard of three women in Merry Widow hats, ca. 1908. Photograph. Collection of Marlis Schweitzer. Cat. 59.

Women were so eager to claim their prize that they began to line up before the show even ended; as it became apparent that not everyone would receive a hat, the crowd grew violent, and women started to push and shove each other in order to get a hold of the newest vogue in millinery. "Battle of the Hats," a print by Marius de Zayas published in the *New York Evening World*, depicts the melee that resulted in which women of all ages, driven by their desire to be fashionable, grappled for the hat popularized by Lily Elsie (fig. 2.15). The pervasiveness of the Merry Widow hat in both Britain and America in the early twentieth century, as evidenced in a photographic postcard of three

women wearing this style, attests to the influence that the theater had over women's fashion choices (fig. 2.16).[20]

In 1911 Lucile designed Lily Elsie's wedding dress for her marriage to Ian Bullough (fig. 2.17). Lucile herself wrote an article detailing Elsie's Empire-style wedding dress in which she explained that it was inspired by one in the wardrobe of Empress Joséphine.[21] Made of white chiffon embroidered with lace and seed pearls, the gown featured a trained overskirt with ermine-trimmed borders. The gown's columnar shape, pale color, delicate fabrics, and applied ornament were very much in keeping with Lucile's aesthetic and the

FIG. 2.17 Foulsham & Banfield. Postcard of Lily Elsie and her husband Ian Bullough, ca. 1911. Photograph. Private collection. Cat. 113.

FIG. 2.18 Lady Duff Gordon, known as Lucile, for the House of Lucile. Detail of wedding dress worn by Alva Bernheimer at her marriage to Bernard F. Gimbel in the Plaza Hotel ballroom, New York, 1912. Silk georgette, silk satin, needle lace, beads, rhinestones, and wax. Museum of the City of New York, Gift of Mrs. Bernard F. Gimbel, 72.97.1a-b. Cat. 57.

ensembles that she had created for Elsie's onstage wardrobe. Because she was one of the most popular actresses of the period, images of Elsie in her wedding dress were published extensively in Britain and the United States (see "The Press" below). In 1912 Alva Bernheimer wore a very similar dress by Lucile when she married Bernard Gimbel, the future board chairman of Gimbel Brothers, at the Plaza Hotel in New York City (fig. 2.18). Like Elsie's dress, Bernheimer's cream-colored georgette gown is extensively trimmed with faux seed pearls on the bodice and includes the same type of pearl belt with streamers and hem treatment. One wonders if Alva Bernheimer knew of Elsie's gown

and requested something similar from Lucile.

Although Lily Elsie is known today as an iconic beauty and a celebrated Edwardian actress, her rise to fame was greatly assisted by the fashions that she wore. Lucile's diaphanous gowns, constructed of tissue-thin layers of silk chiffon and lace, perfectly complemented the actress's willowy figure and graceful bearing and were essential to the formation of Elsie's image as an elegant stage star. —RP

IN THE
PHOTOGRAPHER'S STUDIO

In Edwardian London, Lily Elsie's face was ubiquitous, popularized by an adoring public and a photography studio (Foulsham & Banfield) that was more than ready to meet the demand for her image. Perhaps the best guide through Lily Elsie's career as a photographic icon is her longstanding ardent admirer Cecil Beaton (1904–1980). His own obsession with actresses, glamour, and photography began in 1907 with an Elsie postcard, which, as he later recalled, presented a face that was "the fashionable concept of perfect beauty."[22] Elsie was at the height of her fame in the first decade of the twentieth century, and the popularity of picture postcards was also at its zenith, especially in England, where one to three million were sent through the post daily.[23] By 1910 *The Chicago Examiner* proclaimed Elsie the "most photographed woman in the world," and the enormous volume of her surviving postcards, almost all dating between 1907 and 1911, corroborate this assertion.[24]

The first postcard of Lily Elsie that Beaton encountered was probably similar to one of the actress in *The Merry Widow* from 1907 (see fig. 2.6). "My enthusiasm for Lily Elsie started," he wrote, "when, at the age of three, I discovered on my mother's bed a tinted picture postcard of this swan-like creature with her jewels dotted with sparkling tinsel. The perfection of her profile sent me into transports."[25] It was a story that Beaton would relate time and again in various books, always remarking upon the photograph's particular power to elicit a strong physical and emotional response. This photograph "caused my heart to leap," he wrote, adding: "My passion for Miss Lily Elsie and my interest in photography were thus engendered at the same moment."[26] In his 1971 book *My Bolivian Aunt: A Memoir*, Beaton recalled encountering the masses of postcards used to decorate a room in his aunt's home: "Aunt Jessie … made a somewhat haphazard collection of

picture postcards of current stage-favourites with which she decorated the top of a gilt and pleated silk screen. . . . The latest smiling postcards of my favourite Lily Elsie gave me the terrible desire for ownership which only a collector knows."[27]

Elsie projected the epitome of refined English elegance, becoming the prototypical "English rose" primarily through her photographic representations, which were appreciated in her own time as particularly dignified. A 1910 article in *The Strand* called "The Art of Gesture" contrasted the acting styles of Continental and English actresses, and by extension their photographic personalities. Broken into two parts ("The Continental View" by Spanish actress Carmen Turia and "The English View" by Lily Elsie), the article contains photographs of the actresses in a variety of poses with captions describing the sentiment each was attempting to portray, feelings such as "Oh, what a plight I was in!" and "My dear, I was perfectly astounded!" Although Turia's photographs depict exaggerated poses with wide eyes, animated arms, and toothy grins, Elsie's photographs for the same captions illustrate her characteristically demure demeanor. "If I were asked what is the real charm of the Englishwoman—how does she differ from the Frenchwoman, the Spaniard, or the American?—I would say it is in her repose," Elsie wrote, adding: "I think many Englishwomen would be sorry if all of our sex grew fiery and tumultuous and exchanged a soft and winning grace for the somewhat alarmingly *empressée* manners of our Continental sisters and rivals."[28]

Two cards offer early glimpses of the actress and provide information on the practice of hand-coloring by consumers at home. Sent in 1905, when Elsie was starring in *The Little Michus* at Daly's Theatre, one card is inscribed: "This one has come at last. How do you like it[?] It is very badly painted as it was done in a hurry." Another, exuberantly tinted, shows Elsie in *See-See*, which debuted in 1906 at the Prince of Wales Theatre (fig. 2.19). "That was a pretty card you sent me this morning," wrote the sender, "and I coloured

FIG. 2.19 Foulsham & Banfield. Postcard of Lily Elsie and Leonard Mackay in *See-See*, ca. 1906. Hand-colored photograph with metallic pigment. Private collection. Cat. 82.

FIG. 2.20 Foulsham & Banfield. Autographed postcard of Lily Elsie and Joseph Coyne in *The Merry Widow*, ca. 1907. Photograph. Private collection. Cat. 90.

FIG. 2.21 Foulsham & Banfield. Postcard of Lily Elsie and the company of *The Dollar Princess*, ca. 1909. Photograph. Private collection. Cat. 108.

it pink and brown according to instructions from my friend who went to Sheffield with me on Thursday. He is staying with me to-day and is now busy colouring post cards his first attempt and I must say that he does them very well indeed." As this card makes clear, men as well as women participated in the pastime, which added a personalized touch to mass-produced photographs. Beaton also noted the power of hand-coloring and wrote of his encounter with the seminal Elsie postcard of his youth: "To make the whole effect more unbearably beautiful, the photograph had been tinted; the cheeks and lips of this divine creature were of a translucent pink that I could never

hope to acquire from my box of crayons, and the tulle corsage of her pale yellow dress was spangled with tinsel stardust."[29] In a world of black-and-white photography, color and glitter added a quasi-magical aura to these images, and dramatically highlighted the fashions therein.

If the photographic postcard brought an actress's presence into the home, an autographed image made her presence even more palpable. Autographed cards were clearly desirable to fans who had seen Elsie perform and to those who had not; senders sometimes forewent a message on the back, suggesting that Elsie's autograph alone would have been sufficient as a special gift to a

FIG. 2.22 Foulsham & Banfield. Postcard of Lily Elsie and Lennox Pawle in *The Merry Widow*, ca. 1907. Photograph. Private collection.

FIG. 2.23 Foulsham & Banfield. Postcard of Lily Elsie and Bertram Wallis in *The Count of Luxembourg*, ca. 1911. Photograph. Private collection.

fellow admirer. Signed by Elsie and Joseph Coyne, her costar in *The Merry Widow*, one card may have been an especially cherished souvenir, as it was not sent until 1912, some five years after the play had premiered (fig. 2.20).

New images of stars were eagerly awaited by fans, and women in particular looked forward to the latest postcards for their fashion offerings. Many of Elsie's postcards contain messages expressing the hope that the recipient will "like this one," intimating that they are collectors of her image. On the back of a striking postcard of Elsie in *The Merry Widow*, the sender wrote; "This is not a new one, but still I think it is very good.

Mrs. K was too busy talking to some man to show me where to find any new ones" (see page 126). Sent in July 1908, the card includes a postscript stating: "This is the original Merry Widow hat." By that time, the play had run for hundreds of performances, and postcards from the production featuring Elsie in her Moravian ensemble, as well as more fashionable attire, were ubiquitous. The postscript indicates that the recipient may not have been familiar with the origins of the Merry Widow hat, a term that by 1908 referred generically to a very large hat.

A card featuring Lily Elsie and the company of *The Dollar Princess* exemplifies the type of

FIG. 2.24 Foulsham & Banfield. Postcard of Lily Elsie in a garden, ca. 1911. Photograph. Private collection. Cat. 99.

FIG. 2.25 Foulsham & Banfield. Postcard of Lily Elsie in her Lucile wedding dress, ca. 1911. Photograph. Private collection. Cat. 112.

postcard that appeared in the 1890s, thanks to the innovation of onstage photography (fig. 2.21).[30] Many of Elsie's photographic postcards, all by Foulsham & Banfield, were shot in the theater itself rather than in the studio and have more immediacy than her staged glamour shots, which may have appealed to a different type of collector.[31] The narrative postcards from *The Merry Widow* are obviously posed; it is possible that many, if not all, of these photographs were taken in front of painted backdrops rather than onstage (fig. 2.22). Postcards with scenes from *The Dollar Princess* are much more lively and were evidently taken onstage, as were those taken for *The Count of Lux-*

embourg in 1911 (fig. 2.23 and see fig. A.10). Close examination of many of the cards from the latter production reveals the telltale signs of retouching, including the enhancement of Elsie's makeup.

The numerous images of Elsie in her Lucile frocks firmly established her reputation as one of the designer's muses and, accompanied by a steady stream of publicity, the pictures helped create the notion of Elsie as a fashion plate. Cards such as a 1907 Foulsham & Banfield postcard of the actress (see fig. VI) did not identify the play in which Elsie appeared but instead presented her primarily as a fashion plate in which the consumer might dissect the details of her ensemble.

FIG. 2.26 Rita Martin. Postcard of Lily Elsie (Mrs. Ian Bullough), ca. 1913. Photograph. Private collection. Elsie wears the same dress in fig. 2.5. Cat. 114.

FIG. 2.27 Cecil Beaton (English, 1904–1980). Lily Elsie (Mrs. Bullough), mid-1940s. Bromide print on white card mount. Courtesy of the Cecil Beaton Studio Archive at Sotheby's.

Collectors interested in Elsie and her gowns could be voracious; another card includes the message "Isn't this lovely? Can you get me one like it[?] I have 23 'Dollar Princess' p.c.'s but not this. If you can't get it please send one of her in private dress" (see figs. III and IV).

Even the cards that captured Elsie's "private" moments carried as much information about her public style as they did about her personal pastimes. A few give a somewhat voyeuristic impression of the actress "at home," pursuing the bucolic activities of proper domestic life by tending to, or frolicking in, her garden (fig. 2.24). Her impractical attire in this image reinforces her fashion-plate persona. Postcards that showed the star in her wedding gown, with or without her new husband, ostensibly admitted consumers to an important moment in her private life but served equally to present her as a fashionable theatrical star showing off her Empress Joséphine-inspired Lucile dress (fig. 2.25 and see fig. 2.17). In the space normally reserved for the actress's name and role or play title on these postcards, Elsie's new identity as Mrs. Ian Bullough appears instead, signaling her new "role" in life.

A postcard of Elsie sent in 1913 also features a Lucile gown (fig. 2.26). It illuminates the star's short-lived split personality as theatrical fashion icon and newly minted society dame by including both her professional name, "Miss Lily Elsie," and her married name, "Mrs. Ian Bullough." Her subsequent retirement from the stage meant that she virtually disappeared from public view and was never again a presence in the world of photographic postcards.

By the 1940s, only Cecil Beaton, who had by then struck up a friendship with his childhood idol, could coax the aging star in front of the camera once more, and he photographed her in an original Merry Widow hat in an attempt to re-create the dreamy atmosphere of the postcards of his youth (fig. 2.27).[32] In the photographer's opinion, she "still looked beautiful in the fashions she had worn nearly forty years before."[33] —WD

THE PRESS

Despite being the "most photographed woman in the world," Lily Elsie maintained an unusual level of privacy (fig. 2.28).[34] Unlike many of her peers, Elsie did not actively cultivate a relationship with the press as a means of enhancing her celebrity image; in fact, she was extremely shy and rarely granted personal interviews. One notable exception was an interview with the influential Hearst critic and journalist Alan Dale, published in *Cosmopolitan* in December 1911 (fig. 2.29).[35] In his article, Dale pondered whether Elsie would receive him "without any frills or furbelows" stating, "I pictured her as somewhat haughty, with her pensive penitence as a pose."[36] However, Dale quickly discovered that Elsie was "as unassuming as though her position were still to be secured" and commented that he "felt at home with her at once."[37] By the end of their conversation, Dale came to the conclusion that "this was no pose. Miss Elsie was not acting. This was the real thing."[38] Nonetheless, Elsie's introverted nature did not deter the press from speculating about every aspect of her life, from her failing health to rumored marriages and later her divorce, and from frequently using her well-known and much-loved image to generate

sales. In fact, it would seem that her intense popularity combined with her insistence on keeping out of the public eye encouraged the press in its sensationalist reporting on the actress.

Although reluctant to allow the press access to her private life, Lily Elsie's professional career demanded extensive use of her image in theater-

FIG. 2.28 "A New Picture Every Day in the Year for Lily Elsie." From *The Chicago Examiner*, May 1, 1910, 59, 61, 62. Billy Rose Theatre Division, The New York Public Library for the Performing Arts, Astor, Lenox and Tilden Foundations.

FIG. 2.29 "The Girl Who Made Good." From *Cosmopolitan* (December 1911): 85. Billy Rose Theatre Division, The New York Public Library for the Performing Arts, Astor, Lenox and Tilden Foundations.

related publications such as *The Play Pictorial*. She appeared on the cover of this magazine four times between 1907 and 1911 for each of her major roles: Sonia in *The Merry Widow*, Alice Conder in *The Dollar Princess*, Franzi Steingruber in *A Waltz Dream*, and Angèle Didier in *The Count of Luxembourg* (figs. 2.30, 2.31, 2.32 and see fig. A.11). Inside, the pages were filled with numerous black-and-white photographs of the star in her Lucile gowns and other cast members, presenting highlights of the individual productions.

Elsie's popular appeal and good looks were often lauded by the press, who hailed her as "the most photographed beauty on the Eng-

lish stage."[39] According to one article, the most ardent admirer of the actress was King Manuel of Portugal. In 1909 the young king made a visit to England; on a whim, someone suggested that he go see *The Merry Widow* at Daly's Theatre in London. King Manuel saw the play three times and declared that Lily Elsie was "the most beautiful and the most fascinating woman he had ever seen."[40]

Owing to Elsie's renowned loveliness and charm, the press often sparked rumors about her impending marriages to a bevy of eligible, wealthy men. In the summer of 1910, the *San Jose Evening News* informed their readers that Miss Elsie, who was "in the full flower of her loveliness," was to marry Alfred G. Vanderbilt.[41] There is no way to know if there was any truth to this rumor, but most likely the press fabricated the story to catch readers' attention; it is unclear if Vanderbilt ever saw Elsie perform or met her. Rumors of Elsie's "impending" marriages continued to persist: a piece published in *The Philadelphia Inquirer* on April 16, 1911, reported on Elsie's recovery from surgery, ending with: "[Elsie] finds it necessary to again state that she is not about to be married and that she isn't even engaged."[42]

A few months later, on November 7, 1911, Elsie did indeed marry the Scottish millionaire Ian Bullough (see fig. 2.17). Public interest in her wedding knew no geographical bounds: newspapers all over the world covered the event, reporting on every aspect of her engagement, wedding, and trousseau. Elsie's anticipated retirement from the stage once she became Mrs. Ian Bullough was also a popular topic in the newspapers. The day after her wedding, *The Philadelphia Inquirer* reported: "Although there is a rumor that Mr. Bullough is in consultation with George Edwardes regarding Miss Elsie's reappearance on the stage from time to time, the fact is that he is simply closing up the contracts, for she herself has decided on retirement."[43] The public was convinced that matrimony would bring an end to Elsie's career on the stage, and , although she stopped performing

FIG. 2.30 Foulsham & Banfield. Lily Elsie and Joseph Coyne in
The Merry Widow. Cover of *The Play Pictorial* (August 1907).
Billy Rose Theatre Division, The New York Public Library for the
Performing Arts, Astor, Lenox and Tilden Foundations.

FIG. 2.31 Foulsham & Banfield. Lily Elsie in *The Dollar Princess.* Cover of *The Play Pictorial* (November 1909). Private collection. Cat. 116.

FIG. 2.32 Foulsham & Banfield. Lily Elsie and Bertram Wallis in *The Count of Luxembourg.* Cover of *The Play Pictorial* (July 1911). Private collection. Cat. 118.

soon afterward, the press nonetheless published articles that showed her in her latest "role" as a newly married socialite who took up leisurely pursuits such as fox hunting (fig. 2.33).[44]

Happiness did not last long in Elsie's marrige to Bullough: as early as 1913, newspapers began reporting that the actress was suing her husband for divorce.[45] In fact, they did not divorce until 1930, but that didn't stop speculation that Elsie was unhappy. Some even reported that she was so despondent that she was suffering from a "strange ailment" or even on the brink of death.[46] Like many other actresses of her time, Elsie was a constant figure in the press throughout her career,

as the public longed to read any information they could about the Edwardian stage star. —RP

ADVERTISING

Although Lily Elsie's shyness often prevented her from enthusiastically embracing her role in the public eye, she nonetheless participated, to some degree, in the early twentieth-century phenomenon of testimonial advertising. Like many of her fellow actresses, Elsie "personally" endorsed a number of products, including soap, clothing, nerve tonics, and skin-care and beauty products (figs. 2.34 and 2.35). However, the degree of direct participation that actresses such as Elsie had in the creation of such advertisements likely varied, as personal, sworn testimonials for products often seem canned and advertisers repurposed existing photographs. For example, an ad for Phosferine nerve tonic printed in a 1912 issue of *The Play Pictorial* re-used a Foulsham & Banfield image of Elsie in *A Waltz Dream* that had not only been printed on postcards but had also appeared in the September 15, 1912, issue of American *Vogue* (fig. 2.36).

In 1909, the year that Elsie starred in *The Dollar Princess* at Daly's Theatre, she also appeared in a wordy full-page advertisement for Madame Helena Rubinstein's Valaze Toilet Preparations (fig. 2.37). The design of this advertisement, featured in the issue of *The Play Pictorial* dedicated to this production, mimics the layout of a magazine article, complete with two columns of text, a photo of Elsie in the center, and the title "The Toilet Needs of 'The Dollar Princess.'" The opening paragraph of the advertisement's text establishes Elsie as a woman of great fame and talent, as it references both her breakout role as Sonia in *The Merry Widow* and her more recent role in *The Dol-*

FIG. 2.33 "In Her Latest Rôle: Miss Lily Elsie as a Member of Her Husband's Hunt." From *The Bystander* (November 19, 1913): 405. Billy Rose Theatre Division, The New York Public Library for the Performing Arts, Astor, Lenox and Tilden Foundations.

FIG. 2.34 Postcard of Lily Elsie modeling the Knitroyal Sports Coat, 1915-20. Photograph. Private collection. Cat. 119.

FIG. 2.35 Advertisement for Erasmic soap featuring Lily Elsie. From *The Play Pictorial* (July 1911): vii. Private collection.

FIG. 2.36 Advertisement for Phosferine nerve tonic featuring Lily Elsie. From *The Play Pictorial* (December 1912): xx. Private collection.

always the best, for herself and others." Not surprisingly, the text then states that what she found in her search for the finest was the product featured in this ad, Madame Rubinstein's Valaze Toilet Preparations. According to the ad copy, Elsie has "that perfect complexion that comes from perfect skin health under perfect care" and would never use anything on her complexion that had not been put to "the most scrupulous and exacting tests." Through its association with an actress who is depicted as having discriminating tastes and is naturally beautiful, the reputation of Madame Rubinstein's Valaze skin care was presumably elevated in the eye of the consumer.

The ad also includes a brief personal endorsement from "Miss Elsie" herself, who wrote to Madame Rubinstein to say: "After several months' use of your Valaze, I can frankly say that I have found nothing as beneficial." The copy calls attention to the believability of Elsie's personal support of Valaze skin-care products: "No extravagance of praise, but a simple and moderate statement of experience." Elsie's original handwritten letter, dated November 16, 1909, is reproduced in the center of the page, further augmenting the validity of her endorsement.

Directly above the facsimile of Elsie's note is a half-length portrait of the actress in profile. Wearing a large straw hat adorned with flowers, reminiscent of the Merry Widow style that she popularized, and a simple white blouse with pearls, Elsie looks every bit the "English rose" that this advertisement made her out to be. Beautiful, but not intimidating or overtly sensual, Elsie represented an ideal that all women could try to achieve through the use of Valaze skin products. The text further emphasizes the accessibility of Madame Rubinstein's skin products as well as her personal advice, stating that this "admitted leader of the British beauty cult" is "at all times ready to advise women on matters concerning the care of the complexion" and that, no matter what the circumstances, "she is prepared to advise personally and make no charge for the advice." Madame

lar Princess. The ad copy goes on to describe Elsie's role as Sonia as "never-to-be-forgotten" and the actress herself as "the merriest widow of all," with "infinite grace and charm in her merriment and infinite tenderness behind it."[47] Elsie's fame continued to grow with her part in *The Dollar Princess*, where she is "as invigorating as the sea-breeze, as alluring as a June rose-bud." Elsie's charisma on the stage and her natural beauty, rather than her thespian talents, are highlighted in order to validate her as an aspirational model of attractiveness for the ad's intended female audience.

The advertisement also identifies "Miss Elsie" as "a young lady who has always gone around the world with her eyes wide open, seeking the best,

The Toilet Needs of "The Dollar Princess"

WHEN Miss Lily Elsie created the never-to-be-forgotten part of the Merry Widow, she was the merriest widow of all—the merriest widow conceivable. There was infinite grace and charm in her merriment and infinite tenderness behind it. And now again in the name part of the Dollar Princess she is as invigorating as the sea-breeze, as alluring as a June rose-bud.

She is also a young lady who has gone about the world with her eyes wide open, seeking the best, always the best, for herself and others. Some time ago she found the Valaze Toilet Preparations and these now, of course, have all her suffrages. She has that perfect complexion that comes from perfect skin health under perfect care. She uses nothing for her complexion that she has not put to the most scrupulous and exacting tests.

The other day she wrote to Mme. Rubinstein, who introduced the Valaze preparations to English boudoirs, as follows: "After several months' use of your Valaze, I can frankly say that I have found nothing as beneficial."

(The original of Miss Elsie's letter is reproduced on this page.)

No extravagance of praise, but a simple and moderate statement of experience.

On still another occasion Miss Elsie expressed herself emphatically on the high merit of Valaze Complexion Soap and Face Powder.

One has yet to meet the woman who tried Valaze without prejudice and was dissatisfied with it. It isn't possible. Valaze does what it is intended to do for the complexion better than anything else in the world can do it. It therefore becomes merely a matter of sagacity to test a treatment that thousands of other women have found so beneficial and so good.

Madame Rubinstein, the admitted leader of the British Beauty Cult, is at all times ready to advise women on matters concerning the care of the complexion. It does not matter to her whether they have previously been clients of hers or not. It does not matter how apparently trivial the trouble. She is prepared to advise personally and make no charge for the advice. Where any woman's complexion is concerned, she loves to take trouble. That is her form of enthusiasm and, coupled with the qualifications she possesses for her *metier*, the secret of her tremendous success.

A full and detailed account of Mme. Rubinstein's specialities and of the unique and exclusive methods of complexion treatments employed by her at her famous Maison de Beaute Valaze, 24, Grafton Street, Mayfair, London, will be found in her book, "Beauty in the Making," which deals competently and fully with all complexion defects, and points the way to their prevention and relief. It will be forwarded free on application, when this paper has been mentioned.

The following are the names and prices of some of Mme. Rubinstein's Complexion Specialities: Valaze Skinfood, 4s. 6d., 8s. 6d. and 21s. a jar; Valaze Complexion Soap, 2s. 6d. and 4s. 6d. a cake; Valaze Complexion Powder for greasy and normal skins, or Novena Poudre (for dry skins), at 3s., 5s. 6d. and 10s. 6d. a box; Valaze Lip Lustre, for chapped and pale lips, 2s. 0d. and 3s. 6d.; Dr. Lykuski's Blackhead and Open Pore Cure, 3s. 6d. a box, No. 2. of same for more obstinate cases, 6s. 0d.; Valaze Snow Lotion, a superb Viennese liquid powder, 4s. 0d., 7s. 0d. and 10s. 6d., the same, Special, for greasy skins, 7s. 6d. and 21s. 0d. a bottle; Valaze Liquidine, overcomes redness of nose and cheeks, and adds tone to the skin, 10s. 6d. a bottle.

All correspondence should be addressed to Mme. Rubinstein, Dept. "P.P.," 24, Grafton Street, Mayfair, London.

When communicating with Advertisers kindly mention "THE PLAY PICTORIAL."

ADVT.   XV.

FIG. 2.37 Advertisement for Mme. Rubinstein's Valaze beauty products featuring Lily Elsie. From *The Play Pictorial* (November 1909): xv. Private collection.

Rubinstein's promise of the best care to her customers is followed by a description of a booklet she authored on skin care and a detailed list of all the products available from her line, with prices.

Two years later, in 1911, when Elsie performed in *A Waltz Dream* and *The Count of Luxembourg*, her image appeared in two additional Valaze ads included in *The Play Pictorial* issues focusing on those productions.[48] The first ad features bust-length images of eight popular stage actresses above their testimonials and signatures, with Lily Elsie at the top in one of her easily recognizable Merry Widow hats. The second ad, titled "Let her not Walk in the Sun"—which the copy cites as "Hamlet's advice to Ophelia"—presents a large full-length photograph of Lily in stage costume from *The Count of Luxembourg* above her testimonial. Although the text itself does not refer to or quote the actress, she clearly represents a woman with the ideal "clearness and whiteness of skin" that the use of Valaze promises to consumers.[49]

Lily Elsie's endorsement of Madame Rubinstein's Valaze skin-care products exemplifies the turn-of-the-century phenomenon of actresses' participation in testimonial advertising. Their fans admired them for their beauty, talent, and charm and were likely persuaded to purchase the products they endorsed in hopes of acquiring some of these attributes for themselves. —RP

1   Cecil Beaton, "Lovely Lily Elsie," *The Rise and Fall of the Matinée Idol: Past Deities of Stage and Screen, Their Roles, Their Magic, and Their Worshippers*, ed. Anthony Curtis (New York: St. Martin's Press, 1974), 3.

2   "Miss Lily Elsie: The Merry Widow" *The Times*, December 18, 1962.

3   David Slattery-Christy, *Anything But Merry!: The Life and Times of Lily Elsie* (London: Author House, 2008), 6, 16. There is some uncertainty as to who Elsie's father was and what surname she would have taken at birth. Elsie's mother was Charlotte Elisabeth Barret, known as Lottie; she had worked in cotton mills and as a dressmaker for the performer Nelly Power in the 1870s. Slattery-Christy implies that Lottie was not sure who fathered her daughter (see *Anything But Merry*, 1). Elsie's father could have been William Charles Cotton, known as Billy, who worked as a baggage handler at the Prince of Wales Theatre in Salford, or Bert Hodder, who worked as a flyman at various theaters. According to Slattery-Christy, Lottie had been with Cotton but left him for Hodder, and she returned to Cotton shortly after Elsie's birth. She then married Cotton on March 19, 1891 (p. 18), and Elsie was given his last name at this time. Although Slattery-Christy's work is a sensationalized account of Elsie's life, it is the only published reference that speculates as to the identity of Elsie's father; I was unable to find an interview with the actress in which she discussed her parentage or early childhood.

4   Alan Dale, "The Girl Who Made Good," *Cosmopolitan* (December 1911): 88.

5   Ernest Henry Short and Arthur Compton-Rickett, *Ring up the Curtain: Being a Pageant of English Entertainment Covering Half a Century* (London: Herbert Jenkins, 1938), 153.

6   Dale, "The Girl Who Made Good," 90.

7   Ibid.

8   Elsie said of her performance in *A Waltz Dream*: "The day before the opening I was under the influence of morphin [sic], and it seemed a sure thing that I should not appear. Oh how I willed! I made up my mind that I *would* play. I couldn't contemplate anything else." Dale, "The Girl Who Made Good," 91.

9   "Probate, Divorce, and Admiralty Division (Before Mr. Justice Hill): Decree Nisi for Miss Lily Elsie," *The London Times*, July 16, 1929.

10 Slattery-Christy, *Anything But Merry!*, 192–93.

11 Lady Duff Gordon, *Discretions and Indiscretions* (London: Jarrolds Publishers, 1932), 43.

12 Ibid., 47.

13 Ibid., 47–48.

14 Ibid., 101–2.

15 Ibid., 103.

16 Louise Heilgers, "Delightful Dresses at Daly's," *The Play Pictorial* 10 (1907): 106.

17 Ibid., 107.

18 Marlis Schweitzer, "'Darn That Merry Widow Hat': The On- and Offstage Life of a Theatrical Commodity, circa 1907-1908," *Theatre Survey* 50, no. 2 (2009): 199.

19 Ibid., 191.

20 Schweitzer, "Darn That Merry Widow Hat," 189–221. In this article, Schweitzer explores the full scope of the

social, cultural, and gender implications of the Merry Widow hat.

21 Lady Duff Gordon (Lucile), untitled article in the *Louisville Herald*, December 14, 1911.

22 Beaton, "Lovely Lily Elsie," 3.

23 Veronica Kelly, "Beauty and the Market: Actress Postcards and their Senders in Early Twentieth-Century Australia," *New Theatre Quarterly* 78, no. 20, part 2 (2004): 102.

24 "A New Picture Every Day in the Year for Lily Elsie," *Chicago Examiner*, May 1, 1910. Robinson Locke Scrapbook Collection, New York Public Library for the Performing Arts.

25 Beaton, "Lovely Lily Elsie," 13. Beaton would have been three in 1907, the year of *The Merry Widow*'s premier, making it likely that he first glimpsed a photograph of Elsie in this iconic role.

26 Cecil Beaton, *Photobiography* (New York: Doubleday, 1951), 14.

27 Cecil Beaton, *My Bolivian Aunt: A Memoir* (London: Weidenfeld and Nicolson, 1971), 46.

28 Lily Elsie, "The Art of Gesture: II. The English View," *The Strand* (December 1910): 726, 728.

29 Beaton, *Photobiography*, 14. This postcard may have been hand-colored in the factory rather than at home.

30 David Mayer, "The Actress as Photographic Icon: From Early Photography to Early Film," *The Cambridge Companion to The Actress*, ed. Maggie B. Gale and John Stokes (Cambridge: Cambridge University Press, 2007), 89.

31 The studio was located after 1908 on fashionable Old Bond Street. Michael Pritchard, *A Directory of London Photographers, 1841-1908* (London: PhotoResearch, 1994), 61. The vast majority of Elsie's postcards were published by the Rotary Photographic Company in London.

32 Ibid., 14.

33 Ibid.

34 "A New Picture Every Day in the Year for Lily Elsie." Several of these photographs show Lily Elsie in her stage roles, including Sonia in *The Merry Widow* and Alice Conder in *The Dollar Princess*.

35 Alan Dale, "The Girl Who Made Good," *Cosmopolitan* (December 1911): 85-91. Dale later interviewed Billie Burke for the same magazine; see Alan Dale, "Billie Burke, Comédienne," *Cosmopolitan* (May 1914): 842-44.

36 Ibid., 85.

37 Ibid., 86.

38 Ibid., 90.

39 Untitled article from the *Los Angeles Enquirer* (September 17, 1913). Robinson Locke Scrapbook Collection, New York Public Library for the Performing Arts.

40 "Manuel's Heart with Lily Elsie," *Philadelphia Inquirer*, December 5, 1909.

41 "Alfred Vanderbilt May Wed Actress," *San Jose Evening News*, June 6, 1910.

42 Untitled article from *The Philadelphia Inquirer*, April 16, 1911.

43 "Wealthy Scot to Marry Lily Elsie: Favorite English Actress Will Retire from the Stage Before Long," *The Philadelphia Inquirer*, November 12, 1911.

44 "In Her Latest Rôle: Miss Lily Elsie as a Member of Her Husband's Hunt," *The Bystander* (November 19, 1913): 405.

45 Untitled article from the *Los Angeles Enquirer*, September 17, 1913; Robinson Locke Scrapbook Collection, New York Public Library for the Performing Arts.

46 "Married Rich Gaiety Girls Unhappy," newspaper unknown, December 11, 1912; Robinson Locke Scrapbook Collection, New York Public Library for the Performing Arts. The legitimacy of this article is dubious, given that the author calls Elsie's husband "Ivan Bullough" and states they married in August of the previous year.

47 Advertisement for Mme. Rubinstein's Valaze beauty products. *The Play Pictorial* (November 1909): xv.

48 For the ad in the issue featuring *A Waltz Dream*, see *The Play Pictorial* 17, no. 103 (1911): xi; for the ad in the issue featuring *The Count of Luxembourg*, see *The Play Pictorial* 18, no. 108 (1911): xxi.

49 Ibid.

III
Billie Burke
(1884–1970)

*"The secret of successful dressing is to be original; then
it is no longer a case of following the fashion, but of the
fashion following you, which is much more entertaining.
In nearly all my stage gowns I aim at some quaint
or original idea which invariably catches on and
becomes what is called a fashion."*
—Billie Burke, *The Strand*, May 1907

BILLIE BURKE FAMOUSLY LOVED TO REPEAT THAT HER success as a stage actress had as much to do with the fashions she wore as with her acting talent.[1] Although this quip highlighted Burke's image as a Broadway fashion icon, it diminished the effort it took her to get there. Mary William Ethelbert Appleton Burke was born in 1884 in Washington, D.C. Early in 1883, her father, William Ethelbert Burke, a singing clown in the Barnum and Bailey Circus, had attracted the attention of a forty-year-old widow, Blanche Hodkinson—Billie's mother—and the couple married shortly after.[2] Billie toured the United States with her parents until she was eight years old, when her family set off for London, where her father was eager to try his luck with a show of his own.[3] In her first autobiography, *With a Feather on My Nose*, Burke wrote that her mother pushed her to become an actress—a career Burke claimed that she would not have chosen, owing to her shyness.[4] Burke had her first professional success singing the catchy song "Mamie, I Have a Little Canoe" in the musical *The School Girl* at London's Prince of Wales Theatre in 1903.[5] The song was a hit, and Burke became an overnight celebrity at the age of eighteen. "I remember my excitement," Burke writes, "when I discovered photographers of the West End had their windows full of my pictures—and that they were selling along with those of Lady Randolph Churchill, Queen Alexandra, and the beautiful actress Gertie Millar."[6]

Burke decided to make the transition from musical comedy to theater when Charles Frohman, the Broadway impresario, refused to bring her to the United States to sing in his American production of *The School Girl*. "Réjane, . . . Jane Hading and several of the French actresses who played vacation engagements in London had begun their careers on the lyric stage, and a cherished dream of following them into legitimate comedy was born after seeing them in Paris and London," wrote Burke in an article for *The Theatre*.[7] Frohman rejected Burke twice for American productions but finally solicited the actress in 1907 to star

FIG. 3.1 Sarony Studio (American, 1866–ca. 1930). Billie Burke in *My Wife*, ca. 1907. From *Munsey's Magazine* (March 1908): 812. Private collection.

alongside John Drew in *My Wife*, an English adaptation of the French play *Josette, Ma Femme*. Burke signed a ten-year contract with Frohman in 1907 and, until she broke the contract in 1915, starred in ten plays—not all equally successful.[8] Among the more popular were *My Wife* (1907) (fig. 3.1), *Love Watches* (1908) (fig. 3.2), *The Runaway* (1911) (see fig. A.13), *The "Mind the Paint" Girl* (1912) (see fig. A.14), *The Amazons* (1913), *The Land of Promise* (1913), and *Jerry* (1914) (see figs. 3.E and 3.F). "Having Risen from the Chorus," as the title of an article in *Harper's Bazar* put it, Burke was on her way up "the ladder of hard work that leads to fame and riches."[9]

FIG. 3.2 Sarony Studio. Billie Burke and Cyril Knightley in *Love Watches*, ca. 1908. From *The Theatre* (October 1908): 259. Private collection.

FIG. 3.3 Charlotte "Lallie" Charles (English, 1869–1919). "Married to the Husband Anna 'Held.'" (featuring Billie Burke). From *The Tatler* (May 20, 1914): 240. Private collection. Cat. 160.

Burke's romance with and subsequent marriage to Florenz Ziegfeld (1867–1932) in 1914 set the stage for her next career move as a film actress. Burke starred in her first two films in 1916, *Peggy* and *Gloria's Romance*. Burke's marriage to Ziegfeld also brought her a new level of fame, celebrity, and press. Their secret wedding was a tabloid sensation in the United States and abroad—*The Tatler* published a full-page article on the news with a clever play on words: "Married To The Husband Anna 'Held' An Old London Musical-comedy Favourite who is the Leading Actress on the 'Legitimate' Stage of 'Noo Yark'" (fig. 3.3).[10] (Ziegfeld's former wife was the French actress Anna Held.) The birth of a daughter, Patricia, in 1916 brought Burke's domestic life to public attention. Articles featuring photographs of Burke with her daughter circulated alongside those describing the luxurious estate the Burke-Ziegfeld family owned in Hastings-on-Hudson, New York (see figs. 3.22 and 3.25).[11]

Burke took her career as an actress seriously: she worked continuously through Patricia's childhood and past Ziegfeld's death in 1932 and starred in more than eighty films, as well as performing intermittently in the theater through the 1960s. Burke's marriage to her larger-than-life impresario husband was highlighted in MGM's *The Great*

Ziegfeld (1936), a lavish musical in which Myrna Loy played Billie (fig. 3.4). Burke published *With a Feather on My Nose* in 1949 and an advice book for women, *With Powder on My Nose*, ten years later. During her lifetime, Burke was known for her sweet face, charming roles, and elegant but simple style; today she is perhaps best known for her role as Glinda in *The Wizard of Oz*. "Are you a good witch or a bad witch?" she asks Dorothy, who has just arrived in Oz; as the quintessentially "good witch," Burke was the living embodiment of L. Frank Baum's Witch from the North, "a beautiful woman, who kn[ew] how to keep young in spite of the many years she had lived."[12] Burke died on May 14, 1970 at the age of eighty-five. Her sense of understated stylishness remained a defining characteristic of this actress throughout her long and prolific career. —MBK

FIG. 3.4 Margaret Chute (1886-1948). *Art Imitating Life* (Billie Burke and Myrna Loy publicity photograph for *The Great Ziegfeld*), ca. 1936. Courtesy Getty Images.

FASHION

"I was a new kind of actress," wrote Billie Burke in her autobiography, "carefree, and red-headed, and I had beautiful clothes."[13] Indeed, Burke's public persona was mediated and shaped by the clothes she wore onstage and off. The simple yet elegant columnar silhouettes of the Lucile (Lady Duff Gordon) dresses Burke wore to play Lily Parradell in *The "Mind The Paint" Girl* helped define Burke's personality as youthful, capricious, and energetic and her look as that of a pretty "American Girl" whose good—albeit costly— taste veered toward simpler styles of dress that best suited her figure and features.[14] In a 1908 "Sunday Morning Chat," Burke explained her preference for this straight silhouette in terms of her "natural" acting style: "My gowns are a good deal alike in style. They don't vary much from year to year. I am fond of straight lines, and I think the line from the shoulder in front should be accentuated. Simplicity is the thing in dress as naturalness is in acting."[15]

Under contract beginning in 1907 with the prolific theater manager and "star maker" Charles Frohman, Burke was encouraged to select her own stage clothes and "redress" her roles as she wished, as part of Frohman's plan to blend the spectacle of theater with that of fashion.[16] As such, *The "Mind the Paint" Girl* dress reflects both a fashionable Lucile silhouette as well as Burke's own taste—and endorsement—of such styles to suit both her public and her private image.

Arthur Pinero's stage directions called for Burke's character, Lily Parradell, a famous stage actress and "an entrancing vision of youth, grace, and beauty," to make her first entrance into her living room, "exhausted" after a portrait painting session with the artist "Morgan" on Fitzroy Street.[17] For this scene, Burke wore a floor-length, floral-patterned lace afternoon dress in the Empire revival style (fig. 3.5). Two tiers of delicate lace fall from the slightly raised waist, revealing the lilac-colored silk foundation skirt, which has lilac silk

FIG. 3.5 Lady Duff Gordon, known as Lucile (English, 1863–1935) for the House of Lucile (English, 1894–1920s). Dress worn by Billie Burke in *The "Mind the Paint" Girl*, ca. 1912. Lace, silk faille, silk flowers, chiffon, and wire. Museum of the City of New York, Gift of Mrs. William R. Stephenson, 70.101.10. 3_4. Cat. 121.

FIG. 3.6 Detail of fig. 3.5.

strips and pink and purple ribbon roses along the bottom and a godet of white silk chiffon for ease of movement on the right side. Both tiers are finished with scalloped hems and the top, apron-like tier has two pockets. The lace bodice has a wire-stiffened collar, puffed shoulders, and long net sleeves. The silk underbodice is trimmed with pink ribbon and a corsage of pink and purple silk flowers (orange blossoms and lilacs) between the breasts (fig. 3.6). The back of the bodice fastens with hooks and a lace panel falls from the waist to the upper leg. In the original production, a mauve satin sash, now lost, girdled the figure at the waist.[18]

Lucile mastered this style of sheath dress

between 1910 and 1913: these dresses, like Burke's, were composed of diaphanous layers of lace and chiffon over peach or flesh-pink silk linings and sported seductive leg-baring slits. Pastel shades, silk corsage flowers, net lace, and embroidered chiffon were all hallmarks of Lucile's decorating devices during this period.[19] The provocative nude foundations and high slits "brok[e] down the visual barrier between body and clothes," creating the illusion of *déshabillé* while remaining resolutely modern.[20] For Billie Burke, this Lucile dress represented the easy sensuality and modernity of the character of Lily Parradell, an actress who "sings and dances her way to the heart of

FIG. 3.7 Foulsham & Banfield (English, 1906–20). Marie Löhr and Allan Aynesworth in *The "Mind the Paint" Girl*, 1912. From *The Playgoer and Society Illustrated* 5, no. 30 (1912), 185. Private collection.

an impressionable youth of ancient lineage and becomes a lady of title."[21]

Although Burke wore the creations of other designers such as Madame Hayward on and off stage, the simple and stylish silhouette of this Lucile dress from *The "Mind the Paint" Girl* remained in many ways her signature look.[22] The November 1912 issue of *Vogue* included a one-page feature on Burke with three photographs of the actress in her *"Mind the Paint" Girl* gowns. The description of this particular Lucile dress claimed that it represented the typical "Billie Burke frock" and concluded that "the noteworthy feature of Billie Burke's toilettes is that they achieve real

distinction without sacrificing a bit of the girlishness that is their chief charm."[23] Comparing Burke's gown to the one that Lucile made for the British actress Marie Löhr in the original London production for the same scene reveals not only that Burke had different dresses made for the American version, but also that her choice was a more delicate, graceful, and "younger" iteration of Löhr's sheath gown—and perhaps, a more appropriate costume choice for a character who has just come from having her portrait done (fig. 3.7).[24] Details such as the mauve belt and standing collar were almost certainly added as requests from Burke: mauve was Burke's favorite color, and she believed that standing collars enhanced her neckline.[25]

In the novelization of the play, illustrated with photographs of Billie Burke in costume, Lily Parradell's sartorial choices were justified in terms of her character (fig. 3.8):

> Her gown and her hat were in the fashion of the moment, but without any exaggeration. Her good taste invariably demanded restful colors and she was always ready to subtract a few inches from the diameter of a hat and add them to the length and circumference of a short skirt. But the veriest novice in the mysteries of woman's dress could see that her clothes were costly. Jeyes understood without being told that a quarter's pay would not meet the bills for Lily Parradell's simple morning outfit. But that reflection did not disturb him—it was only reasonable that the leading lady of the Pandora Theater should be well and expensively attired.[26]

The same observation could be applied to Burke onstage and off: countless photographs, postcards, and illustrations show that Burke's outfits were fashionable and expensive yet retained a quiet unfussiness and subdued refinement that gave her the effortless, modern charm of the "American" actress that she was. A full-length portrait of Burke dating to about 1918 by painter

FIG. 3.8 Sarony Studio. Billie Burke and Bernard Merefield in *The "Mind the Paint" Girl*, 1912. From the Miss Billie Burke Edition of the novelization of *The "Mind-the-Paint" Girl*. Private collection. Cat. 151.

FIG. 3.9 Sigismund de Ivanowski (Russian, 1874-1937). *Billie Burke*, ca. 1918. Oil on canvas. Museum of the City of New York, Gift of The Actors' Fund of America, 67.40.

Sigismund de Ivanowski captures the actress wearing the quintessential "Billie Burke dress": a pale lace and silk columnar silhouette with a high waist, not unlike the Lucile dress Burke wore for her portrait painting session as her character Lily Parradell (fig. 3.9). If Burke described her own sartorial philosophy as that of "simplicity," she also conceded to viewing her fashionable dresses as investments to impress managers, secure roles in big productions, and seduce the crowd. Frohman and later Ziegfeld paid the bills for Burke's expensive dresses; they, like Burke, understood that her choice of dress was as crucial as her acting skills to ensure her popularity and longevity as an actress and trendsetter. As Burke so aptly noted, the female audience's primary interest in a stage production was the fashions it featured, "regardless of the brain or wit of the play or the intelligent effort of the players."[27] Hence, the pastel Lucile sheath dress that Burke wore in *The "Mind the Paint" Girl* fulfilled Burke's criteria for a "smart gown": it suited her complexion and figure, met her preference for ease and elegance, and was constructed and embellished according to the demands of couture—a quality whose expense was not lost on the audience, and whose worth reflected Burke's own pride and confidence in her role as fashion icon. —MBK

FIG. 3.10 Postcard of *Billie Burke*, ca. 1903–7. Photograph.
Private collection. Cat. 126.

FIG. 3.11 Verso of fig. 3.10.

IN THE
PHOTOGRAPHER'S STUDIO

Postcard production in the United States increased after 1900 and reached its pinnacle in 1906, with more than 750 million postcards sold and sent.[28] Postcards of Billie Burke, like those of Lily Elsie and Jane Hading, were sold as a way to market the actresses, by advertising the fashions they wore and spurring interest in their plays. A cheaper alternative to high-end cabinet cards, souvenir programs, or fashion and theater magazines, postcards of actresses were mass consumed and discussed as part of social discourse. The senders

and receivers who engaged with the medium by hand-coloring the images of the actresses or by commenting on the subjects portrayed revealed the special relationship that existed between the actress and her audience. On postcards of Burke, for instance, senders commented on her "sweet" features and approachability and acknowledged the practice of building collections of similar postcards. Similarly, the hand-colored and glittered embellishments on some of these show an appropriation of Burke's image and fashions to suit the creative fancy of the sender.

In 1907 "May" wrote to "Miss L. Owen" hoping that "you will like this one," a reference to the

FIG. 3.12 Postcard of Billie Burke, ca. 1910. Photograph. Private collection. Cat. 146.

FIG. 3.13 Postcard of Billie Burke, ca. 1907–10. Photograph. Private collection. Cat. 138.

postcard of Billie Burke in a high-necked dotted net blouse with lace appliqués and large hat (figs. 3.10 and 3.11). Likewise, "Gertie" rhetorically asked her friend if "Billie Burke looks sweet here?" regarding a photograph of the actress, her head posed pensively over gloved hands, large lace and net hat perched on top of her head (see page 152). In 1910 "Miss Taylor" remarked that a smiling and young Billie Burke wearing a perky satin bow brought to mind an acquaintance ("Doesn't this remind you of Mrs. Tonge?"), while a certain "J. H." remarked to a friend that a fur-clad Burke "is very sweet looking" and "so lovely" that he or she could "hardly choose between" the image of Billie Burke

or that of another actress, Mabel Greene (figs. 3.12 and 3.13).

Commenting on Burke's appearance gave the correspondents a mutual vocabulary with which to share their thoughts about the images and signifiers they considered fashionable, charming, and "sweet." Although their observations refer to Burke's general appearance rather than a particularly stylish hat or dress worn in the photograph, fashion was an integral part of crafting the Burke image the photographs marketed (fig. 3.14). The cabinet cards, postcards, and many of the photographs that appeared in the theater and fashion magazines showed Burke posing formally

FIG. 3.14 Alfred, Ellis and Walery (English, 1900–1918). Postcard of Billie Burke, ca. 1907. Photograph. Private collection. Cat. 142.

FIG. 3.15 Postcard of Billie Burke, ca. 1907. Photograph. Private collection. Cat. 135.

in a studio or more informally in a studio setting while wearing the simple yet elegant ensembles that defined her style, such as a practical tailored suit (or skirt) worn with a shirtwaist blouse, which was an integral component of American women's fashion by the turn of the twentieth century (fig. 3.15). Indeed, two hand-colored postcards of Burke highlight first the fashion and then her face—the fringed and pleated green silk dress with spreading white collar and the glitter-decorated deep blue-green velvet suit with large white fur collar, lapels, and muff are brought to the foreground, making Burke's face a secondary emphasis (figs. 3.16 and 3.17). Whether she stared

sweetly into the camera or contemplatively into the distance, while wearing softly draped off-the-shoulder dresses, Burke's poses were intended to convey the image of a young and charming ingénue, as opposed to Hading's overt theatricality or Elsie's wistful sensuality (fig. 3.18). These postcards encapsulate the three facets of Billie Burke's public image as a woman, actress, and style icon.

Although Burke's image was already commercialized in England after her first big hit in 1903, the photographs of her taken by the Sarony Studio after her arrival in the United States confirmed Burke's status as a fashionable actress in the eyes of her American audience. The most sought-after

FIG. 3.16 Dover Street Studio (English, active ca. 1906–12). Postcard of Billie Burke, ca. 1907. Hand-colored photograph. Private collection. Cat. 137.

FIG. 3.17 Richard Brown (British, active ca. 1890). Postcard of Billie Burke, ca. 1907. Hand-colored photograph with glitter. Private collection. Cat. 136.

photographer in America in the late nineteenth century, Napoleon Sarony captured virtually every actor and actress working on the New York stage, as well as society ladies, politicians, and businessmen.[29] Sarony died in 1896, but his studio continued after his death. The Sarony Studio photographed Burke in both costume and fashionable dress (fig. 3.19). These images were then disseminated on cabinet cards, in fashion magazines, and in advertisements. Selling the rights to these photographs was such a profitable enterprise for the studio that Sarony paid the biggest stars to sit for them: Sarony himself paid the British actress and well-known beauty Lillie Langtry $5,000 for her picture.[30] A star in the making after her return to the United States in 1907, Burke was unlikely to have been paid for her portraits. Eager for free publicity, many actresses signed away the rights to their portraits for nothing, knowing that the profit they gained came from recognition rather than royalties.[31] Just the distinction of having her portrait taken by Sarony was enough for *Munsey's Magazine* to mention under Burke's photographs that this image was indeed "her *latest* photograph by Sarony, New York" (emphasis mine) (fig. 3.20).[32]

Burke always expressed delight at seeing her picture in the stores and homes of her fans. An anecdote recounted in her autobiography is

MISS BILLIE BURKE   T 242

FIG. 3.18 Postcard of Billie Burke, ca. 1905. Photograph.
Private collection.

FROM THE
JOHN H. JAMES
COLLECTION
256 FIFTH AVENUE,
NEW YORK.

FIG. 3.19 Sarony Studio. Cabinet card of Billie Burke, ca. 1908.
Billy Rose Theatre Division, The New York Public Library for the
Performing Arts, Astor, Lenox and Tilden Foundations. Cat. 139.

revealing in its perception of both the significance of her fame and its fleeting nature. Entering a suitor's room around the time of her breakthrough performance in *The School Girl* (1903), Burke remarked on the "enchanting" decoration: "He had a shelf around the four walls of his sitting room and every inch of that shelf was occupied by a different picture of me. But then, I fancy he changed this gallery from time to time, depending upon his visitor."[33] Burke understood that her image was a powerful tool of seduction but recognized that its place of honor was subject to the fickle whims of her audience. Burke's ability to maintain her presence in the press throughout her long career owed

a great deal not only to her "sweet image," but also to her popularity as a fashion icon portrayed in the thousands of photographs diffused of the actress on cabinet cards and postcards and in the theater and fashion magazines of the day. —MBK

THE PRESS

"These are real photographs. They purport to represent phases of the actual home life of five eminent actresses. They are intended to discredit those cynics whose hobby it is to spread the delusion that stage folk in their hours of ease haunt gilded restaurants and consume unlimited quantities of

lobster à la Newburg. We confess to a certain skep-
ticism. Hitherto we, also, thought of them as spend-
ing their leisure moments in luxurious apartments,
reading their press notices and autographing their
pictures—while some hired dignitary did the cook-
ing. However the camera—so it is alleged—never
lies, and here we have the camera's evidence."
—"In Roles They Never Play," *Vanity Fair*
(April 1914)

Beginning with her appearance on the cover of
The Theatre in 1908, the year after her arrival
in the United States from London, Burke had a
strong presence in the American press (fig. 3.21).
Contemporary coverage of Billie Burke's personal

and professional lives offers a prime example of
the public's fascination with actresses at the turn
of the twentieth century. Additionally, articles on
Burke's life at home exemplify actresses' eager
embrace of the press as a means of bolstering
their newfound respectability and showing their
adoring fans that, when not on stage, they were
also ordinary wives and mothers. Numerous such
pieces on Burke appeared in newspapers, fashion
magazines, and theater periodicals and covered
everything from her career on the stage to her
home life with her husband and daughter. By
revealing details of her private life, Burke was able
to present herself as a typical caring mother and
accomplished hostess who just happened to be a

FIG. 3.20 Sarony Studio. "Billie Burke, Starring in Pinero's Latest
Play, 'The Mind-the-Paint Girl.'" From *Munsey's Magazine*
(1912): 343. Private collection. Cat. 157.

FIG. 3.21 Billie Burke. Cover of *The Theatre* (March 1908).
Private collection. Cat. 155.

Copyright Byron   BILLIE BURKE ON THE TERRACE OF HER HOME, "BURKELEIGH CREST," AT HASTINGS-ON-THE-HUDSON

FIG. 3.22 Byron Studio (American, 1892-present). "The Lady of Burkeleigh Crest" (featuring Billie Burke). From *The Theatre* (January 1913): 28. Private collection. Cat. 159.

famous stage star, and thus she upheld her image as a sweet, all-American girl. Burke's perpetually youthful appearance and "genuine" nature led one author to describe her as a "dainty, impudently pretty, very human sprite, bubbling over with a hundred charms."[34] In articles on the actress, her charisma and charm were mentioned more often than her dramatic abilities. Burke's personality that she conveyed in interviews, rather than the talents she demonstrated on stage, seems to have been the main attraction for her fans.

Burke offered reporters a glimpse into her life at home many times throughout her stage career. In an article from the August 1913 issue of *Harper's Bazar,* entitled "Under My Own Vine and Fig Tree," Burke recalled how she came to move from a stuffy apartment in the city to a spacious estate in a suburb of New York, which she later named Burkeleigh Crest. The piece begins with a note from the editor: "Miss Billie Burke has always

been identified on the stage with the sweet domestic type. It is interesting to know that these characteristics are not assumed, that in her home life she shows the same qualities as in her many endearing impersonations."[35] This reported correlation between her personas on stage and her everyday self made Burke appear accessible and authentic to her fans, more like a good friend than a distant celebrity.

The Theatre also published photographs of Burke at home in several issues. In the first issue of 1913, Ada Patterson's article, "The Lady of Burkeleigh Crest," recounted an interview with Burke and described both the actress's persona "at home" and her estate in great detail.[36] Residing in an imposing stone mansion among stately trees, Japanese huts, and tiny bridges over streams with an adopted "sister" named Cherry and her three poodles, Tutti, Frutti, and Sammie, Burke appears playful, unaffected, and able to benefit from her

FIG. 3.23 Moffett Studio (American, 1905–present). *A New Portrait of Billie Burke.* From *The Theatre* (January 1913): 29. Private collection. Cat. 159.

FIG. 3.24 Sarony Studio. Billie Burke in a walking costume. From *The Theatre* (November 1908): 301. Private collection. Cat. 156.

wealth while remaining unspoiled. Patterson writes that Burke is an "informal hostess" who enjoys the outdoors and appreciates "the heart of quiet, and the companionship of real people and things."[37] Photographs of Burke on the first page of the spread show her standing on the steps of her home and sitting on a bench with her three dogs (fig. 3.22). Despite Patterson's efforts to present Burke as an ordinary young woman with extremely good fortune, a full-page photograph of the actress in a floor-length fur coat and oversized muff betrays her extraordinary star status to all (fig. 3.23).

The June 1914 issue of *The Theatre* includes an article entitled "Prominent Players in Their Homes" featuring several actors and actresses. Burke, described as "a player of fluff," is photographed playing fetch with one of her dogs under a large tree, casually lounging in an armchair, and standing at a window, staring out wistfully. These images give the impression of spontaneity, suggesting a real intimacy with the subject, "Miss Burke." Additionally, the domestic facet of her persona is further cemented through a drawing at the top left corner of the page, of a woman in silhouette, holding a broom, presumably meant to represent Burke and to imply that she too does housework. Readers of periodicals such as *Harper's Bazar* and *The Theatre* were intensely curious

FIG. 3.25 Billie Burke and her daughter, Patricia. From *Harper's Bazar* (February 1917): 55.

of red silk"), what she ate for breakfast ("scrambled eggs and a bit of crisp bacon, some butterless toast, with marmalade and a cup of coffee, all preceded by a glass of orange juice"), and the contents of her wardrobe.[39] Patterson describes "neat white-painted closets, with gossamer-like gowns of blue and pink and white" and a "double row of tiny boots all wrinkleless on their trees" (fig. 3.24).[40] When Burke was asked how many dresses she owned, her mother interjected, saying that the actress traveled with twenty-two private trunks, all packed and unpacked by a maid.[41]

Although her fans may have never achieved the sartorial abundance that Burke enjoyed, some aspects of her family life would have been more familiar to the public. Two years after her marriage to Florenz Ziegfeld in 1914, Burke had a daughter, Patricia. Images of Patricia and Billie were printed in a number of fashion magazines, including *Harper's Bazar* (fig. 3.25). The caption for this Sarony photograph, which depicts Burke leaning over her baby's crib, notes Patricia's likeness to her mother and even refers to her as a "future leading lady."[42] By offering the public access to her personal life, albeit through a careful presentation of herself in print and photographs, Billie Burke encouraged the press's descriptions of her as a sincere all-American girl. Pictures of her at home with her daughter allowed her fans to relate to Burke in her roles as wife and mother, while simultaneously allowing them to fantasize about her wealth and fame.

The multitude of articles on Burke, published in a wide variety of periodicals and newspapers, indicates that the actress actively cultivated her relationship with media. She crafted an identity that deliberately blurred the differences between her public and private personas and communicated to her admirers that, despite her status as a popular and highly successful actress, she was heartfelt and unpretentious. Even today, the image of Billie Burke as a star who remained down-to-earth and unaffected by her fame persists. —RP

about what actresses were like, not only in their professional lives on the stage but also in their private lives at home. The public wanted to know details of celebrities' lives so they could compare them to their own, even though they were sure to be vastly different.[38]

Even the most mundane facts about Burke's life were written about with enthusiasm. In "A Sunday Morning Chat with Billie Burke" from the November 1908 issues of *The Theatre*, the author, Ada Patterson, diligently records exactly how Burke sat during their interview ("with her spine straight and her feet straight out before her"), what she wore (a "gray silk kimono with facings

ADVERTISING

"I tell you this: Clean linen, brushed hair, showers, soap and water add considerably to the bliss of married life. I'm constantly amazed when I talk to young people—they are frank and tell everything— to learn how much they know about Sex and how little about soap."
—Billie Burke, *With Powder on My Nose*, 1959

Although Billie Burke spent much of her early life in England, her celebrity was predicated upon a certain concept of Americanness that she reinforced with stage roles in *Jerry* (1914) and *Gloria's Romance* (1915), as well as in the many articles written about her private life. In contrast to Jane Hading's serious hauteur and Lily Elsie's enigmatic seductiveness, Burke embodied the "independent and confident, talkative, well educated, energetic, cheerful, forthright, ambitious, athletic, and pretty" archetype of the American Girl.[43] Cleanliness was a virtue coded as inherently American, and Burke's near obsession with hygiene and appearance made her an ideal candidate for skin-care endorsements, which make up the bulk of the advertising material studied here. In addition, although Burke's image was certainly used for traditional pictorial advertising such as cigarette cards, she evinced a high level of personal agency (or at least the indication thereof) by actively participating in testimonial advertising, which featured her voice in addition to her face and/or full-length figure (fig. 3.26).[44] Burke's advertising appeal, unlike Hading's and Elsie's, began with her personality rather than her image.

Over the course of her long career, Burke was consistently praised for her youthful appearance, a fact she acknowledged in her 1959 memoir *With Powder on My Nose*. She wrote that being a woman required remaining "as attractive as possible," to which she added: "As for my age, I am pleased but not overwhelmed when people tell me that I don't look mine. I don't and I darn well know it. This is no accident. I have worked at it for years."[45] Although

FIG. 3.26 Ogden's Guinea Gold Cigarettes trade card featuring Billie Burke, ca. 1907. Photograph. Private collection. Cat. 164.

Burke also nostalgically praised the Ziegfeld Follies girls for having natural peaches-and-cream complexions ("Remember, in those days, a complexion had to come with the girl, not from Rexall or Miss Arden," she wrote), cosmetics and skin creams were heavily advertised and used throughout the late nineteenth and early twentieth centuries.[46] This area of the market formed a large part of many actresses' advertising personae, and Burke was no exception to this trend.

An advertisement for Pond's cold and vanishing creams appeared in *Ladies' Home Journal* in March 1918 (fig. 3.27).[47] Against a lavender backdrop that complements the pink dresses and cheeks of the

FIG. 3.27 Advertisement for Pond's cold and vanishing creams featuring Billie Burke (oval frame at left). From *Ladies' Home Journal* (March 1918): 89. Private collection. Cat. 165.

FIG. 3.28 Draycott Galleries (English, active early 20th century). Postcard of Billie Burke, ca. 1908. Photograph. Private collection. Cat. 141.

women in the illustration, Burke and fellow actress Hazel Dawn compete with three columns of dense text that extols the scientific credentials of the Pond's formula and cites the many famous women who use it. At the time, *Ladies' Home Journal* was one of the top publications in the country, commanding higher advertising rates than any other women's magazine, and along with Burke's film debut and the birth of her daughter, this ad had enhanced her already well-established celebrity.[48] Although the large, full-color image that makes up the top half of the advertisement is not explicitly identified as Burke, it clearly alludes to the salient aspects of the actress's image: her mass of auburn

hair, distinctive profile, and wide-eyed expression, traits echoed in postcards such as that in figure 3.28. By placing a jar of the advertised vanishing cream in her hands, the advertisement effectively demonstrated Burke's endorsement, but it went a step further by including a testimonial from Burke, just below her oval picture in the lower left corner, that reads: "Billie Burke, whose beautiful skin is the envy of everyone who sees her, says: 'No one appreciates Pond's Vanishing Cream more than I.'"

Burke's endorsement of such a product would seem to be somewhat at odds with her own earlier portrayal of her beauty as the result of a simple hygiene and exercise regimen, which she described

FIG. 3.29 Advertisement for Mineralava Beauty Clay featuring Billie Burke (second from right). From *Cosmopolitan* (December 1922): 171. General Research Division, The New York Public Library, Astor, Lenox and Tilden Foundations.

FIG. 3.30 Advertisement for Rogers & Thompson's Soirée Silk featuring Billie Burke. From *The Theatre* (September 1916): 165. Private collection. Cat. 163.

in a 1911 article called "My Simple Rules for Beauty" published in *The Delineator*. She claimed that "beauty is something you can not buy save with infinite pains," and although she advocated the use of cleansing and whitening creams, she noted that if any woman "indulges herself and pampers herself, and then tries to cover the effects of her slothfulness with artificial remedies, there is something in the whole procedure as revolting as it is useless."[49] However, as theater historian Marlis Schweitzer has shown, skin creams were regarded differently from such cosmetics as rouge, powder, and lipstick, which were considered artificial means of covering up one's defects. No

matter how outlandish their claims, skin creams were viewed as a healthful way of enhancing or restoring one's natural beauty and thus posed no apparent contradiction to the squeaky-clean and healthy all-American image Burke projected.[50]

Although testimonials from ordinary users (or "some pleased customer out in Peoria," in the words of one advertising executive) were also used in advertisements of the time, statements from famous actresses were considered much more effective in generating sales.[51] An advertisement for Mineralava Beauty Clay featuring a "Quartet of Beauty," which included Billie Burke, appeared in *Cosmopolitan* in 1922 (fig. 3.29).[52] The copy boasted that the famous cream is "endorsed by thousands of grateful women as the one perfect corrective" for a number of skin ailments, but it is the four actresses who dominate the advertisement. Shown in profile, Burke declares, "Mineralava has kept my skin in a state of radiant health," a phrase that again ties Burke to a connotation of American health and vigor. In this case, the text of the ad takes the form of an article with a byline, a common device that was also deftly employed by Hading in her promotion of cosmetics (see the section on Jane Hading and advertising).

While the advertisements for skin-care products in which Burke appeared highlight the "clean" and "youthful" aspects of the actress's personality, her promotion of Rogers & Thompsons's Soirée Silk emphasizes her glamorous side. An advertisement that appeared in *The Theatre* in 1916 shows Burke from the back, in profile yet again, in an Empire-waist gown with delicate floral embellishments (fig. 3.30). The Sarony Studio photograph underscores the level of quality that this ad attempted to project. Burke's testimonial in this case is brief: "I am delighted with my gown of Soirée Silk. It is truly beautiful both in texture and coloring," but the inclusion of her signature adds a personalizing touch.

Burke would go on to endorse numerous other goods throughout her long career, such as Cutex nail polish (1928), Lux soap (1931), Enna Jetticks shoes (1935), and Royal Gelatin (1941), but it was her early advertisements for beauty products that laid the foundation for an enduringly appealing image.[53] Tellingly, all of these later advertisements were testimonial in nature, capitalizing on Burke's charming and approachable personality as much as on her looks, a pattern that the ads for Pond's, Mineralava, and Soirée Silk established when Burke's star was first on the rise. —WD

1   Billie Burke, *With a Feather on My Nose* (New York: Appleton-Century-Crofts, 1949), 79.
2   Grant Hayter-Menzies, *Mrs. Ziegfeld: The Public and Private Lives of Billie Burke* (Jefferson NC: McFarland & Company, 2009), 13–14.
3   Burke, *With a Feather on My Nose*, 8–12.
4   Ibid., 16–17.
5   Ibid., 28.
6   Ibid., 28–29.
7   Billie Burke, "Personal Reminiscences," *The Theatre* (September 1916): 123.
8   Leslie Midkiff DeBauche, "Testimonial Advertising Using Movie Stars in the 1910s: How Billie Burke Came to Sell Pond's Vanishing Cream in 1917," *Marketing History at the Center*, ed. Blaine Branchik (Durham NC: Charm Association, 2007), 149.
9   Charles Belmont Davis, "Having Risen from the Chorus," *Harper's Bazar* (December 1913): 40.
10 *The Tatler*, May 20, 1914, 240.
11 Photograph of Burke and Patricia from *Harper's Bazar* (February 1917): 55.
12 L. Frank Baum, *The Wonderful Wizard of Oz* (Chicago: George M. Hill Co., 1900), 215.
13 Burke, *With a Feather on My Nose*, 79.
14 DeBauche, "Testimonial Advertising," 150.
15 Ada Patterson, "A Sunday Morning Chat with Billie Burke," *The Theatre* (November 1908): 304.
16 Marlis Schweitzer, *When Broadway Was the Runway* (Philadelphia: University of Pennsylvania Press, 2009), 65–66.
17 Arthur Pinero, *The "Mind the Paint" Girl: A Comedy in Four Acts* (Teddington: The Echo Library, 2008), 16.
18 The sash has since been replaced but an article about the dress in *Vogue* describes the original color; see *Vogue* (November 15, 1912): 42.
19 Valerie D. Mendes and Amy de la Haye, *Lucile Ltd. London, Paris, New York and Chicago, 1890s–1930s* (London: V&A Publishing, 2009), 188.
20 *Designing the It Girl: Lucile and Her Style*, exh. cat. (New York: FIT, The School of Graduate Studies, 2005), 3.
21 "Applause and Boos After Pinero Play," *New York Times*, February 18, 1912.
22 Janet Loring, "Costuming on the New York Stage from 1895 to 1915 with Particular Emphasis on Charles Frohman's Companies," PhD diss., State University of Iowa, 1960, 142.
23 *Vogue* (November 15, 1912): 42.
24 "The Mind the Paint Girl," *The Playgoer and Society Illustrated* 5, no. 30 (1912): 185.
25 Billie Burke, "The Actress and Her Clothes," *Saturday Evening Post* (February 20, 1909): 12.
26 Louis Tracy, *The "Mind the Paint" Girl* (New York: Edward J. Clode, 1912), 65–66.
27 Burke, "The Actress and Her Clothes," 12.
28 Aline Ripert and Claude Frère, *La carte postale, son histoire, sa fonction sociale* (Paris: CNRS, 1983), 65. This places the USA behind Germany in postcard consumption but ahead of England.

29 Ben Bassham, *The Theatrical Photographs of Napoleon Sarony* (Kent OH: Kent State University, 1978), 3.

30 Ibid., 4.

31 Ibid.

32 "Billie Burke, Starring in Pinero's Latest Play, 'The-Mind-the Paint Girl," *Munsey's Magazine* (1912): 343.

33 Burke, *With a Feather on My Nose*, 32.

34 "The Players," *Everybody's Magazine* (July–December 1908): 846.

35 Billie Burke, "Under My Own Vine and Fig Tree," *Harper's Bazar* (August 1913): 19.

36 Ada Patterson, "The Lady of Burkeleigh Crest," *The Theatre* (January 1913): 28–30.

37 Ibid., 30.

38 DeBauche, "Testimonial Advertising," 150.

39 Ada Patterson, "A Sunday Morning Chat," 300–304.

40 Ibid., 304.

41 Ibid.

42 *Harper's Bazar* (February 1917): 55.

43 DeBauche, "Testimonial Advertising," 147.

44 Note that the ensemble Burke wears in this card is the same one in a postcard, see fig. 3.15.

45 Billie Burke, with Cameron Shipp, *With Powder on My Nose* (New York: Coward-McCann, 1959), 18.

46 Ibid., 36. Advertising for cosmetic and grooming products began in America in the 1880s and almost immediately employed actresses to sell products. For a brief explanation of the early days of this phenomenon, see Victoria Sherrow, *For Appearance' Sake: the Historical Encyclopedia of Good Looks, Beauty, and Grooming* (Westport CT: Oryx Press, 2001): 2–5.

47 The ad campaign had begun in December of the previous year. See DeBauche, "Testimonial Advertising," 150.

48 Ibid., 147.

49 Billie Burke, "My Simple Rules for Beauty," *The Delineator* (June 1911): 510.

50 Marlis Schweitzer, "'The Mad Search For Beauty': Actresses, Cosmetics, and the Middle-Class Market," *Testimonial Advertising in the American Marketplace: Emulation, Identity, Community*, ed. Marlis Schweitzer and Marina Moskowitz (New York: Palgrave Macmillan, 2009): 123–150, esp. 138–42.

51 DeBauche, "Testimonial Advertising," 153. The author cites C. B. McCuaig's article "Making the Testimonial Earn Its Keep" from the February 8, 1917 edition of *Printers' Ink*.

52 The other actresses in this quartet were Marjorie Rambeau, Julia Sanderson, and Irene Bordoni. The advertisement ran on page 15 of the December 1922 issue of *Cosmopolitan*.

53 These advertisements are readily available individually for sale online to collectors, and it was therefore not always possible to determine in which periodicals they originally appeared. The Royal Gelatin ad appeared in the June 1941 issue of *Good Housekeeping*, whereas the Cutex advertisement appeared in the September 1928 issue of *McCall's Magazine*, page 71. For further corroboration of these campaigns, see DeBauche, "Testimonial Advertising," 154.

Checklist of the Exhibition

JANE HADING AND FASHION

1. Woman's hat
Ruland, New York and Paris (American, active late 19th-early 20th century)
New York, ca. 1895
Lace, silk velvet, ostrich feathers, beads, and metal pins
Height: 7 in. (17.8 cm), crown diameter: 7 in. (17.8 cm)
Label: "Ruland 40 West 28th Street/ NY & Paris"
Museum of the City of New York, Gift of Mrs. Robert Hartshorne, 41.155.30

2. Evening gown
Charles Poynter (English, 1853-1929)
For the House of Redfern (English, 1881-1929)
Paris, ca. 1904
Silk taffeta, silk satin, silk plissé chiffon, machine-made Brussels lace, iridescent sequins, and beads
Center back: 66 in. (167.6 cm)
Label: "Breveté Redfern / Paris / By Special Appointment to H.I.M.— Empress of Russia / By Special Appointment to H.R.H.—Princess of Wales"
Museum of the City of New York, Gift of Mrs. Ruth Fahnestock and Mrs. Faith Fahnestock Paine, 41.339.15
See fig. 1.9

3. *La Vie parisienne* (April 1, 1893)
Open to page 182, showing "Toilettes de Mme Jane Hading dans 'Les Effrontés' créations de la Maison Laferrière"
Magazine (closed): 12 x 15⅞ in. (30.5 x 40.3 cm)
Library, Bard Graduate Center: Decorative Arts, Design History, Material Culture; New York
See fig. 1.5

4. *Le Théatre* (September 1898): inside back cover
"Tournées Artistiques de Madame Jane Hading: Les Chapeaux"
Reutlinger Studio (French, 1850-1937)
Halftone
11¾ x 15 in. (29.8 x 40.3 cm)
Private collection

5. *Le Rire* (November 3, 1900): back cover
"Jane Hading ou la 'Demi-Vierge' Rêvée"
Leonetto Cappiello (Italian, active in Paris, 1875-1942)
Lithograph
Magazine (closed): 9⅞ x 12⅞ in. (25 x 32.7 cm)
Private collection
See fig. 1.7

6. *Femina* (April 15, 1901)
Open to pages 126-27, showing "Une Journée chez un grand Couturier (Redfern)"
Halftone
Magazine (closed): 11¾ x 14¾ in. (29.8 x 37.5 cm)
Private collection
See fig. VIII

7. *Paris Review* (April 1902)
"Les Succès de Redfern au Théâtre/ The Theatrical successes of Redfern"
Halftone
Magazine (closed): 11¾ x 15¾ in. (29.8 x 40 cm)
Private collection

8. Postcard of Jane Hading
Paul Boyer (French, active late 19th-early 20th century)
ca. 1899
Hand-colored photograph with metallic gold pigment
3½ x 5⁹⁄₁₆ in. (8.9 x 14.1 cm)
Private collection
See fig. 1.16

9. Postcard of Jane Hading in *La Pompadour*
Reutlinger Studio (French, 1850-1937)
Published by La Société Industrielle de Photographie (S.I.P.), Paris
ca. 1901
Hand-colored photograph
3½ x 5⅜ in. (8.9 x 13.7 cm)
Message (on recto): "Douter, c'est mourir / Jane Hading / 1903" [autographed]
Translation: "To doubt is to die"
Private collection
See fig. 1.13

10. Postcard of Jane Hading in *La Pompadour*
Reutlinger Studio (French, 1850-1937)
Published by La Société Industrielle de Photographie (S.I.P.), Paris
ca. 1901
Hand-colored photograph with glitter
3¾ x 5⅞ in. (9.5 x 15 cm)
Recipient: Mlle M. Pierrou, 9 Rue de Fauraz [?], 4e Paris
Private collection

11. Jane Hading in *La Châtelaine*
Reutlinger Studio (French, 1850-1937)
Published by La Société Industrielle de Photographie (S.I.P.), Paris
ca. 1902
Hand-colored photograph with glitter and metallic gold pigment
3¹³⁄₁₆ x 6 in. (9.7 x 15.2 cm)
Postmark: [location illegible] February [?], 1904
Recipient: Mademoiselle Marie Cartherinot, Institution Jeanne d'Arc, Chinon, Indre-et-Loire
Message (on recto): "Reçois, ma chère Marie, les plus doux baisers de sa petite, Jeanne"
Translation: "Accept, my dear Marie, the sweetest kisses from her little one, Jeanne"
Private collection
See fig. 1.6

12. Postcard of Jane Hading in *L'Alibi*
Reutlinger Studio (French, 1850-1937)
Published by P.C.
ca. 1908
Hand-colored photograph
3¾ x 6 in. (9.5 x 15.2 cm)
Recipient: Mlle Jane [H?]illoutreix, Colonies de vacances, St. Sébastien, Creuse
Message: "Limoges 31/8/09 / Bons souvenirs, F. Moreau"
Translation: "Limoges 31/8/09 / Fond memories, F. Moreau"
Private collection
See fig. X

JANE HADING IN THE PHOTOGRAPHER'S STUDIO

13. Cabinet card of Jane Hading
Van Der Weyde Studio (English, 1878-1902)
Sold by Charles L. Ritzman, 945 Broadway and 171½ Fifth Avenue, N.Y. [stamp on verso]
London, ca. 1885
6½ x 4 in. (16.5 x 10.2 cm)
Billy Rose Theatre Division, The New York Public Library for the Performing Arts, Astor, Lenox and Tilden Foundations
See fig. v

14. Cabinet card of Jane Hading
Van Bosch Studio (French, active 1880s-90s)
Sold by Charles L. Ritzman, 945 Broadway and 171½ Fifth Avenue, N.Y. [stamp on verso]
Paris, ca. 1885
6½ x 4 in. (16.5 x 10.2 cm)
Billy Rose Theatre Division, The New York Public Library for the Performing Arts, Astor, Lenox and Tilden Foundations
See fig. 1.18

15. Cabinet card of Jane Hading
Van Bosch Studio (French, active 1880s-90s)
Paris, ca. 1885-89
6½ x 4 in. (16.5 x 10.2 cm)
Billy Rose Theatre Division, The New York Public Library for the Performing Arts, Astor, Lenox and Tilden Foundations
See fig. 1.19 and page 92

16. Cabinet card of Jane Hading
Van Bosch Studio (French, active 1880s-90s)
Sold by Maison Martinet, Albert Hautecoeur, 18 Bd. des Capucines [stamp on verso]
Paris, ca. 1889
4¼ x 6⁷/₁₆ in. (10.8 x 16.4 cm)
Private collection

17. Cabinet card of Jane Hading
Nadar Studio (French, active ca. 1854-1910)
Sold by Dr. Joshua J. Roth, 5 Union Square, New York, Importer, Dealer & Publisher of Etchings and Engravings and Photographs of Celebrities and

Views from All Parts of The World [stamp on verso]. Dr. Joshua J. Roth, Fine Arts, Stationery, Books, & c., 327 5th Ave., N.Y. [sticker on verso]
Paris, ca. 1889
6½ x 4 in. (16.5 x 10.2 cm)
Billy Rose Theatre Division, The New York Public Library for the Performing Arts, Astor, Lenox and Tilden Foundations

18. Cabinet card of Jane Hading in *Nos Intimes*
Reutlinger Studio (French, 1850-1937)
Sold by Meyer Bros. & Co. Booksellers, Stationers, 13 West 24th Street, New York [sticker on verso]
Paris, ca. 1891
6½ x 4 in. (16.5 x 10.2 cm)
Billy Rose Theatre Division, The New York Public Library for the Performing Arts, Astor, Lenox and Tilden Foundations
See fig. 1.20

19. Cabinet card of Jane Hading in *Nos Intimes*
Reutlinger Studio (French, 1850-1937)
Sold by Hazebroucq, Ingénieur-Opticien, 23, Rue de la Paix, 23, Paris. [stamp on verso]
Paris, ca. 1891
6½ x 4 in. (16.5 x 10.2 cm)
Billy Rose Theatre Division, The New York Public Library for the Performing Arts, Astor, Lenox and Tilden Foundations
See fig. A.3

20. Cabinet card of Jane Hading in dress by Maison Laferrière
Reutlinger Studio (French, 1850-1937)
Sold by Hazebroucq, Ingénieur-Opticien, 23, Rue de la Paix, 23, Paris. [stamp on verso]
Paris, ca. 1898
6½ x 4 in. (16.5 x 10.2 cm)
Billy Rose Theatre Division, The New York Public Library for the Performing Arts, Astor, Lenox and Tilden Foundations

21. Postcard of Jane Hading
Reutlinger Studio (French, 1850-1937)
Published by The Rotary Photographic Company (London, active from ca.1889)
ca. 1898
Photograph
1¾ x 5³/₈ in. (4.4 x 13.7 cm)

Postmark: Nairn | April 25, 1904
Recipient: Miss E. Gibbs, Douglas St., Nairn
Message (on recto): "Your image when 20"
Message (on verso): From "one you know Ta Ra Ra"
Private collection
See fig. 1.22

22. Postcard of Jane Hading
Reutlinger Studio (French, 1850-1937)
Published by La Société Industrielle de Photographie (S.I.P.), Paris
ca. 1898-1904
Photograph
3⁹/₁₆ x 5½ in. (9 x 14 cm)
Postmark: La Rochette | July 11, 1904
Recipient: Mademoiselle A. [Feubrier?], La Rochette, Savoie
Message (on recto): "Mon Meilleur souvenir [rest illegible]"
Translation: "My Best remembrance"
Private collection
See fig. 1.23

23. Postcard of Jane Hading in *Plus que Reine*
Reutlinger Studio (French, 1850-1937)
Published by Kunzli Frères Editeurs, (French, active ca. 1900-1910)
ca. 1899
Photograph
3¾ x 5⁷/₈ in. (9.5 x 15 cm)
Postmark: June [illegible], 1900
Recipient: Madame Paul Gérard, Quai de Brabant 38, Charleroi
Message (on recto): "Ma chère Lucile, je suis très heureuse d'apprendre ton retour et je viens t'envoyer à venir passer [l'après?] dîner le Mercredi ou Jeudi avec nous. Fais moi savoir le jour que tu choisis et reçois mille bons baisers. Loulou"
Translation: "My dear Lucile, I am very happy to hear of your return and I just sent you to come spend [the after?] dinner on Wednesday or Thursday with us. Let me know what day you choose and accept a thousand kisses. Loulou"
Private collection
See fig. 1.24

24. Book postcard of Jane Hading in *Plus que Reine*
Reutlinger Studio (French, 1850-1937)
Published by La Société Industrielle de Photographie (S.I.P.), Paris

ca.1899
Hand-colored photograph with metallic pigment
1⅞ x 6 in. (4.8 x 15.2 cm)
Recipient: Madame Gautier, Amiens
Message (on recto): "Marthe/9 [illegible] 04"
Private collection

25. Postcard of Jane Hading in
Plus que Reine
Reutlinger Studio (French, 1850-1937)
Published by La Société Industrielle de Photographie (S.I.P.), Paris
ca.1899
Hand-colored photograph with metallic pigment
3¾ x 5⅞ in. (9.5 x 15 cm)
Private collection

26. Postcard of Jane Hading in
Plus que Reine
Reutlinger Studio (French, 1850-1937)
Published by La Société Industrielle de Photographie (S.I.P.), Paris
ca.1899
Hand-colored photograph with metallic gold pigment
3¾ x 5⅞ in. (9.5 x 15 cm)
Private collection
See fig. A.4

27. Postcard of Jane Hading in
La Pompadour
Reutlinger Studio (French, 1850-1937)
Published by La Société Industrielle de Photographie (S.I.P.), Paris
ca.1901
Hand-colored photograph with glitter
3¾ x 6 in. (9.5 x 15.2 cm)
Private collection
See fig. 1.25

28. Postcard of Jane Hading in
La Pompadour
Reutlinger Studio (French, 1850-1937)
Published by La Société Industrielle de Photographie (S.I.P.), Paris
ca.1901
Hand-colored photograph
3¾ x 6 in. (9.5 x 15.2 cm)
Postmark: La Fresne, Gironde | September 17, 1907
Recipient: Mlle Margot, Jaillard Au Bastard, La Frèsne, Gironde
Message: "Eh bien a tu rêfflechi [sic] fais moi savoir de oui ou de non assez tôt mais je pense que se [sic] serra [sic] oui Bonjour a tous Ton ami [Louis?]"

Translation: "And so did you think it over let me know if yes or no soon but I think that it will be yes Hello to all Your friend [Louis?]"
Private collection

29. Postcard of Jane Hading in
La Pompadour
Reutlinger Studio (French, 1850-1937)
Published by La Société Industrielle de Photographie (S.I.P.), Paris
ca.1901
Hand-colored photograph
3¾ x 5⅞ in. (9.5 x 15 cm)
Recipient: M Distinta, Sig^ra Concetta [Sponnprivato?]
Message (on recto): "Ricordati di me [illegible] / 24-10-04 [?]"
Translation: "Remember me 24-10-04 [?]"
Private collection

30. Postcard of Jane Hading in
La Pompadour
Reutlinger Studio (French, 1850-1937)
Published by La Société Industrielle de Photographie (S.I.P.), Paris
ca.1903
Hand-colored photograph
3¾ x 5⅞ in. (9.5 x 15 cm)
Private collection
See fig. A.5

31. Postcard of Jane Hading in
La Pompadour
Reutlinger Studio (French, 1850-1937)
Published by La Société Industrielle de Photographie (S.I.P.), Paris
ca.1901
Photograph
3¾ x 5⅞ in. (9.5 x 15 cm)
Postmark: January 15, 1904
Sender unknown
Recipient: Monsieur Auguste Chollet, a [sic] St Saturnin-de Séchaud., commune-du-Port-d'Anvaux , Ch. Snfre
Message (on recto): "Bonnes amitiés"
Translation: Best wishes
Private collection

32. Postcard of Jane Hading
Reutlinger Studio (French, 1850-1937)
Published by Kunzli Frères Editeurs (French, active ca.1900-1910)
ca.1902
Photograph
3¾ x 6 in. (9.5 x 15.2 cm)
Postmark: Briey, Meurthe-et-Moselle

| November 4, 1904
Recipient: Monsieur et Madame Gargatte, Sociéte génerale, Briey, Meurth et Moselle
Message (on recto): "Bons Baisers Madeleine"
Translation: "Sweet Kisses Madeleine"
Private collection

33. Postcard of Jane Hading
Reutlinger Studio (French, 1850-1937)
Published by La Société Industrielle de Photographie (S.I.P.), Paris
ca.1902
Photograph
3¾ x 6 in. (9.5 x 15.2 cm)
Private collection

34. Postcard of Jane Hading
Reutlinger Studio (French, 1850-1937)
Published by Kunzli Frères Editeurs (French, active ca.1900-1910)
ca.1902
Hand-colored photograph with glitter and applied ornaments (now missing)
3¾ x 5⅞ in. (9.5 x 15 cm)
Recipient: Monsieur A. Besse, Institut à Buxy, Saône-et-Loire
Message: "Mon cher Antoine, j'ai neuf élèves! Au moment de la récréation papa est arrivé en ce moment il pêche à la rivière. Il veut que j'envoie mes élèves à midi, et que je parte avec lui pour Neuviè. je le ferai peut-être, car vraiment ma classe est vide, et je n'ai aucun goût à la faire. Je vous embrasse bien des fois, Votre Eugenie"
Translation: "My dear Antoine, I have nine students! Papa arrived during recess and he's now fishing in the river. He wants me to send my students home at noon and leave with him for Neuvié. I might do it since my class is really empty and I have no desire to teach it. I send you much love. Your Eugenie"
Private collection
See fig. 1.26

35. Cabinet card of Jane Hading
Reutlinger Studio (French, 1850-1937)
Paris, ca.1897-1904
4½ x 7 in. (11.4 x 17.8 cm)
Private collection

JANE HADING AND THE PRESS

36. *Le Théatre* (May 1899): cover
"Mme Jane Hading (Rôle de Joséphine)"
Paul Boyer (French, active late 19th-

early 20th century)
Published by Jean Boussod, Manzi,
Joyant & Cie. (French, 1898-1921)
Lithograph
Magazine (closed): 11¾ x 15 in. (29.8
x 40.3 cm)
Private collection
See fig. 1.28

37. *Le Théâtre* (November 1900):
cover
"Théatre de l'Athénée.— Mme Jane
Hading"
Paul Nadar (French, 1820-1910)
Published by Jean Boussod, Manzi,
Joyant & Cie. (French, 1898-1921)
Halftone
Magazine (closed): 11¾ x 15 in. (29.8
x 40.3 cm)
Private collection
See frontispiece

38. *Le Théâtre* (June 1901): cover
"Théatre de l'Athénée. —Mme Jane
Hading"
Paul Nadar (French, 1856-1939)
Published by Jean Boussod, Manzi,
Joyant & Cie. (French, 1898-1921)
Lithograph
Magazine (closed): 11¾ x 15 in. (29.8
x 40.3 cm)
Private collection
See fig. A.6

39. *Le Théâtre* (December 1901): cover
"Porte-Saint-Martin—La Pompadour—
Mme Jane Hading—Rôle de Madame
de Pompadour"
Reutlinger Studio (French, 1850-1937)
Published by Boussod, Manzi, Joyant
& Cie. (French, 1898-1921)
Lithograph
Magazine (closed): 11¾ x 15 in. (29.8
x 40.3 cm)
Library, Bard Graduate Center:
Decorative Arts, Design History,
Material Culture; New York
See fig. 1.29

40. *Le Théâtre* (June 1908): cover
"Mme Jane Hading, du Théâtre
National de l'Odéon"
Reutlinger Studio (French, 1850-1937)
Published by Jean Boussod, Manzi,
Joyant & Cie. (French, 1898-1921)
Lithograph
Magazine (closed): 11¾ x 15 in. (29.8
x 40.3 cm)
Private collection
See fig. 1.30

41. *Comœdia illustré* (January 1, 1909):
cover
"Jane Hading qui vient de créer avec
succès *la Femme X...*"
Henri Manuel (1874-1947) and Larcher
Edited by Michel de Brunoff (French)
Lithograph
Magazine (closed): 10¼ x 13 in.
(26 x 33 cm)
Private collection
See fig. 1.33

JANE HADING AND ADVERTISING

42. Duke's Cigarettes trade card:
"Jane Hading, Ostiaks, Russia"
On verso: "Portraits of Our Leading
Actors and Actresses in the Costumes
of All Nations, from 600 B.C. to the
present time."
Printed by Knapp & Co.,
Lithographers, New York
ca. 1888-89
Chromolithograph
1½ x 3 in. (3.8 x 7.6 cm)
Private collection
See fig. 1.34

43. Melia Cigarettes trade card:
Jane Hading in *La Mégère Apprivoisée*
ca. 1900
Hand-colored photograph
1⅛ x 2⅞ in. (2.9 x 7.3 cm)
Private collection
See fig. 1.37

44. Ogden's Guinea Gold Cigarettes
trade card: Jane Hading in *La
Pompadour*
ca. 1901
Photograph
1½ x 2⅜ in. (3.8 x 6 cm)
Private collection

45. Ogden's Guinea Gold Cigarettes
trade card: Jane Hading
ca. 1901
Photograph
1½ x 2⅜ in. (3.8 x 6 cm)
Private collection

46. Chocolat Poulain trade card:
Mme Jane Hading in *L'Œil crevé*
ca. 1881
Chromolithograph
2¾ x 4½ in. (7 x 11.4 cm)
Private collection

47. Chocolat Guérin-Boutron
trade card: "260. Jane Hading, dans

l'Aventurière."
Printed by Delmasure, Paris
ca. 1900
Halftone with hand-applied metallic
gold pigment
2⅛ x 4⅜ in. (5.4 x 11.1 cm)
Private collection
See fig. 1.35

48. Lefèvre-Utile biscuit trade card:
"Jane Hading, *Plus que Reine*, Acte V.
Les Larmes"
Reutlinger Studio (French, 1850-1937)
Printed by J. E. Goosens, Paris & Lille
ca. 1899
Chromolithograph with embossing
and applied halftone
4 x 7¼ in. (10.2 x 18.4 cm)
Private collection
See fig. 1.36

49. Félix Potin trade card: Jane
Hading
Reutlinger Studio (French, 1850-1937)
ca. 1900
Photograph
1¾ x 3¼ in. (4.4 x 8.3 cm)
Private collection

50. *Le Gaulois du Dimanche* (June
12-13, 1909): back cover
Advertisement for Eau de Jeunesse
Jane Hading
Georges Redon (French, 1869-1943)
Halftone
Magazine (closed): 11 x 14½ in. (27.9
x 36.8 cm)
Collection of William DeGregorio

51. *La Gazette du Bon Ton* (ca. 1913)
Advertisement for Eau de Jeunesse
Jane Hading
Pierre Brissaud (French, 1885-1964)
Lithograph
8¼ x 10¼ in. (21 x 26 cm)
Private collection
See fig. 1.39

52. *La Gazette du Bon Ton* (June 1913)
Advertisement for Parfum Jane
Hading aux Roses d'Orient
Georges Lepape (French, 1887-1971)
Lithograph
8¼ x 10¼ in. (21 x 26 cm)
Private collection
See fig. 1.41

53. **Woman's hat**
Joseph G. Darlington and Co.,
Philadelphia
United States, ca. 1908-10
Straw, silk flowers and leaves
Height: 18 in. (45.7 cm); brim diameter: 9 in. (22.9 cm)
Label: "Joseph G. Darlington and Co.
Chestnut St. Philadelphia"
Philadelphia Museum of Art, Gift of
an anonymous donor 1964-123-74
See fig. 2.8

54. **Woman's hat**
Lady Duff Gordon, known as Lucile
(English, 1863-1935)
House of Lucile (English, 1894-1920s)
New York, ca. 1910
Silk and cotton velvet, and egret
feathers
Brim: 19½ x 16¼ in. (49.5 x 41.3 cm)
Label: "Lucile Ltd./37 and 39 West
57th St./NEW YORK"
Courtesy of Jan Glier Reeder
See fig. 2.11

55. **Woman's hat**
James G. Johnson & Co. (American,
active early 20th century)
Newark, NJ, ca. 1910
Black horsehair lace over wire and
bird of paradise
Crown: 4 in. (10.2 cm); brim diameter:
19 in. (48.3 cm)
Label: "Made by James G. Johnson &
Co. of Newark N.J."
Philadelphia Museum of Art, Gift of
Susie McClure 1958-5-1
See fig. 2.9

56. **Woman's hat**
Suzanne Talbot (French, 1917-1947)
France (Paris), ca. 1914-18
Straw, silk velvet, and ostrich feathers
Brim diameter: 19 in. (48.3 cm)
Label: "Suzanne Talbot, 14 Rue Royale,
Paris"
Philadelphia Museum of Art, Gift of
Mrs. Richard Greenwood 1956-106-5
See fig. 2.10

57. **Wedding dress**
Lady Duff Gordon, known as Lucile
(English, 1863-1935)
For the House of Lucile (English,
1894-1920s)
New York, 1912
Silk georgette, silk satin, needle lace

(*point d'Alençon*), beads, rhinestones,
and wax
Center back: 53 in. (134.6 cm)
Label: "Lucile Ltd. 17 West 36th
Street. New York"
Museum of the City of New York, Gift
of Mrs. Bernard F. Gimbel, 72.97.1a-b
See fig. 2.18

58. **Merry Widow hat parody
postcard: "She stood on the bridge at
midday, boys, / Imagine a fix like that,
/ We couldn't get by, hard as we'd try, /
By that Merry Widow Hat."**
Published by I. Grollman (American,
active early 20th century)
1908
Halftone
3¾ x 5⅞ in. (9.5 x 15 cm)
Postmark: Waterloo, Iowa | February
7, 1910
Recipient: Mrs. Mabell Emry,
[Pashville?], La
Message: "Hellow Sister how are you
all coming I wrote you a letter last
week well Mabell is I a bout [sic] dead
I would like to see you afel [sic] bad I
am going to Doctor to morrow dont
say anything to the [illegible] about
[illegible?]. From Carrie."
Collection of Marlis Schweitzer

59. **Postcard of three women in
Merry Widow hats**
ca. 1908
Photograph
3⅜ x 5⅜ in. (8.6 x 13.7 cm)
Collection of Marlis Schweitzer
See fig. 2.16

60. **Merry Widow hat parody
postcard: "If two is company and
three's a crowd, / You needn't be
bothered by that; / Just shut the
third one out, girls, / Use your Merry
Widow Hat."**
Published by I. Grollman (American,
active early 20th century)
1908
Halftone
3¾ x 5⅞ in. (9.5 x 15 cm)
Postmark: Philadelphia | September
1, 1908
Recipient: Miss E. Craig, Havre-de
Grace, Md., c/o Rural De[f?].
Message [on recto]: "How is your old
merry widow did you take it down
with you, I am still wearing mine If
you see any nice lead pencils down
there send me one up"

Message [on verso]: "although I think
I would like duck shooting, I would
much rather be doing this / H.H."
Collection of Marlis Schweitzer

61. **Merry Widow hat parody
postcard: "What takes four hands
to lift it? / What's larger than your
flat? / What's detested by all men? /
Why—that Merry Widow Hat."**
Published by I. Grollman (American,
active early 20th century)
1908
Halftone
3¾ x 5⅞ in. (9.5 x 15 cm)
Postmark: [location illegible] | August
21, 1908
Recipient: Lena D. Moor, Lincoln Ill.
Message: "Friday P.M. I am going
home in the morn. & will ans. your
letter as soon as I can after I get settled. How is your mother? [illegible]"
Collection of Marlis Schweitzer
See fig. 2.14

62. **Merry Widow hat parody
postcard: "Say, honest, girls, it's
beastly / To wear a thing like that.
/ And make us tag along like pups
behind / Your Merry Widow Hat."**
Published by I. Grollman (American,
active early 20th century)
1908
Halftone
3½ x 5½ in. (8.9 x 14 cm)
Collection of Marlis Schweitzer

63. **Merry Widow hat parody
postcard: "Although he looks quite
pleasant, / Don't think he feels like
that, / For all the while he's thinking /
'Darn that Merry Widow Hat!'"**
Published by I. Grollman (American,
active early 20th century)
1908
Halftone
3¾ x 5⅞ in. (9.5 x 15 cm)
Postmark: Sheffield, Kansas |
September 2, 1908
Recipient: Miss Sara Biehler,
Frederick, Kan.
Message: "Hello Sara / Read your card
and was glad to here [sic] you had
control of your Eyes. I don't think I
will effect them very soon 'D.' said he
dident [sic] know anything about that
mule team, guess you must bin [sic]
dreaming, guess I will [s/r?]ing off for
this time / C.H."
Private collection

64. Merry Widow hat parody postcard: "When the elevator's crowded / What's the use to wait for that? / Just make a parachute / Of your Merry Widow Hat."
Published by I. Grollman (American, active early 20th century)
1908
Halftone
3¾ x 5⅞ in. (9.5 x 15 cm)
Postmark: York | November 18, 1908
Recipient: Miss Marguerite Storms [?], Shrewsbury, Pa.
Message: "I think this will be the case with me when I get my large hat. I have not heard anything about that, remember what I told you: expect to come home about Friday, or Sat. will see you then / A.V. [illegible] / 605 E. Market St."
Private collection

65. Merry Widow hat parody postcard: "'Tis a shame,' the lady sighed, / 'To bear a load like that.' / But the woman cried in anger / 'That's my Merry Widow Hat.'"
Published by I. Grollman (American, active early 20th century)
1908
Halftone
3¾ x 5⅞ in. (9.5 x 15 cm)
Postmark: [location illegible] | March 23, 1908
Recipient: Mrs. Henry Scott, Nicholson, Pa.
Message: "Dear Sis, haven't had time too [sic] write hardly to breathe, never mind the [illegible] until Mother comes up. Tell her she had better come up & help me keep my birthday. I am going to have Mrs Newman down to spend the day with me, [illegible] very to Bing Sas & had some teeth filled Gle[n?] has been sick but is all right now (Emma)"
Private collection

66. Merry Widow hat parody postcard: "I've all the cash that I can use, / This will of Hubby's fixes that, / There's none to growl next time I choose / To get a Merry Widow Hat."
Published by I. Grollman (American, active early 20th century)
1908
Halftone
3¾ x 5⅞ in. (9.5 x 15 cm)
Postmark: Youngston | August 15, 1908

Recipient: Miss Lizzie Moran, Whallonsburg, N. York
Message: "Hello! Lizzie / How are all the Brookfield people It is very warm here today. wish could see you all. / Marion"
Postscript: "What do you think of this hat?"
Private collection
See fig. 2.12

67. Merry Widow hat parody postcard: "Ah, Sweetheart don't you know / What I am driving at? / Why, my love for you is as big / As—your Merry Widow Hat."
Published by I. Grollman (American, active early 20th century)
1908
Halftone
3¾ x 5⅞ in. (9.5 x 15 cm)
Postmark: Chicago, Ill. | February 13 [or 18], 1909
Recipient: Miss Susan Rose, Box 8 Route #3, Laporte, Ind.
Message: "Dear Friend / I received your letter and I shall come to Laporte either Saturday after-noon or Sunday as I don't know how soon I can get off from work but you can rest easy that I will be there I have a slight cold but I guess I shall be all right by Saturday / Cousin / Joe"
Private collection

68. Merry Widow hat parody postcard
Published by I. Grollman (American, active early 20th century)
1908
Halftone
3¾ x 5⅞ in. (9.5 x 15 cm)
Postmark: Chicago, Ill. | February 19, 1909
Recipient: Miss Susan Rose, Box 8 Route #3, Laporte, Ind.
Message: "Dear Friend, / This is the last card I shall address to Miss Susan Rose I expect as I suppose it will have to be otherwise don't you think so / Joe"
Private collection

69. Merry Widow hat parody postcard: "Alone here on the piazza, / I can't miss a chance like that, / But Gee, I wonder who it is / 'Neath that Merry Widow Hat."
Published by I. Grollman (American, active early 20th century)
1908

Halftone
3¾ x 5⅞ in. (9.5 x 15 cm)
Postmark: Chicago, Ill. | February 1, 1909
Message: "Dear Friend, I received your postal, and to-day I heard you are well again but next time be more careful and don't dance so long at a surprise Gee I wished I was there I am hopeing [sic] you shall be in good health again when this postal reaches you Regards to you and folks from Joe"
Private collection

70. Merry Widow hat parody postcard: "We all agree that barn doors / Would scarce suit the modern flat, / Yet how much more convenient / For the Merry Widow Hat."
Published by I. Grollman (American, active early 20th century)
1908
Halftone
3¾ x 5⅞ in. (9.5 x 15 cm)
Private collection

71. Merry Widow hat parody postcard: "Ah beg yuh pahdon, Miss, / But dis haint no place fo' dat, / De freight elevator back dere'll / Take yuh Merry Widow Hat."
Published by I. Grollman (American, active early 20th century)
1908
Halftone
3¾ x 5⅞ in. (9.5 x 15 cm)
Postmark: [location illegible] | April 6, 1909
Recipient: Lillian Bert, Dix, Nebr.
Message: "Dear Lillian / How are you we are well Do you go to school we are going to have vacation next week. write soon / From Lilla"
Private collection

72. Merry Widow hat parody postcard: "No wonder she's alone, / But who's to blame for that. / He thought it was a rose bush, / That Merry Widow Hat."
Published by I. Grollman (American, active early 20th century)
1908
Halftone
3¾ x 5⅞ in. (9.5 x 15 cm)
Postmark: Chicago, Ill. | February 11, 1909
Recipient: Miss Susan Rose
Message: "2/11/09 / Dear Friend Susan:- / As I did not hear wheather

[sic] you are well again I am thinking that perhaps you are not well as yet and I hope that is not the case as I only like to hear good news when I hear anything from you. Regards to you and all / from Joe"
Private collection

73. Merry Widow hat parody
postcard: "He wished to take her arm, / (Now what do you think of that.) / She had to cut a 'Man'-hole / In her Merry Widow Hat."
Published by I. Grollman (American, active early 20th century)
1908
Halftone
3¾ x 5⅞ in. (9.5 x 15 cm)
Private collection
See fig. 2.13

74. Merry Widow hat parody
postcard: "No wonder she's alone, / But who's to blame for that. / He thought it was a rose bush, / That Merry Widow Hat."
Published by I. Grollman (American, active early 20th century)
1908
Halftone
3¾ x 5⅞ in. (9.5 x 15 cm)
Postmark: Ellsworth, Kans. | September 15, 1908
Recipient: Miss Sarah Biehler, Frederick, Kans.
Message: "Ellsworth 9/14 / Hello Sarah what you no [sic] about the other side / J.W.D."
Private collection

75. Merry Widow hat parody
postcard: "Who would think that he'd be killed / By a little shock like that? / Why 'twas nothing but the bill / For my Merry Widow Hat."
Published by I. Grollman (American, active early 20th century)
1908
Halftone
3¾ x 5⅞ in. (9.5 x 15 cm)
Postmark: Chicago, Ill. | February 19, 1909
Recipient: Miss Susan Rose, Box 8 Route #3, Laporte, Ind.
Message: "Dear Friend:- / I shall try my utmost to get the 1.40 train to-morrow but if I don't I surely will get the 1.40 Sunday. I hope everything is OK / Joe"
Private collection

76. Merry Widow hat parody
postcard: "No Admission / To the Surf--- / The Merry Widow / Invades the Beach."
Published by H. Sollott, Philadelphia
ca. 1908
Lithograph
3½ x 5½ in. (8.9 x 14 cm)
Collection of Marlis Schweitzer

77. Merry Widow hat parody
postcard: "Merry Widow I Ran Into In _____"
Published by Kansas City Postcard Co., Kansas City
1908
Lithograph
3¾ x 5⅞ in. (9.5 x 15 cm)
Postmark: Kansas City, MO | February 28, 1909
Recipient: Mr. Everett Deweese, Butler MO., Route 8.
Message: "I'll send you this card in perseverance of old times. Its too bad about you and Walter being so good. I'd like to see if you're so good as all that - How is everything down there? from Rhoda"
Collection of Marlis Schweitzer

78. Merry Widow Wiles postcard: "A 'Merry Widow' hat covers a multitude of sins—sometimes.—"
Walter Wellman (American, 1879-1949)
ca. 1908
Lithograph
3⅝ x 6 in. (9.2 x 15.2 cm)
Postmark: [location illegible] | October 7, 1908
Recipient: Miss Margaret P[oom?], Basking Ridge, N.J.
Private collection

79. Merry Widow Wiles postcard: "Wanted! A Merry Widower."
Walter Wellman (American, 1879-1949)
ca. 1908
Lithograph
3⅝ x 6 in. (9.2 x 15.2 cm)
Recipient: Miss Margaret Edna Harris, Harrisburg, [Mon?]
Message: "[We?] have called our party off as Arthur could not be here. Resp. / Mrs. Howell. R. Fr. H. No. 1."
Private collection

LILY ELSIE IN THE PHOTOGRAPHER'S STUDIO

80. Postcard of Lily Elsie
Published by W. McKenzie & Co., London
ca. 1904
Series: The Artistic Series
Photograph
3¾ x 5¾ in. (9.5 x 14.6 cm)
Postmark: Harrogate | July 30, 1904
Recipient: Miss Constance Baug, The Lodge, Aslockton, North
Message: "It is very hot here am going to try to get in to see Arthur Roberts at the Kursaal in the Darling of the Guards. Been & enjoyed it very much"
Private collection

81. Postcard of Lily Elsie
Published by Ralph Dunn & Co., (English, active ca. 1900-1910)
ca. 1905
Hand-colored photograph
3¾ x 5⅞ in. (9.5 x 15 cm)
Postmark: Dundee | December 2, 1905
Recipient: Miss L. Easson, 6 Lawrence St., Dundee
Message: "2-12-05 Dear Lizzie, This one has come at last. How do you like it. It is very badly painted as it was done in a hurry. Best wishes from Q. Soulas"
Private collection

82. Postcard of Lily Elsie and Leonard Mackay in *See-See*
Foulsham & Banfield (English, 1906-20)
Published by The Rotary Photographic Company (English, active from ca. 1889)
ca. 1906
Hand-colored photograph with metal-lic pigment
3¾ x 5⅞ in. (9.5 x 15 cm)
Postmark: Leicester | June 15, 1907
Recipient: Miss Worthington, 54 Selwyn St, Kirkdale, Liverpool
Message: "That was a pretty card you sent me this morning and I coloured it pink and brown according to instruc-tion from my friend who went to Sheffield with me on Thursday, he is staying with me to-day and is now busy colouring postcards his first attempt and I must say that he does them very well indeed. I will send you a photograph that I took of him and his friend who are both servers at our church. He has been to all the lovely

churches in England as he is a traveler. It is quite a lovely day to-day. Swept the path is a little easier / Laurie"
Private collection
See fig. 2.19

83. Postcard of "Stage Favorites: Miss Edna May, Miss Gabrielle Ray, Miss Madge Crichton, Miss Madge Lessing, Miss Billie Burke, Miss Lily Elsie"
Published by The Rotary Photographic Company (English, active from ca.1889)
ca.1906
Composite photograph
3¾ x 5⅞ in. (9.5 x 15 cm)
Postmark: Stockton-on-Tees | June 2,1906
Secondary postmark: BFDALE | June 3,1906
Recipient: Miss Silo, 117 High Street, Holywood, Nr Belfast, Ireland.
Message: "Weather keeping fine I'm now staying in Stockton I shall be here for a week perhaps longer This is a very nice little town. Hope [illegible] is well. Regards to Jasper Love from yours / Dolly."
Private collection
See fig. 1

84. Postcard of Lily Elsie in *The Merry Widow*
Foulsham & Banfield (English, 1906-20)
Published by The Rotary Photographic Company (English, active from ca.1889)
ca.1907
Photograph
3¾ x 5⅞ in. (9.5 x 15 cm)
Postmark: London E.D. | January 23, 1908
Recipient: Miss E. Isaacs, 11 St Peter's Rd, Mile End, E.
Message: "Dear Est / Hoping you feel better to-day I could not get one to go the other way / With Love / Jules."
Private collection
See fig. A.9

85. Sheet music: "The Merry Widow"
Music: Franz Lehár (Austrian, 1870-1948)
Arrangement: H.M. Higgs (English, 1855-1929)
Published by Chappell & Co., Ltd., London, New York & Melbourne
ca.1907
Chromolithograph
Dimensions (closed): 8¼ x 11 in. (21 x 28.6 cm)

Collection of Marlis Schweitzer
See fig. 2.7

86. *The Merry Widow Souvenir Book*
Talbot Hughes (English, 1869-1942)
Author: Adrian Ross (English, 1859-1933)
Published by William Heinemann, London
1908
Chromolithograph
7¼ x 9⅞ in. (18.4 x 25.1 cm)
Collection of Marlis Schweitzer

87. Postcard of Lily Elsie in *The Merry Widow*
Foulsham & Banfield (English, 1906-20)
Published by The Rotary Photographic Company (English, active from ca. 1889)
ca.1907
Photograph
3⅝ x 5½ in. (9.2 x 14 cm)
Postmark: South Kensington | October 15,1907
Recipient: Miss C Dobbs, Overstrand Hall, Cromer
Message: "54 Onslow Gdns / S. Kensington / Dear Cis, Thank you for PPC. I expect you think I am a long time answering it. I like your photo very much it is nice I hope you are quite well love Edie."
Private collection

88. Postcard of Lily Elsie in *The Merry Widow*
Foulsham & Banfield (English, 1906-20)
Published by The Rotary Photographic Company (English, active from ca.1889)
ca.1907
Hand-colored photograph
3⅝ x 5½ in. (9.2 x 14 cm)
Private collection
See fig. 2.6

89. Postcard of Lily Elsie in *The Merry Widow*
Foulsham & Banfield (English, 1906-20)
Published by The Rotary Photographic Company (English, active from ca.1889)
ca.1907
Photograph
3⅝ x 5½ in. (9.2 x 14 cm)
Autograph (on recto): Lily Elsie
Private collection
See fig. 2.1

90. Postcard of Lily Elsie and Joseph Coyne in *The Merry Widow*
Foulsham & Banfield (English, 1906-20)
Published by The Rotary Photographic Company (English, active from ca.1889)
ca.1907
Photograph
3⅝ x 5½ in. (9.2 x 14 cm)
Recipient: Mr. N. Richardson, 94 Grant Avenue, Smithdown Rd, Sefton Pk, Liverpool
Message: "To Dear old Will / With best wishes for a Bright + Happy Xmas and a very Prosperous New Year. From Tom Constantine / 1912"
Private collection
See fig. 2.20

91. Postcard of Lily Elsie in *The Merry Widow*
Foulsham & Banfield (English, 1906-20)
Published by The Rotary Photographic Company (English, active from ca.1889)
ca.1907
Hand-colored photograph
3¾ x 5⅞ in. (9.5 x 15 cm)
Private collection

92. Postcard of Lily Elsie in *The Merry Widow*
Foulsham & Banfield (English, 1906-20)
Published by The Rotary Photographic Company (English, active from ca.1889)
ca.1907
Photograph
3⅝ x 5½ in. (9.2 x 14 cm)
Postmark: London S.W. | July 21,1908
Recipient: Mrs Barnes, 6 Crowncourt, Pall Mall, London
Message (on verso): "Dear G, This is not a new one, but still I think it is very good. Mrs K was too busy talking to some man to show me where to find any new ones / Love from Hilda"
Postscript: "This is the original Merry Widow hat."
Message (on recto): "Hilda / 21/4/08"
Private collection
See page 126

93. Postcard of Lily Elsie
Foulsham & Banfield (English, 1906-20)
Published by The Rotary Photographic Company (English, active from ca.1889)
ca.1907
Photograph

3¾ x 5⅞ in. (9.5 x 15 cm)
Private collection
See fig. VI

94. Postcard of Lily Elsie
Foulsham & Banfield (English,
1906-20)
Published by The Rotary Photographic
Company (English, active from ca.1889)
ca.1907
Photograph
3¾ x 5⅞ in. (9.5 x 15 cm)
Postmark: Birmingham | August 3,
1907
Recipient: Mrs G. O. Fathers, c/o Mr
Jefferies, 6 Pier Terrace, Lowestoft
Message (on verso): "Dear Edith /
Many thanks for card. Hope you are
having a nice time. Did you get any
gloves? for me so please ask mother
to pay you for them. My love to you all
/ Ethel[?]"
Postscript: "We have heard of all your
domes[?] from Miss Burley."
Message (on recto): "Ethel[?]"
Private collection

95. Postcard of Lily Elsie
ca.1907
Hand-colored photograph with glitter
3¾ x 5⅞ in. (9.5 x 15 cm)
Postmark: Whittleford, Nuneaton |
December 22, 1906 [or 1908]
Recipient: Miss P. Randle, Montipelier
House, Hartshill, Atherstone
Message: "Thanks awfully for P.C
did'nt receive it till I got home from
Hartshill, hope you will like this one
From / JS"
Postscript: "PS / Please mind the
miseltoe [sic] You [illegible] it you did
awfully much so"
Private collection

96. Postcard of Lily Elsie
Foulsham & Banfield (English,
1906-20)
Published by The Rotary Photographic
Company (English, active from ca.1889)
ca.1908
Photograph
3¾ x 5⅞ in. (9.5 x 15 cm)
Postmark: London S.W. | April 7, 1908
Recipient: Miss Cissie Cox, 227
Shirland Road, Maida Hill, W.
Message: "Surely they have put the
wrong name under this photograph.
I've heard from J. about concert to-
night and shall be outside Friendly at
10 to 8 p.m. I'm very sorry, dear, that

I am too busy to let you have a letter
to-day. Yours, Will"
Postscript: "I suppose you've almost
settled down now at home"
Private collection

97. Postcard of Lily Elsie
Foulsham & Banfield (English,
1906-20)
Published by The Rotary Photographic
Company (English, active from ca.1889)
ca.1909
Photograph
3¾ x 5⅞ in. (9.5 x 15 cm)
Private collection

98. Postcard of Lily Elsie in
A Waltz Dream
Published by The Rotary Photographic
Company (English, active from ca.1889)
ca.1909
Photograph
3¾ x 5⅞ in. (9.5 x 15 cm)
Postmark: London | November 18,
1912
Recipient: Miss A. Murley, 28
Cambridge Rd., Bromley, Kent
Message: "Fleet St / Novbr-18 / Dear
A / Very pleased to hear from you &
to hear you feel better I trust you may
keep well dear. I have not heard from
anyone but you since I saw you last
only one letter from Mrs Watts that
brought my cloak up Rose went away
& left no address before she came
away I thought Mrs Baxter could have
written but as not done so never mind
dear No! I have not prepared for Xmas
yet only made some mince meat hope
to hear from you soon all send [love?]
/ Yr / true friend / Ma.P."
Postscript: "[illegible] you dear"
Private collection

99. Postcard of Lily Elsie
Foulsham & Banfield (English,
1906-20)
Published by The Rotary Photographic
Company (English, active from ca.1889)
ca.1911
Photograph
3¾ x 5⅞ in. (9.5 x 15 cm)
Private collection
See fig. 2.24

**100. Postcard of Lily Elsie and Robert
Michaelis in *A Waltz Dream***
Foulsham & Banfield (English,
1906-20)
Published by The Rotary Photographic

Company (English, active from ca.1889)
ca.1911
Photograph
3⅝ x 5½ in. (9.2 x 14 cm)
Postmark: Thornton-Heath, Surrey |
March 8, 1911
Recipient: Miss Winifred Welch, H5
Argyle Road, Alford, R[illegible]
Message: "March 8th 1911. Thornton
Heath / Dear Winnie, How do you like
this card. Isn't he sweet? Tell Kitty I
am patiently awaiting her letter. Love
to all from all / Elsie"
Private collection
See fig. 2.3

101. *The Graphic* (February 1911)
Tear sheet showing " 'The Waltz
Dream' at Daly's Theatre"
3½ x 5½ in. (8.9 x 14 cm)
Private collection

**102. Postcard of Lily Elsie:
"Birthday Greetings"**
Published by The Rotary Photographic
Company (English, active from ca.1889)
ca.1906-1909
Composite photograph with glitter
3¾ x 5⅞ in. (9.5 x 15 cm)
Message [across entire verso]: "To
dear Grandpa wishing you many
happy returns of the day from Ethel"
Private collection

103. Postcard of Lily Elsie in
The Dollar Princess
Foulsham & Banfield (English,
1906-20)
Published by The Rotary Photographic
Company (English, active from ca.1889)
ca.1909
Photograph
3¾ x 5⅞ in. (9.5 x 15 cm)
Private collection

104. Postcard of Lily Elsie in
The Dollar Princess
Foulsham & Banfield (English,
1906-20)
Published by The Rotary Photographic
Company (English, active from ca.1889)
ca.1909
Photograph
3⅝ x 5½ in. (9.2 x 14 cm)
Postmark: Cardiff | February 9, 1910
Recipient: Miss M. Lloyd., 110 Carlisle
St., Splott, Local.
Message: "Dear M. as you see I am
keeping my promise, but I shall want
one in return before I send another

one. Thanks so much for last P.C. I liked it very much. Love from Edith 8/2/10."
Private collection

105. Postcard of Lily Elsie in *The Dollar Princess*
Foulsham & Banfield (English, 1906-20)
Published by The Rotary Photographic Company (English, active from ca.1889)
ca.1909
Photograph
3⅝ x 5½ in. (9.2 x 14 cm)
Postmark: Whitley Bay R.S., Northumberland | July 1, 1910
Recipient: Miss L. Watson, 11 Ashfield Terrace East., Newcastle-on-Tyne
Message: "30 June/10 / The day will soon be here. / Bill"
Private collection

106. Postcard of Lily Elsie in *The Dollar Princess*
Foulsham & Banfield (English, 1906-20)
Published by The Rotary Photographic Company (English, active from ca.1889)
ca.1909
Photograph
3⅝ x 5½ in. (9.2 x 14 cm)
Postmark: Cardiff | June 7, 1910
Recipient: Miss M. Lloyd, 110 Carlysle St, Splotlands., Cardiff
Message: "Tuesday. / Dear Marie / I will come down to your house on Thursday as it is my easy night for homework. I will come down about half past six will that do? I am ashamed of myself have failed P. [Ts.?]. Thanks so much for P.C. It was very pretty / Love Phyllis"
Private collection
See fig. XI

107. Postcard of Lily Elsie in *The Dollar Princess*
Foulsham & Banfield (English, 1906-20)
Published by The Rotary Photographic Company (English, active from ca.1889)
ca.1909
Photograph
3⅝ x 5½ in. (9.2 x 14 cm)
Postmark: Atherton, Manchester | May 9, 1910
Recipient: Miss G. Telbout, 3 Marlborough Rd., Exeter.
Message: "Is'nt this lovely? Can you get me one like it? I have 23 'Dollar

Princess' p.cs but not this. If you can't get it please send one of her in private dress. / Annie Orrell"
Private collection
See fig. III

108. Postcard of Lily Elsie and the company of the *The Dollar Princess*
Foulsham & Banfield (English, 1906-20)
Published by The Rotary Photographic Company (English, active from ca.1889)
ca.1909
Photograph
3¾ x 5⅞ in. (9.5 x 15 cm)
Postmark: London | [date illegible]
Recipient: Miss K. Morris, Farlight, Kenilworth Rd, H. Leonardo or [illegible]
Message: "I hope that you will like this took just 2 hrs. to get up here."
Private collection
See fig. 2.21

109. Postcard of Lily Elsie
Claude Harris (English, active early 20th century)
Published by J. Beagles & Co. (English, 1881-1939)
ca.1910
Photograph
3¾ x 5⅞ in. (9.5 x 15 cm)
Recipient: Miss Eardley, 9 Willow Rod, Aylesbury Bucks
Message: "My dear Nellie - What on earth has happened to you - I do hope you are not ill. How is the hair business progressing? Fred is out of the army, so you can imagine how pleased I feel. We are endeavoring to get a flat but I fear it will be a terrible job. I hope to leave business in March. I am most anxious to hear what you are going to do. I am having a day or two away from bus: we are buying civilian clothes for Fred & doing a theatre or two - he is very excited. Write soon. Much love from both. Yours affect / Queenie"
Postscript: "Excuse awful writing but it is Fred's pen"
Stamped on verso: "Bill Hopkins Collection / Notting Hill Gate / London / 21 Kensington Park Road W11"
Private collection

110. Postcard of Lily Elsie in *The Count of Luxembourg*
Foulsham & Banfield (English, 1906-20)

Published by The Rotary Photographic Company (English, active from ca.1889)
ca.1911
Photograph
3⅝ x 5½ in. (9.2 x 14 cm)
Message [in upper left corner, verso]: "1911. / Lottie Davis"
Private collection

111. Postcard of Lily Elsie in *The Count of Luxembourg*
Foulsham & Banfield (English, 1906-20)
Published by The Rotary Photographic Company (English, active from ca.1889)
ca.1911
Photograph
3⅝ x 5½ in. (9.2 x 14 cm)
Postmark: Glasgow | May 14, 1913
Recipient: Miss Macfarlane, Kilgraston, Bridge-of-Weir
Message: "I am so sorry I haven't had time to write you but will do so fully when I get to Belfast. My address is: Gordon House, Annadale, Belfast. Nellie & I cross tonight at present I am in town in a big hurry. Much love from / Alice."
Private collection
See fig. 2.4

112. Postcard of Lily Elsie in her wedding dress / (Mrs. Ian Bullough)
Foulsham & Banfield (English, 1906-20)
Published by The Rotary Photographic Company (English, active from ca.1889)
ca.1911
Photograph
3¾ x 5⅞ in. (9.5 x 15 cm)
Private collection
See fig. 2.25

113. Postcard of Mr. and Mrs. Ian Bullough / (Miss Lily Elsie)
Foulsham & Banfield (English, 1906-20)
Published by The Rotary Photographic Company (English, active from ca.1889)
ca.1911
Photograph
3¾ x 5⅞ in. (9.5 x 15 cm)
Private collection
See fig. 2.17

114. Postcard of Miss Lily Elsie / (Mrs. Ian Bullough)
Rita Martin (English, 1875-1958)
Published by J. Beagles & Co. (English,

1881-1939)
ca. 1913
Photograph
3¾ x 5⅞ in. (9.5 x 15 cm)
Postmark: London | July 8, 1913
Recipient: Miss Gladys Swanson,
c/o Miss Forrester, Jackson Street,
Coalville, W[est?] Leicester
Message: "3 Church Lane, /
Walthamstow / N.E. / 8th July, 1913 /
Dear Gladys / Thanks for card. I hope
you are having a nice time. Dad is get-
ting along alright now. Give my love
to Miss Forrester. Also remember me
to the other B[ounder?]. Your loving
Brother, D."
Private collection
See fig. 2.26

LILY ELSIE AND THE PRESS

115. *The Play Pictorial* (August 1907)
Open to page 80-81, showing Lily
Elsie in *The Merry Widow*
Halftone
Magazine (closed): 9 x 12½ in.
(22.9 x 31.8 cm)
Private collection

116. *The Play Pictorial* (November
1909): cover
Lily Elsie in *The Dollar Princess*
Lithograph
Magazine (closed): 9½ x 12½ in.
(24.1 x 31.8 cm)
Private collection
See fig. 2.31

117. *The Play Pictorial* (February 1911):
cover
Lily Elsie in *A Waltz Dream*
Lithograph
Magazine (closed): 9½ x 12½ in.
(24.1 x 31.8 cm)
Private collection
See fig. A.11

118. *The Play Pictorial* (July 1911):
cover
Lily Elsie and Bertram Wallis in
The Count of Luxembourg
Lithograph
Magazine (closed): 9½ x 12½ in.
(24.1 x 31.8 cm)
Private collection
See fig. 2.32

LILY ELSIE AND ADVERTISING

119. Postcard of Lily Elsie modeling
the Knitroyal Sports Coat
Published by The Rotary Photographic
Company (English, active from ca. 1889)
ca. 1915-20
Photograph
3⅛ x 5⅞ in. (8 x 15 cm)
Private collection
See fig. 2.34

120. Postcard of Lily Elsie modeling
the Knitroyal Sports Coat
Published by The Rotary Photographic
Company (English, active from ca. 1889)
ca. 1915-20
Hand-colored photograph
3⅛ x 5¾ in. (8 x 14.6 cm)
Private collection

BILLIE BURKE AND FASHION

121. Dress worn by Billie Burke in
The "Mind the Paint" Girl
Lady Duff Gordon, known as Lucile
(English, 1863-1935)
House of Lucile (English, 1894-1920s)
New York, 1912
Machine-made lace (Brussels *point de
gaze*), silk faille, silk flowers, chiffon,
and wire
Center back: 58 in. (147.3 cm)
Label: "Lucile Ltd. 37 & 39 West 57th
St. New York"
Museum of the City of New York,
Gift of Mrs. William R. Stephenson,
70.101.10
See fig. 3.5

122. Billie Burke in *The "Mind the
Paint" Girl*
Sarony Studio (American, 1866-ca.
1930)
New York, 1912
Studio Signature
9 x 12½ in. (22.9 x 28.6 cm)
Museum of the City of New York, The
Burns Mantle Collection, Gift of Mrs.
Robert Burns Mantle, 48.210.727
See fig. A.14

123. Billie Burke at her home on
Mt. Vernon (inscribed on verso)
Byron Studio (American,
1892-present)
New York, 1912
Photograph
8 x 10¼ in. (20.3 x 26 cm)
Private collection

124. *The Stage Quarterly* (September
1914)
Open to page 17, showing "Miss Billie
Burke, Star of 'Jerry'"
Halftone
12 x 9¼ in. (25.7 x 17.8 cm)
Billy Rose Theatre Division, The
New York Public Library for the
Performing Arts, Astor, Lenox and
Tilden Foundations

125. Billie Burke in *Jerry*
George Grantham Bain (American,
1865-1944)
"[illegible] The Bain News Service /
from George Grantham Bain / [8?] 2
Union Square East, NY / Apr 16, 1914
[stamp on verso]"
Copyrighted by Charles Frohman
New York, 1914
Photograph
5 x 7 in. (12.7 x 17.8 cm)
Private collection
See fig. 3.F

BILLIE BURKE IN THE
PHOTOGRAPHER'S STUDIO

126. Postcard of Billie Burke
Published by The Rotary Photographic
Company (English, active from ca. 1889)
ca. 1903-7
Photograph
3⅝ x 5½ in. (9.2 x 14 cm)
Postmark: Ferndale, Pontypridd | April
25, 1907
Recipient: Miss L. Owen, Porth Hotel,
Porth
Message: "Hope you arrived safe &
hope you will like this one / With love
/ May"
Private collection
See fig. 3.10

127. Postcard of Billie Burke
Published by Misch & Stock (English,
ca. 1890-1913) (printed in Saxony)
ca. 1903-7
Color lithograph
3⅝ x 5½ in. (9.2 x 14 cm)
Recipient: Mr. G. Elephant, Mrs.
Giraffe, High Street, Handcross, Nr.
Crawley, Sussex
Message: "Believe not each accusing
tongue, / As most weak person do /
But still believe that story wrong, /
Which ought not to be true. / Good
birthday advice"
Private collection

128. Postcard of Billie Burke
Published by Raphael Tuck and Sons
(English, ca. 1870–ca. 1940)
ca. 1904
Photograph
3¾ x 5¾ in. (9.5 x 14.6 cm)
Private collection

129. Postcard of Billie Burke
Published by Ralph Dunn & Co.,
(English, active from ca. 1900-10)
ca. 1904-7
Photograph
3⅝ x 5½ in. (9.2 x 14 cm)
Recipient: Miss N. Firth
Message: "Did you say Violets"
[in purple pencil]
Private collection

130. Postcard of Billie Burke
Published by Philco Publishing Co.
(English, 1906-34)
ca. 1906
Photograph
3¾ x 5¾ in. (9.5 x 14.6 cm)
Recipient: Miss Flo. [Reough?],
Iddesleigh, Redditch
Message: "When are you going to
write me again it seems ages since
I had a letter hope you haven't quite
forgotten 'poor me.' How are you
enjoying this cool weather, I shall
be nothing but a grease [spot?] if it
continues much longer. The concerts
have begun in the Gardens this week,
went Monday evening, it was a treat.
Hope you will have a jolly time this
weekend. Yours lovingly Gertie"
Postscript: Don't you think Billie
looks sweet - here?"
Private collection
See page 152

131. Postcard of Billie Burke
Published by The Rotary Photographic
Company (English, active from ca.
1889)
ca. 1905
Photograph
3⅝ x 5½ in. (9.2 x 14 cm)
Postmark: Lark [Lane?], Liv[erpool?] |
February 18, 1905
Sender: Gertie, 35 Hertford Rd., Bootle
Recipient: Mr. Geo Lloyd, 171 Carlisle
St, Roath, Cardiff
Message [on verso]: "Dear Geo, Have
been expecting photo but have not
received it yet. I had mine taken but
look an awful sight so won't send
one. Am having some more taken

on Monday. Are you well? I hope so.
When are you sending it? Soon I
hope in haste. Yours very sincerely,
Gertie"
Message [on recto]: "I went to the
Panto to see this Lady on Monday in
Aladin. GW."
Private collection

132. Postcard of Billie Burke
Draycott Galleries (English, active
early 20th century)
Published by Davidson Bros. (English,
1901-11)
ca. 1905-6
Photograph
3⅝ x 5½ in. (9.2 x 14 cm)
Postmark: Cambridge | September
12, 1906
Recipient: Miss Shrubbs, 90 Townsend
Terrace, Richmond, Surrey, S.W.
Message: "Dear M. I hope you enjoyed
the theatre last even. Thanks very
much for letters. It's raining a little
here [now?] ma chèrie [sic]. Am long-
ing for Friday even. I'm feeling very
well indeed as for ma chèrie [sic]. Give
my love to M + A & with fondest love
to your dear self. From yours ever
[illegible]."
Private collection

133. Postcard of Billie Burke
Bassano Studio (English, 1850-1963)
Published by Davidson Bros. (English,
1901-11)
ca. 1907
Photograph
3¾ x 5¾ in. (9.5 x 14.6 cm)
Postmark: [location illegible] | August
28, 1907
Recipient: Master A. Golden,
Echline House, 30 Princes Road, Gt.
Yarmouth, Norfolk
Message: "Shipley / My Dear Alan,
Thanks very much for your pretty p.c.
I am glad you are enjoying yourself.
Aunt Martha"
Private collection

134. Postcard of Billie Burke
Published by Philco Publishing Co.
(English, 1906-34)
ca. 1907
Photograph
3⅝ x 5½ in. (9.2 x 14 cm)
Postmark: London | June (or July?)
14, 1907
Recipient: Miss Edith Sheaf, 91
Geneva Rd, Brixton, S.W.

Message: [illegible shorthand]
Private collection

135. Postcard of Billie Burke
Published by The Rotary Photographic
Company (English, active from ca. 1889)
ca. 1907
Photograph
3⅝ x 5½ in. (9.2 x 14 cm)
Private collection
See fig. 3.15

136. Postcard of Billie Burke
Richard Brown (English, active ca. 1890)
Published by Philco Publishing Co.
(English, 1906-34)
ca. 1907
Hand-colored photograph with glitter
3⅝ x 5½ in. (9.2 x 14 cm)
Private collection
See fig. 3.17

137. Postcard of Billie Burke
Dover Street Studio (English, active
ca. 1906-12)
Published by The Rotary Photographic
Company (English, active from ca. 1889)
ca. 1907
Hand-colored photograph
3⅝ x 5½ in. (9.2 x 14 cm)
Private collection
See fig. 3.16

138. Postcard of Billie Burke
Published by Aristophot Co. Ltd.
(English, active early 20th century)
ca. 1907-10
Photograph
3⅝ x 5½ in. (9.2 x 14 cm)
Recipient: Mr. L. Earle Rice, Jefferson,
Md.
Message: "Oct 30-10 / How do you
like this one? Yes our tastes differ
somewhat on actress pictures but not
in views for I like all you send me very
much indeed. This is my favorite out
of the lot I think she is very sweet
looking and Mabel Greene too I think
she is lovely I can hardly choose
between them. Yes I liked Madge
Lessing best of the others. Didn't
intend to keep you waiting so long
this time will do better next. J.H."
Private collection
See fig. 3.13

139. Cabinet card of Billie Burke
Sarony Studio (American, 1866-ca.
1930)
New York, ca. 1908

6½ x 4 in. (16.5 x 10.2 cm)
Billy Rose Theatre Division, The
New York Public Library for the
Performing Arts, Astor, Lenox and
Tilden Foundations
See fig. 3.19

140. Cabinet card of Billie Burke
Sarony Studio (American, 1866–
ca. 1930)
New York, ca. 1908
6½ x 4 in. (16.5 x 10.2 cm)
Billy Rose Theatre Division, The
New York Public Library for the
Performing Arts, Astor, Lenox and
Tilden Foundations

141. Postcard of Billie Burke
Draycott Galleries (English, active
early 20th century)
Published by Davidson Bros. (English,
1901–11)
ca. 1908
Photograph
3⅝ x 5½ in. (9.2 x 14 cm)
Postmark: [location illegible] | June
[or July?] 5, 1908
Recipient: Mrs. N. Openshaw,
Baltimore House [?], Heywood, Bury
Message: "Dear Nellie, Thanks for
PPC. I had one from [illegible] on
Tuesday. Hope your Mother is better
With BOL [Bags of Love?] / Ada"
Private collection
See fig. 3.28

142. Postcard of Billie Burke
Alfred, Ellis & Walery (English,
1900–1908)
Published by Regal Art Publishing Co.,
London
ca. 1907
Photograph
3⅝ x 5½ in. (9.2 x 14 cm)
Postmark: Croydon | May 25, 1907
Recipient: Miss Weller, 57 Leslie
Grove, East Croydon
Message: "Dear Miss Weller, Thought
you would like this for your Album /
Edie"
Private collection
See fig. 3.14

143. Postcard of Billie Burke
Published by Davidson Bros.,
(English, 1901–11)
ca. 1908
Photograph
3⅝ x 5½ in. (9.2 x 14 cm)
Postmark: Halifax | February 12, 1908

Recipient: J.E. Middleton, Esqr,
Redmire Cottage, Cleveland Rd,
Crumpsall, Manchester
Message: "Dearest Ellis, Think of it;
your exam will be over tomorrow. Oh!
Dear me, the callers have been innu-
merable, these last two days. Fondest
love to all. Yours, Mattie."
Private collection

144. Postcard of Billie Burke
Published by The Rotary Photographic
Company (English, active from ca. 1889)
ca. 1909
Photograph
3⅝ x 5½ in. (9.2 x 14 cm)
Postmark: [location illegible] |
December 24, 1909
Recipient: Mrs. Goss "Rozel", 10
Manor Rd, Forest Hill
Message: "To dear Mother wishing
her a very happy Christmas. From
Muriel"
Private collection

145. Postcard of Billie Burke
Published by The Rotary Photographic
Company (English, active from ca. 1889)
ca. 1909
Photograph
3⅝ x 5½ in. (9.2 x 14 cm)
Postmark: Bury | March 11, 1909
Recipient: Miss N. Openshaw,
Ashleigh, Holcomb Brook, N. Bury
Message: "Dear N. This Is what I
ought to have sent you for your birth-
day. Hope you will like it. Much love
from Annie."
Postscript: "I have had an invitation
to Miss Graham's wedding."
Private collection

146. Postcard of Billie Burke
Published by The Rotary Photographic
Company (English, active from ca. 1889)
ca. 1910
Photograph
3⅝ x 5½ in. (9.2 x 14 cm)
Postmark: South-Shore, Blackpool |
June [or July?] 18, 1910
Recipient: Miss Taylor, 13 Hough
Lane, Tyldesley, n. Manchester
Message: "Sat. Doesn't this remind
you of Mrs. [T?]onge? Lovely day.
Wish you were here. Love from Nan"
Private collection
See fig. 3.12

147. Postcard of Billie Burke in
The Belle of Mayfair

Bassano Studio (English, 1850–1963)
Published by Davidson Bros. (English,
1901–11)
ca. 1906
Photograph
3¾ x 5¾ in. (9.5 x 14.6 cm)
Postmark: Leicester | March 13, 1912
Recipient: Mdlle. Pierette Pialle, Mr.
Drucker, Raitz, Bei Brünn, Austria
Message: "Many thanks for your card.
I am so glad to here [*sic*] you were well.
I hope you like Austria. — It is just
like spring here. Hunting I am sorry to
say has nearly finished. I have 2 ponies
1 is nearly a horse. England is in the
middle of a coal strike & I am afraid
if it is not soon settled it will become
serious. I shall look forward to hear
how you like Austria. I am learning
German I have a frau come 2 a week.
With love from us all your A.C.L."
Private collection

**148. Postcard of Billie Burke and
Farren Soutar in** *The Belle of Mayfair*
Bassano Studio (English, 1850–1963)
Published by Davidson Bros. (English,
1901–11)
ca. 1906
Photograph
3¾ x 5¾ in. (9.5 x 14.6 cm)
Private collection
See fig. VII

**149. Postcard of Billie Burke and
Farren Soutar in** *The Belle of Mayfair*
Bassano Studio (English, 1850–1963)
Published by Davidson Bros. (English,
1901–11)
ca. 1906
Photograph
3¾ x 5¾ in. (9.5 x 14.6 cm)
Postmark: [?]ostone, Middlesex | May
12, 1907
Recipient: Miss Clarke, 23 Station
Rd., Berkhamsted, Herts.
Message: "Dear May, How are you?
Enjoying life eh! Love to all from Min"
Private collection

150. Postcard of Billie Burke in
The Belle of Mayfair
Alfred, Ellis & Walery (English,
1900–1908)
Published by J. Beagles & Co. (English,
1881–1939)
ca. 1904–7
Photograph
3¾ x 5¾ in. (9.5 x 14.6 cm)
Private collection

151. The "Mind the Paint" Girl
("Miss Billie Burke Edition")
Novelization of the Sir Arthur
Pinero play by Louis Tracy (English,
1863-1928)
Open to page 38 showing "Lily Gives
Her Friend, Vincent Bland, A Personal
Check to Make Up His Losses at the
Races"
Photographs by Sarony Studio
(American, 1866-ca. 1930)
Published by Edward J. Clode,
New York, 1912
Book (closed): 5⅝ x 8¼ in.
(14.3 x 21 cm)
Private collection
See fig. 3.8

152. Billie Burke and company on
stage in The "Mind the Paint" Girl
White Studios (American, active
1903-39)
New York, 1912
Photograph
12 x 15 in. (30.5 x 38.1 cm)
Private collection

153. Scrapbook of news clippings
of Billie Burke
ca. 1912-36
9½ x 11 ¼ in. (22.9 x 28.6 cm)
Billy Rose Theatre Division, The
New York Public Library for the
Performing Arts, Astor, Lenox and
Tilden Foundations, Flo Ziegfeld-
Billie Burke papers, 1907-1984

154. Contact sheet photographs
of Billie Burke
New York, ca. 1910
Photograph
7¼ x 9¼ in. (18.4 x 23.5 cm)
Stamped on verso: "Culver Service
/ 206 East 42nd Street / New York /
[illegible]" with additional paper label,
"Culver Service / Photos Research /
205 E. 42nd St. New York City"
Private collection
See fig. IX

BILLIE BURKE AND THE PRESS

155. The Theatre (March 1908): cover
Billie Burke
Lithograph
Magazine (closed): 10⅝ x 14½ in. (27
x 36.8 cm)
Private collection
See fig. 3.21

156. The Theatre (November 1908)
Open to pages 300-301, showing "A
Sunday Morning Chat with Billie
Burke"
Sarony Studio (American, 1866-ca.
1930)
Halftone
Magazine (closed): 10⅝ x 14½ in.
(27 x 36.8 cm)
Private collection
See fig. 3.24

157. Munsey's Magazine (1912 [?])
Page 343, "Billie Burke, Starring in
Pinero's Latest Play, 'The Mind-the-
Paint Girl'" [single page only]
Sarony Studio (American, 1866-
ca. 1930)
Halftone
10⅛ x 7 in. (25.7 x 17.8 cm)
Private collection
See fig. 3.20

158. Sheet music: "The 'Mind the
Paint' Girl"
Music by Jerome D. Kern (American,
1885-1945)
Lyrics by Sir Arthur Pinero
(1855-1934)
ca. 1912
13½ x 10½ in. (34.3 x 26.7 cm)
Museum of the City of New York
(Broadway Production Files)

159. The Theatre (January 1913)
Open to pages 28-29, "The Lady of
Burkeleigh Crest"
Halftone
Magazine (closed): 10⅝ x 14½ in.
(27 x 36.8 cm)
Private collection
See fig. 3.22

160. The Tatler (May 20, 1914)
Page 240, showing "Married to the
Husband Anna 'Held'" [single page
only]
Lallie Charles, née Charlotte Elizabeth
Martin (English, 1869-1919)
Halftone
10¼ x 14⁹/₁₆ in. (26 x 37 cm)
Private collection
See fig. 3.3

161. Postcard of Billie Burke in
Gloria's Romance
Sarony Studio (American, 1866-
ca. 1930)
ca. 1916
Photograph

3⅝ x 5½ in. (9.2 x 14 cm)
Printed on verso: "DON'T MISS
the opening chapters of the GREAT
"SERIAL-NOVEL," the great-
est achievement in the art of
Cinematography, featuring THE
CHARMING COMEDY ACTRESS—
MISS Billie Burke in Gloria's Romance
/ The "Super-Serial," in twenty chap-
ters. From the well-known "Novel" by
Mr. and Mrs. RUPERT HUGHES. The
Opening Chapters of this Great Serial
will COMMENCE on THURSDAY,
NOVEMBER 22nd, at the Harehills
Picture House. Secured at Enormous
Cost! A Two Hundred Thousand
Pounds (£200,000) Production."
Private collection

162. The Theatre (September 1916)
Open to page 122-23, "Personal
Reminiscences By Billie Burke"
Sarony Studio (American, 1866-ca.
1930)
Halftone
Magazine (closed): 10⅝ x 14½ in.
(27 x 36.8 cm)
Private collection

BILLIE BURKE AND ADVERTISING

163. Advertisement for Rogers &
Thompson's Soirée Silk featuring
Billie Burke
From The Theatre (September 1916):
165
Sarony Studio (American, 1866-ca.
1930)
Halftone
10⅝ x 14½ in. (27 x 36.8 cm)
Private collection
See fig. 3.30

164. Ogden's Guinea Gold Cigarettes
trade card: Billie Burke
ca. 1907
Photograph
1⅝ x 2⅜ in. (4.1 x 6 cm)
Private collection
See fig. 3.26

165. Advertisement for Pond's Cold
and Vanishing Creams featuring
Billie Burke
From The Ladies' Home Journal
(March 1918): 89
Lithograph
11⅝ x 16¾ in. (29.5 x 42.5 cm)
Private collection
See fig. 3.27

Selected Performances

JANE HADING

1876
Ruy-Blas
Théâtre Michel, Marseilles
Author: Victor Hugo
Character: La Reine
Notes: Opera bouffe.

Fille de Roland
Théâtre Michel, Marseilles
Author: Henri de Bornier
Notes: Opera bouffe.

La Fille de Madame Angot
Author: Charles Lecocq
Character: Clairette
Notes: Opera bouffe.

Grand-Mogol
Author: Edmond Audran
Notes: Opera bouffe.

1877
La Chaste Suzanne
Théâtre du Palais-Royal, Paris
Author: Paul Ferrier
Character: Suzanne
Notes: Opened July 4;
35 performances.

Bérengère et Anatole
Théâtre du Palais-Royal, Paris
Author: Paul Poirson
Notes: Previously performed at the
Théâtre de la Renaissance; opened
August 14; 19 performances.

La Petite Mariée
Théâtre du Palais-Royal, Paris
Authors: Eugène Leterrier, Albert
Vanloo (book); Charles Lecocq (music)
Character: Graziella
Notes: Opened September 20;
26 performances.

1878
Paris-Canard
Théâtre du Palais-Royal, Paris
Authors: Saint-Agnan, Choler, Hector
Cremieux
Character: Rosabelle
Notes: Opened July 24;
17 performances.

Tant plus ça change
Théâtre du Palais-Royal, Paris
Authors: Edmond Gondinet,
Pierre Véron
Character: Anatole
Notes: Opened December 28;
4 performances.

Actéon
Théâtre du Palais-Royal, Paris
Authors: Emmanuel Théaulon, Félix-
Auguste Duvert, Adolphe de Leuven
Character: Clytie
Notes: Opened January 24; 27
performances.

1879
La Jolie Persane
Théâtre de la Renaissance, Paris
Authors: Eugène Leterrier, Albert
Vanloo (book); Charles Lecocq (music)
Character: Namouna
Notes: 67 peformances.

Héloïse et Abélard
Théâtre de la Renaissance, Paris
Authors: Henry Litolff, M. Clairville,
William Busnach
Character: Héloïse
Notes: Opened February 20; 5
performances.

Les Rendez-vous bourgeois
Théâtre de la Renaissance, Paris
Author: François Benoît Hoffmann
Character: Reine
Notes: Revival of one-act opera
bouffe that originally premiered at
the Opéra-Comique in 1807; opened
March 11; 25 performances.

1880
Belle Lurette (fragments)
Théâtre des Variétés, Paris
Author: Jacques Offenbach
Character: Belle Lurette
Notes: Matinee organized by
Le Figaro on November 18 in honor
of Offenbach.

Belle Lurette
Théâtre de la Renaissance, Paris
Authors: Jacques Offenbach, Ernest
Blum, Édouard Blau, Raoul Toché
Character: Belle Lurette
Notes: Offenbach's last piece, suppos-
edly written especially for Hading;
67 performances (originated the role).

1881
L'Œil crevé
Théâtre de la Renaissance, Paris

FIG. A.1 Postcard of the Théâtre du Vaudeville and the Boulevard des Italiens, ca. 1905.
Hand-colored photograph. Private collection.

FIG. A.2 Paul Nadar (French, 1856–1939). Jane Hading in *Héloïse et Abélard*, ca. 1879. From *Le Théatre* (November 1900): 14. Private collection.

Authors: M. Hervé, Hector Crémieux
Character: Fleur de noblesse
Notes: Revival; opened September 24; 59 performances.

1883
Le Maître de Forges
Théâtre du Gymnase, Paris
Author: Georges Ohnet
Character: Claire de Beaulieu
Costume Designer: Jane Hading
Notes: Opened December 15; about 300 performances (originated the role).

1885
Le Prince Zilah
Théâtre du Gymnase, Paris
Author: Jules Claretie
Character: Marsa
Costume Designer: Maison Félix
Notes: Opened February 28; 103 performances (originated the role).

Sapho
Théâtre du Gymnase, Paris
Author: Alphonse Daudet
Character: Fanny Legrand
Notes: Opened December 18; 15 performances (originated the role).

1886
Frou-Frou
Théâtre du Gymnase, Paris
Authors: Henri Meilhac, Ludovic Halévy

Character: Frou-Frou
Costume Designer: Magnier et Bruck
Notes: Opened October 7; 43 performances. Lead played alternately by Mmes Delaporte, Marie Legault, Sarah Bernhardt, and Hading.

1887
La Comtesse Sarah
Théâtre du Gymnase, Paris
Author: Georges Ohnet
Character: Sarah
Notes: Opened January 15; 104 performances (originated the role).

1888
Le Maître de Forges
Palmer's Theatre, New York; Academy of Music, Montreal
Author: Arthur W. Pinero (adaptation from Georges Ohnet's original)
Character: Claire de Beaulieu
Costume Designer: Laferrière
Notes: Hading performed in theaters in South America before debuting in New York. On this tour, Hading played *Magda*, *La Dame aux Camélias*, and *Le Maître de Forges* in English in the Americas and England. *Le Maître de Forges* played the matinees on October 20 and 22.

L'Aventurière
Palmer's Theatre, New York
Author: Émile Augier
Character: Clorinde
Costume Designer: Laferrière
Notes: October 10, matinee of October 13, farewell night performance October 27; Hading also gave a matinee performance of this play in Brooklyn on November 1.

Gringoire
Palmer's Theatre, New York
Author: Theodore de Banville
Character: Loyse
Costume Designer: Laferrière
Notes: October 11.

Frou-Frou
Palmer's Theatre, New York
Authors: Henri Meilhac, Ludovic Halévy
Character: Frou-Frou
Costume Designer: Laferrière
Notes: October 15, matinee of October 24 (by popular demand).

Camille (La Dame aux Camélias)
Palmer's Theatre, New York
Author: Alexandre Dumas fils
Character: Marguerite Gauthier [sic]
Costume Designer: Laferrière
Notes: October 22, grand farewell matinee on October 27.

Mlle. de la Sieglière
Palmer's Theatre, New York
Author: Jules Sandeau
Character: Hélène
Costume Designer: Laferrière
Notes: October 24.

L'Étrangère
Palmer's Theatre, New York
Author: Alexandre Dumas fils
Character: Catherine de Septmonts
Costume Designer: Laferrière
Notes: October 25 and 26.

Jean Marie
Palmer's Theatre, New York
Author: André Theurlet
Character: Thérèse
Costume Designer: Laferrière
Notes: Matinee of October 26; Hading also recited Victor Hugo's *La Fiancée du Timbalier*. That night, there was a special benefit for the victims of the recent Cuban hurricane, organized by the Sociedad Literaria Hispano-Americana.

Le Maître de Forges
Academy of Music, Montreal
Author: Arthur W. Pinero (adaptation from Georges Ohnet's original)
Character: Claire de Beaulieu
Costume Designer: Laferrière
Notes: Hading opened on November 5 in Montreal.

Mlle. de la Sieglière
Academy of Music, Montreal
Author: Jules Sandeau
Character: Hélène
Costume Designer: Laferrière
Notes: November 7.

Gringoire
Academy of Music, Montreal
Author: Theodore de Banville
Character: Loyse
Costume Designer: Laferrière
Notes: November 9.

Le Député de Bombignac
Academy of Music, Montreal
Author: Alexandre Bisson
Character: Marquise de Cernais (?)
Costume Designer: Laferrière
Notes: November 9.

L'Aventurière
Academy of Music, Montreal
Author: Émile Augier
Character: Clorinde
Costume Designer: Laferrière
Notes: Matinee of November 10.

Don Caesar de Bazan
Academy of Music, Montreal
Authors: Jules Massenet, Adolphe
d'Ennery, Jean Henri Dumanoir, Jules
Chantepie
Character: Maritana
Costume Designer: Laferrière
Notes: November 10; a note in the
New York Times on November 10 indi-
cates that the company was to open in
Philadelphia on November 12.

Le Maître de Forges
Albaugh's Grand Opera House,
Washington, D.C.
Author: Arthur W. Pinero (adaptation
from Georges Ohnet's original)
Character: Claire de Beaulieu
Costume Designer: Laferrière
Notes: Opened November 20.

L'Aventurière
Albaugh's Grand Opera House,
Washington, D.C.
Author: Émile Augier
Character: Clorinde
Costume Designer: Laferrière
Notes: November 21.

Camille (La Dame aux Camélias)
Albaugh's Grand Opera House,
Washington, D.C.
Author: Alexandre Dumas fils
Character: Marguerite Gautier
Costume Designer: Laferrière
Notes: Played the finale matinee on
November 24.

Don Caesar de Bazan
Albaugh's Grand Opera House
Authors: Jules Massenet, Adolphe
d'Ennery, Jean Henri Dumanoir, Jules
Chantepie
Character: Maritana
Costume Designer: Laferrière

Notes: Played finale evening performance on November 24.

Le Maître de Forges
McVicker's Theatre, Chicago
Author: Arthur W. Pinero (adaptation
from Georges Ohnet's original)
Character: Claire de Beaulieu
Costume Designer: Laferrière
Notes: Opened November 27.

L'Aventurière
McVicker's Theatre, Chicago
Author: Émile Augier
Character: Clorinde
Costume Designer: Laferrière
Notes: Matinee of November 28.

Frou-Frou
McVicker's Theatre, Chicago
Authors: Henri Meilhac, Ludovic
Halévy
Character: Frou-Frou
Costume Designer: Laferrière
Notes: November 28.

Camille (La Dame aux Camélias)
McVicker's Theatre, Chicago
Author: Alexandre Dumas fils
Character: Marguerite Gautier
Costume Designer: Laferrière
Notes: Matinee of November 29.

1889
Les Surprises du Divorce
Palmer's Theatre, New York
Author: Alexandre Dumas fils
Character: Catherine de Septmonts
Costume Designer: Laferrière
Notes: February 18.

Denise
Palmer's Theatre, New York
Author: Alexandre Dumas fils
Character: Denise
Costume Designer: Laferrière
Notes: February 20.

L'Aventurière
Gaiety Theatre, London
Author: Émile Augier
Character: Clorinde
Costume Designer: Madame
Lebouvier
Notes: Opened May 27.

Camille (La Dame aux Camélias)
Gaiety Theatre, London
Author: Alexandre Dumas fils

Character: Marguerite Gautier
Costume Designer: Madame
Lebouvier

Gringoire
Gaiety Theatre, London
Author: Theodore de Banville
Character: Loyse
Costume Designer: Madame
Lebouvier

L'Étrangère
Gaiety Theatre, London
Author: Alexandre Dumas fils
Character: Catherine de Septmonts
Costume Designer: Madame
Lebouvier

1890
Le Député Leveau
Théâtre du Vaudeville, Paris
Author: Jacques Lemaire
Character: La Marquise
Notes: Opened October 16; 70
performances.

1891
Nos Intimes
Théâtre du Vaudeville, Paris
Author: Victorien Sardou
Character: Cécile
Costume Designer: Laferrière
Notes: Opened October 22 (reprise);
82 performances.

1892
Le Prince d'Aurec
Théâtre du Vaudeville, Paris
Author: Henri Lavedan
Character: Princesse d'Aurec
Notes: Opened June 1; 100 perfor-
mances (originated the role).

1892
Thérèse Raquin
Théâtre du Vaudeville, Paris
Author: Émile Zola
Character: Thérèse
Notes: Played a charity gala on
May 20.

1893
Les Effrontés
Comédie-Française, Paris
Author: Émile Augier
Character: La Marquise
Costume Designer: Laferrière
Notes: Hading was a junior pension-
naire at the Comédie-Française that

year; 43 performances with the most representations of the year at the Comédie-Française.

Les Effrontés
Unknown theater, London
Author: Émile Augier
Character: La Marquise
Costume Designer: Laferrière
Notes: Performed sometime in June.

L'Aventurière
Hooley's Theatre, Chicago
Author: Émile Augier
Character: Clorinde
Notes: Opened October 2.

Mlle. de la Sieglière
Hooley's Theatre, Chicago
Author: Jules Sandeau
Character: Hélène
Notes: October 3.

Nos Intimes
Hooley's Theatre, Chicago
Author: Victorien Sardou
Character: Cécile
Notes: October 4.

Tartuffe
Hooley's Theatre, Chicago
Author: Molière
Notes: October 5.

La Dame aux Camélias
Hooley's Theatre, Chicago
Author: Alexandre Dumas fils
Character: Marguerite Gautier
Notes: October 6.

La Mégère Apprivoisée
Hooley's Theatre, Chicago
Author: Paul Delair (adaptation of *The Taming of the Shrew*)
Character: Catherine
Notes: Performed week of October 9.

Le Gendre de Monsieur Poirier
Hooley's Theatre, Chicago
Authors: Émile Augier, Jules Sandeau
Character: Antoinette (?)
Notes: Performed week of October 9.

Frou-Frou
Hooley's Theatre, Chicago
Authors: Henri Meilhac, Ludovic Halévy

FIG. A.3 Reutlinger Studio (French, 1850–1937). Cabinet card of Jane Hading in *Nos Intimes*, ca. 1891. Billy Rose Theatre Division, The New York Public Library for the Performing Arts, Astor, Lenox and Tilden Foundations. Cat. 19.

Character: Frou-Frou
Notes: Performed week of October 10.

Thermidor
Hooley's Theatre, Chicago
Author: Victorien Sardou
Character: Fabienne
Notes: Performed week of October 16.

L'Ami Fritz
Hooley's Theatre, Chicago
Authors: Émile Erckmann, Alexandre Chatrian, Alfred Hennequin
Notes: After four weeks in Chicago, the company was to play for two weeks in San Francisco, one week in New Orleans, four days in Washington, one week in Philadelphia, one week in Montreal, one week in Boston, and then New York.

1894
L'Aventurière
Abbey's Theatre, New York
Author: Émile Augier
Character: Clorinde

Thermidor
Abbey's Theatre, New York

Author: Victorien Sardou
Character: Fabienne

Nos Intimes
Abbey's Theatre, New York
Author: Victorien Sardou
Character: Cécile

La Mégère Apprivoisée
Abbey's Theatre, New York
Author: Paul Delair (adaptation of *The Taming of the Shrew*)
Character: Catherine

Adrienne Lecouvreur
Abbey's Theatre, New York
Authors: Eugène Scribe, Ernest Legouvé
Character: Adrienne Lecouvreur
Notes: Benefit for Hading.

L'Aventurière
Comédie-Française, Paris
Author: Émile Augier
Character: Clorinde
Notes: Revival opened November 5.

1895
Les Demi-Vierges
Théâtre du Gymnase, Paris
Author: Marcel Prévost
Character: Maud de Rouvre
Notes: Opened May 21; 129 performances (originated the role).

Hommage à Alexandre Dumas
Théâtre du Gymnase, Paris
Author: Alexandre Dumas fils
Character: Recitation
Notes: Opened December 6; 8 performances.

Marcelle
Théâtre du Gymnase, Paris
Author: Victorien Sardou
Character: Marcelle
Notes: Opened December 21; 11 performances (originated the role); earned the largest profit of the year on December 31: 6,705 francs.

La Princesse de Bagdad
Théâtre du Gymnase, Paris
Author: Alexandre Dumas fils
Character: Lionette
Notes: Revival; 50 performances.

Une Idylle tragique
Théâtre du Gymnase, Paris
Author: Paul Bourget
Character: Ely
Notes: Opened December 23;
11 performances.

1897
La Jeunesse de Louis XIV
Théâtre du Gymnase, Paris
Author: Alexandre Dumas fils
Character: Marie
Costume Designer: Madame Carlier
(millinery)
Notes: Opened December 4;
33 performances.

La Montagne enchantée
Théâtre de la Porte-Saint-Martin,
Paris
Authors: Émile Moreau,
Albert Cabré
Notes: Opened April 12; 34 perfor-
mances; music by André Messager
and Xavier Leroux.

Les Jocrisses de l'amour
Théâtre du Vaudeville, Paris
Authors: Théodore Barrière, Lambert
Thiboust
Character: Léontine
Notes: Revival; 37 performances.

1898
L'Étrangère
European Tour
Author: Alexandre Dumas fils
Character: Catherine de Septmonts
Costume Designers: Laferrière (cos-
tumes); Madame Carlier (millinery)

La Princesse de Bagdad
European Tour
Author: Alexandre Dumas fils
Character: Lionette
Costume Designers: Laferrière (cos-
tumes); Madame Carlier (millinery)

L'Aventurière
European Tour
Author: Émile Augier
Character: Clorinde
Costume Designers: Laferrière (cos-
tumes); Madame Carlier (millinery)

Adrienne Lecouvreur
European Tour
Authors: Eugène Scribe,
Ernest Legouvé

Character: Adrienne Lecouvreur
Costume Designers: Laferrière (costumes); Madame Carlier (millinery)

La Visite de Noces
European Tour
Author: Alexandre Dumas fils
Character: Mme De Morance
Costume Designers: Laferrière (cos-
tumes); Madame Carlier (millinery)

Le Maître de Forges
European Tour
Author: Georges Ohnet
Character: Claire de Beaulieu
Costume Designers: Laferrière (cos-
tumes); Madame Carlier (millinery)

Le Sphinx
European Tour
Author: Octave Feuillet
Costume Designers: Laferrière (cos-
tumes); Madame Carlier (millinery)

Sapho
European Tour
Authors: Alphonse Daudet, Adolphe
Bellot
Character: Fanny Legrand
Costume Designers: Redfern (cos-
tumes), Madame Carlier (millinery)

Le Retour de Jérusalem
European Tour
Author: Maurice Donnay
Character: Henriette de Chauzé
Costume Designers: Redfern (cos-
tumes), Madame Carlier (millinery)

Le Duel
European Tour
Author: Henri Lavedan
Character: La Duchesse de Chailles
Costume Designers: Redfern (cos-
tumes), Madame Carlier (millinery)

La Châtelaine
European Tour
Author: Alfred Capus
Character: Thérèse de Rives
Costume Designers: Redfern (cos-
tumes), Madame Carlier (millinery)

La Dame aux Camélias
European Tour
Author: Alexandre Dumas fils
Character: Marguerite Gautier
Costume Designers: Laferrière (cos-
tumes); Madame Carlier (millinery)

1899
Plus que Reine
Théâtre de la Porte-Saint-Martin,
Paris
Author: Émile Bergerat
Character: Empress Joséphine
Costume Designers: Goupy (cos-
tumes); Madame Carlier (millinery)
Notes: Opened April 4; 75
performances.

FIG. A.4 Reutlinger Studio. Postcard of
Jane Hading in *Plus que Reine*, ca. 1899.
Hand-colored photograph with metallic
gold pigment. Private collection. Cat. 26.

1900
L'Enchantement
Théâtre du Gymnase, Paris
(under the direction of le
Théâtre de l'Odéon)
Author: Henry Bataille
Character: Isabella
Costume Designer: Redfern
Notes: Opened May 10;
40 performances.

Les Demi-Vierges
Théâtre de l'Athénée, Paris
Author: Marcel Prevost
Character: Maud de Rouvre
Notes: Opened September 29
(revival).

1901
Le Vertige
Théâtre de l'Athénée, Paris

Author: Michel Provins
Character: Andrée de Roville
Costume Designer: Redfern

FIG. A.5 Reutlinger Studio. Postcard of Jane Hading in *La Pompadour*, ca. 1901. Hand-colored photograph. Private collection. Cat. 30.

La Pompadour
Théâtre de la Porte-Saint-Martin, Paris
Author: Émile Bergerat
Character: Mme de Pompadour
Costume Designer: Redfern

1902
La Châtelaine
Théâtre de la Renaissance, Paris
Author: Alfred Capus
Character: Thérèse de Rives
Costume Designer: Redfern
Notes: Opened October 25; 78 performances; the most profitable matinee of the year is played on opening day (earning 9,178 francs).

Le Maître de Forges
Coronet Theatre, London
Author: Georges Ohnet
Character: Claire de Beaulieu
Notes: This brief tour of London probably took place in early May; Hading may also have appeared on the London stage at the Coronet Theatre in 1903, but the exact productions (apart from *Sapho*) and schedule are unknown.

Frou-Frou
Coronet Theatre, London

Authors: Henri Meilhac, Ludovic Halévy
Character: Frou-Frou

L'Étrangère
Coronet Theatre, London
Author: Alexandre Dumas fils
Character: Catherine de Septmonts

Le Vertige
Coronet Theatre, London
Author: Michel Provins
Character: Andrée de Roville

La Princesse de Bagdad
Coronet Theatre, London
Author: Alexandre Dumas fils
Character: Lionette

Maud (i.e., Les Demi-Vierges)
Coronet Theatre, London
Author: Marcel Prevost
Character: Maud de Rouvre

Le Maître de Forges
Théâtre du Parc, Brussels
Author: Georges Ohnet
Character: Claire de Beaulieu
Notes: May 18.

Frou-Frou
Théâtre du Parc, Brussels
Authors: Henri Meilhac, Ludovic Halévy
Character: Frou-Frou
Notes: May 19.

L'Étrangère
Théâtre du Parc, Brussels
Author: Alexandre Dumas fils
Character: Catherine de Septmonts
Notes: May 20.

Le Vertige
Théâtre du Parc, Brussels
Author: Michel Provins
Character: Andrée de Roville
Notes: May 21.

La Princesse de Bagdad
Théâtre du Parc, Brussels
Author: Alexandre Dumas fils
Character: Lionette
Notes: May 22.

1905
Le Maître de Forges
Théâtre de la Gaîté, Paris
Author: Georges Ohnet

Character: Claire de Beaulieu
Notes: Opened April 28; 55 performances.

1906
Serge Panine
Théâtre de la Gaîté, Paris
Author: Georges Ohnet
Character: Mme Desvarennes
Costume Designer: Redfern
Notes: Opened January 9; 25 performances; with Jean Coquelin.

L'Attentat
Théâtre de la Gaîté, Paris
Authors: Alfred Capus, Lucien Descaves
Character: Marcelle
Costume Designers: Redfern (costumes); Madame Carlier (millinery)
Notes: Opened March 9, 40 performances; with Jean Coquelin.

1907
Le Retour de Jérusalem
European Tour
Author: Maurice Donnay
Character: Henriette (first act) and Judith (second and third acts)
Costume Designers: Redfern (costumes), Madame Carlier (millinery)
Notes: Toured with the actor Le Bargy, traveled to Anvers, Brussels, Lille, Roubaix, Mulhouse, Strasbourg, Lyon, Marseilles-Nîmes, Montpellier, Barcelona, Madrid, Lisbon, Porto,

FIG. A.6 Paul Nadar (French, 1856–1939). Jane Hading in *Le Vertige*. Cover of *Le Théâtre* (June 1901). Private collection. Cat. 38.

Bordeaux-Toulouse, Marseilles, and London (where she appeared in June at the Coronet Theatre).

Le Marquis de Priola
European Tour
Author: Henri Lavedan
Character: Mme de Valleroy
Costume Designers: Laferrière (costumes), Madame Carlier (millinery)

La Châtelaine
European Tour
Author: Alfred Capus
Character: Thérèse de Rives
Costume Designer: Madame Carlier (millinery)

FIG. A.7 Photographie Nouvelle. Jane Hading in *La Châtelaine*. Cover of *Le Théatre* (November 1902). Private collection.

Le Demi-Monde
European Tour
Author: Alexandre Dumas fils
Character: La Baronne Suzanne d'Ange
Costume Designers: Laferrière (costumes), Madame Carlier (millinery)

Une Visite de Noces
European Tour
Author: Alexandre Dumas fils
Character: Mme de Morance
Costume Designer: Madame Carlier (millinery)

Sapho
European Tour
Authors: Alphonse Daudet,

Adolphe Bellot
Character: Fanny Legrand
Costume Designer: Madame Carlier (millinery)

L'Étrangère
European Tour
Author: Alexandre Dumas fils
Character: Catherine de Septmonts
Costume Designers: Laferrière (costumes), Madame Carlier (millinery)

1908
L'Alibi
Théâtre de l'Odéon, Paris
Author: Gabriel Trarieux
Character: Madeleine Laroche
Costume Designer: Redfern
Notes: 29 performances (originated the role).

1908
La Femme X...
Théâtre de la Porte-Saint-Martin, Paris
Author: Alexandre Bisson
Character: Jacqueline
Notes: Opened December 15; 21 performances; with Jean Coquelin.

1910
Le Feu du Voisin
Théâtre Michel, Marseilles
Author: Francis de Croisset
Character: Raymonde

1911
La Femme nue
Théâtre de la Porte-Saint-Martin, Paris
Author: Henry Bataille
Character: Princesse de Chabran
Costume Designer: Redfern
Notes: 73 performances.

1912
La Crise
Théâtre de la Porte-Saint-Martin, Paris
Authors: Paul Bourget, André Beaunier
Character: Giselle
Notes: Opened May 3; 41 performances.

1913
La Chienne du Roi
Théâtre Sarah Bernhardt, Paris
Author: Henri Lavedan

Character: Mme Du Barry
Notes: Opened February 8; 94 performances.

1916
Le Maître de Forges
Théâtre Apollo, Bordeaux
Author: Georges Ohnet
Character: Claire de Beaulieu
Notes: October 22 (it is unknown whether this was a one-off performance or part of a short run).

LILY ELSIE

1896
Little Red Riding Hood
Queens Theatre, Manchester; UK Tour
Character: Title role
Notes: Lily Elsie's first performance, at the age of 10; show ran six weeks and then toured for six more.

Arabian Nights
Queens Theatre, Manchester, UK Tour
Character: Queen Mirza

1898
King Klondike
Britannia Theatre, Hoxton
Character: Arielle, Spirit of the Air
Notes: Lily Elsie's first London appearance.

1900
McKenna's Flirtation
UK Tour
Author: E. Selden
Character: Chorus
Notes: Toured for one year.

1901
Silver Slipper
Lyric Theatre, London
Authors: Owen Hall (book), Leslie Stuart (music)
Character: Chorus

Dick Whittington
Camden Theatre, London
Notes: Christmas pantomime

1902
The Forty Thieves
Coronet Theatre, London

Character: Morgiana
Notes: Christmas pantomime

1903
Blue Beard
Coronet Theatre, London
Notes: Christmas pantomime

Three Little Maids
Prince of Wales Theatre,
London; UK Tour
Author: Paul Rubens
Character: Hilda Branscombe
Costume Designer: Wilhelm
Notes: Choreographed by Willie
Warde; 348 performances; Lily Elsie
left after seven weeks.

A Chinese Honeymoon
Royal Strand Theatre, London
Authors: George Dance (book),
Howard Talbot (music)
Character: Princess Soo-Soo
Costume Designer: Nathan, from
designs by Comelli
Notes: Opened October 5, 1901;
choreography by Will Bishop and Fred
Farren; first musical to run for more
than 1,000 (1,075) performances.

Madame Sherry
Apollo Theatre, London
Authors: C. E. Hands (English
libretto), Adrian Ross (English
lyrics), Hugo Felix (music)
Character: Chorus

1904
Lady Madcap
Prince of Wales Theatre, London
Authors: Paul Rubens and Percy
Greenbank (book), Paul Rubens
(music)
Character: Gwenny Holden
(chorus part)
Costume Designer: Percy Anderson
Notes: Opened December 17;
354 performances; Elsie may have
performed in a touring production of
this play.

The Cingalee (alternate title:
Sunny Ceylon)
Daly's Theatre, London
Authors: James Tanner (book), Lionel
Monckton (music), Adrian Ross and
Percy Greenbank (lyrics)
Character: Lady Patricia Vereker
Costume Designer: Percy Anderson
Notes: Opened March 5, 1904, and
closed March 11, 1905; 391 perfor-
mances. Elsie may have performed in
a touring production of this play.

1905
The Little Michus (alternate title *Les
P'tites Michu*)
Daly's Theatre, London
Authors: Henry Hamilton (book?),
Percy Greenbank (lyrics)
Character: Madame du Tertre
Notes: English adaptation of French
operetta (1897) by André Messager,
Albert Vanloo, and Georges Duval;
401 performances.

1906
The Little Cherub (alternate
title *The Girl on the Stage*)
Prince of Wales Theatre, London
Authors: Owen Hall (book), Adrian
Ross (lyrics), Ivan Caryll (music)
Character: Lady Agnes Congress
Costume Designer: Percy Anderson
Notes: Opened January 13, 1906;
revised and reproduced at the same
theater as *The Girl on Stage 5* for 29
performances in May
and June 1906.

See-See
Prince of Wales Theatre, London
Authors: Charles Brookfield (book),
Adrian Ross (lyrics), Sidney Jones
(music)
Characters: See-See, Hummingbird
Costume Designers: Mrs. Freed,
B. J. Simmons
Notes: Opened June 20, 1906.

The New Aladdin
Gaiety Theatre, London
Authors: Adrian Ross, Percy
Greenbank, W.H. Risque, George
Grossmith, Jr. (lyrics), Ivan Caryll,
Lionel Monckton (music)
Character: Lally
Costume Designer: Wilhelm
Notes: 203 performances.

1907
The Merry Widow
Daly's Theatre, London
Authors: Franz Lehár (music), Basil
Hood (libretto and lyrics), Adrian
Ross (lyrics)
Character: Sonia
Costume Designers: Lucile Ltd. (other
costumes by Maison Pascaud and
Percy Anderson)
Notes: Opened June 8, 1907; adapted
from *Die lustige Witwe* by Victor Leon
and Leo Stein; 778 performances.

1909
The Dollar Princess
Daly's Theatre, London
Authors: Basil Hood (libretto and
lyrics), Adrian Ross (lyrics)
Character: Alice Conder
Costume Designers: Lucile Ltd.
(costumes); Maison Lewis, Zyrot &
Cie (millinery).
Notes: Opened September 25. Adapted
from *Die Dollarprinzessin* (1907) by

FIG. A.8 Postcard of the Gaiety Theatre, London, ca. 1909. Hand-colored photograph.
Private collection.

FIG. A.9 Foulsham & Banfield (English, 1906–20). Postcard of Lily Elsie in *The Merry Widow*, ca. 1907. Photograph. Private collection. Cat. 84.

Fritz Grünbaum, Alfred Maria Millner, and Leo Fall; 428 performances.

1911

A Waltz Dream
Hicks Theatre, London
Authors: Basil Hood (libretto and lyrics), Adrian Ross (lyrics)
Character: Franzi Steingruber
Costume Designer: Lucile Ltd.
Notes: Opened January 7; revival of first English production at Hicks Theatre, March 1908; Adapted from *Ein Walzertraum* (1907) by Oscar Straus, Felix Dörmann, and Leopold Jackson.

The Count of Luxembourg
Daly's Theatre, London
Authors: Basil Hood, Adrian Ross (libretto and lyrics), Franz Lehár (music)
Character: Angèle Didier
Costume Designers: Lucile Ltd. (costumes); Mrs. Ansell, London (millinery)
Notes: Opened May 20. Adapted from *Der Graf von Luxemburg* (1909) by Alfred Maria Millner and Franz Lehár; Lily Elsie's understudy, Daisy Irving, took over the role when Elsie left the stage to get married.

The Critic
His Majesty's Theatre, London
Character: Ellena
Notes: Gala Performance to celebrate the coronation of King George V.

1915

Mavourneen
His Majesty's Theatre, London
Character: Lady Patricia O'Brien
Notes: Charity production.

1916

Shakespeare's Legacy
Theatre Royal, London
Author: J. M. Barrie
Character: Mrs. Bantry
Notes: One-day "playlet" on April 14 for charity, Women's Munitions Workers.

National Anthem
The London Coliseum
Notes: One-day charity performance on June 9 for the Star and Garter Building fund of British Women's Hospital; Lily Elsie was one of several performers.

Admirable Chrichton
Wyndham's Theatre, London
Character: Lady Catherine Lazenby
Notes: Charity production.

1917

Sir Charles and Lady Wyndham's Entertainment to our Wounded Soldiers

FIG. A.11 Foulsham & Banfield. Lily Elsie in *A Waltz Dream*. Cover of *The Play Pictorial* (February 1911). Private collection. Cat. 117.

Criterion Theatre, London
Notes: One-day charity performance on March 5; Lily Elsie was one of several performers.

Pamela
Palace Theatre, London
Authors: Arthur Wimperis (book), Frederic Norton (songs)
Character: Pamela Durham
Costume Designer: Lucile Ltd. (costumes and headdresses); Zirot & Cie., London (millinery)
Notes: Opened December 10; played for 172 performances.

FIG. A.10 Foulsham & Banfield. Postcard of Lily Elsie and Joseph Coyne in *The Dollar Princess*, ca. 1909. Photograph. Private collection.

1925

Midnight Matinee
Apollo Theatre, London
Notes: Charity benefit on June 22 for
Middlesex Hospital Reconstruction
Fund produced by Jack Hulbert.

1927

The Blue Train
King's Theatre, Southsea and Prince
of Wales Theatre, London
Authors: Reginald Arkell, Dion
Titheradge (book), Robert Stolz, Ivry
St. Helier (music), Reginald Arkell
(lyrics)
Character: Eileen Mayne
Notes: Opened March 14 at
King's Theatre; opened May 10
at Prince of Wales Theatre;
116 performances.

1928

The Truth Game
Globe Theatre, London; Daly's
Theatre, London; UK tour
Authors: Ivor Novello
Character: Rosine Browne
Costume Designer: Norman Hartnell
Notes: Opened October 1928
at the Globe Theatre; Lily Elsie's final
stage appearance was in this produc-
tion, which ended its run
at Daly's Theatre.

BILLIE BURKE

1894

The Amazons
Lyceum Theatre, New York
Authors: Sir Arthur Wing Pinero
Character: Lady Thomasin

1903

The School Girl
Prince of Wales Theatre, London
Authors: Leslie Stuart (composer),
Paul Rubens (additional songs), Henry
Hamilton, Paul M. Potter (book),
Charles H. Taylor (lyrics)
Character: Mamie Reckfeller
Notes: 333 performances.

1906

The Belle of Mayfair
Vaudeville Theatre, London
Authors: Leslie Stuart (music), Basil
Hood and Charles Brookfield (book)

FIG. A.12 Byron Studio, (American,
1892-present). Exterior of the Empire
Theatre, New York, ca. 1902. Photography
Collection, Miriam and Ira D. Wallach
Division of Art, Prints and Photographs,
The New York Public Library; Astor, Lenox
and Tilden Foundations.

Notes: Opened April 11; 416
performances; Burke replaced
Phyllis Dare.

1907

My Wife
Empire Theatre, New York
Author: Michael Morton
Character: Beatrice "Trixie" Dupre
Notes: 129 performances.

1908

Love Watches
Lyceum Theatre, New York
Authors: Robert de Flers, Gaston
Armand de Caillavet (book); Gladys
Unger (book adaptation)
Character: Jacqueline
Notes: 172 performances.

1910

Mrs. Dot
Lyceum Theatre, New York
Author: W. Somerset Maugham
Character: Mrs. Worthley
Notes: 72 performances.

Suzanne
Lyceum Theatre, New York
Authors: Frantz Fonson, Fernand
Wicheler (book); C. Haddon
Chambers (book adaptation)

Character: Suzanne
Notes: 64 performances.

1911

The Philosopher in the Apple Orchard
Lyceum Theatre, New York
Author: E. Harcourt Williams (based
on the story by Anthony Hope)
Notes: 35 performances.

The Runaway
Lyceum Theatre, New York
Author: Pierre Veber, Henri de
Grosse (book); Michael Morton (book
adaptation)
Character: Colette
Notes: 64 performances.

1912

The "Mind the Paint" Girl
Lyceum Theatre, New York
Author: Sir Arthur Wing Pinero
Costume Designer: Lucile Ltd.
Notes: 136 performances. New York
production of Pinero's play that was
first performed at the Duke of York's
Theatre, London, in February 1912.

1913

The Amazons
Lyceum Theatre, New York
Author: Sir Arthur Wing Pinero
Notes: Revival; 48 performances.

FIG. A.13 Sarony Studio (American,
1866-ca. 1930). Billie Burke in *The
Runaway*. From *Munsey's Magazine*
(April 1911): 119. Private collection.

FIG. A.14 Sarony Studio. Billie Burke in *The "Mind the Paint" Girl*, 1912. Signed photograph. Museum of the City of New York, The Burns Mantle Collection, Gift of Mrs. Robert Burns Mantle, 48.210.727. Cat. 122.

1914
The Land of Promise
Lyceum Theatre, New York
Author: W. Somerset Maugham
Notes: 76 performances.

Jerry
Lyceum Theatre, New York
Author: Catherine Chisholm
Character: Jerry
Costume Designer: Lucile Ltd.
Notes: 41 performances.

1917
The Rescuing Angel
Lyceum Theatre, New York
Author: Clare Kummer
Character: Angela Deming
Notes: 32 performances.

1918
A Marriage of Convenience
Henry Miller's Theatre, New York
Author: Sydney Grundy
Character: Louise de Torigny,
Comtesse de Candale
Notes: 53 performances.

1919
Caesar's Wife
Liberty Theatre, New York
Author: W. Somerset Maugham
Character: Violet
Notes: 81 performances.

1921
The Intimate Strangers
Henry Miller's Theatre, New York
Author: Booth Tarkington
Character: Isabel
Notes: 91 performances.

1922
Rose Briar
Empire Theatre, New York
Author: Booth Tarkington
Character: Rose Briar
Notes: 88 performances.

1924
Annie Dear
Times Square Theatre, New York
Author: Clare Kummer
Character: Annie Leigh
Costume Designer: Frances
Notes: 103 performances.

1927
The Marquise
Biltmore Theatre, New York
Author: Noël Coward
Character: The Marquise,
Eloise de Kestournel
Notes: 80 performances.

1928
The Happy Husband
Empire Theatre, New York
Author: Harrison Owen

Character: Dot Rendell
Notes: 72 performances.

1929
Family Affairs
Maxine Elliot's Theatre,
New York
Authors: Earle Crooker,
Lowell Brotano
Character: Estelle Wheaton
Notes: 7 performances.

1930
The Truth Game
Ethel Barrymore Theatre,
New York
Author: Ivor Novello
Character: Evelyn Brandon
Notes: 107 performances.

1943
This Rock
Longacre Theatre, New York
Author: Walter Livingston Faust
Character: Cecily Stanley
Notes: 37 performances.

1944
Mrs. January and Mr. X
Belasco Theatre, New York
Author: Zoë Akins
Character: Mrs. January
Costume Designer: Adrian
Notes: 43 performances.

Bibliography

"Alfred Vanderbilt May Wed Actress." *San Jose Evening News*, June 6, 1910.

"All About Billie Burke." *New York Telegraph*, November 9, 1907.

"A New Picture Every Day in the Year for Lily Elsie." *Chicago Examiner*, May 1, 1910.

Aronson, Arnold. *Looking Into the Abyss: Essays on Scenography*. Ann Arbor: The University of Michigan Press, 2005.

Auster, Albert. *Actresses and Suffragists: Women in the American Theatre, 1890-1920*. New York: Praeger Publishers, 1984.

Bailey, Peter. "'Naughty but Nice': Musical Comedy and the Rhetoric of the Girl, 1892-1914." In *The Edwardian Theatre: Essays on Performance and the Stage*, 36-60. Edited by Michael R. Booth and Joel H. Kaplan. Cambridge: Cambridge University Press, 1996.

Banes, Margaret Illington. "The Mad Search for Beauty: And the Slight Chance that the Average Actress Can Guide the Average Woman." *Green Book Magazine* (May 1912): 956.

Banner, Lois W. *American Beauty*. Chicago: University of Chicago Press, 1983.

Banta, Martha. *Imaging American Women: Ideas and Ideals in Cultural History*. New York: Columbia University Press, 1987.

Bassham, Ben. *The Theatrical Photographs of Napoleon Sarony*. Kent OH: Kent State University, 1978.

Baum, L. Frank. *The Wonderful Wizard of Oz*. Chicago: Geo. M. Hill Co., 1900.

Beaton, Cecil. "Lovely Lily Elsie." In *The Rise and Fall of the Matinée Idol: Past Deities of Stage and Screen, Their Roles, Their Magic, and Their Worshippers*, 3-13. Edited by Anthony Curtis. New York: St. Martin's Press, 1974.

___. *My Bolivian Aunt: A Memoir*. London: Weidenfeld and Nicolson, 1971.

___. *Photobiography*. New York: Doubleday, 1951.

Beaton, Cecil, and Madeleine Ginsburg. *Fashion: An Anthology*. London: Victoria and Albert Museum, 1971.

"Beautiful Madame Hading: She Chats Gayly About Her Life and Aspirations." *The World*, October 10, 1888.

Belasco, David. "Seeing Four Thousand Stage-Struck Women Every Year." *New York Times*, September 5, 1909, 3.

Bentley, Lillian L. "Does Red Make Us Nervous?" *Ladies' Home Journal* (March 1908): 20.

Berlanstein, Lenard R. "Cultural Change and the Acting Conservatory in Late-Nineteenth-Century France." *The Historical Journal* 46 (2003): 583-97.

___. *Daughters of Eve: A Cultural History of French Theater Women from the Old Regime to the Fin-de-Siècle*. Cambridge MA: Harvard University Press, 2001.

___. "Historicizing and Gendering Celebrity Culture: Famous Women in Nineteenth-Century France." *Journal of Women's History* 16 (Autumn 2004): 65-91.

___. "Ready for Progress? Opinion Surveys on Women's Roles and Opportunities in Belle Epoque France." *French Politics, Society, and Culture* 27 (Spring 2009): 1-22.

___. "Selling Modern Femininity: *Femina*, a Forgotten Feminist Publishing Success in Belle Epoque France." *French Historical Studies* 30 (Fall 2007): 623-50.

Blumberg, Joan Jacobs. *The Body Project: An Intimate History of American Girls*. New York: Random House, 1997.

Boime, Albert. "The Case of Rosa Bonheur: Why Should a Woman Want to Be More Like a Man?" *Art History* 4 (December 1981): 384-409.

Bonnefont, Gaston. *Les Parisiennes chez elles: Nos grandes artistes.* Paris: Ernest Flammarion, 1897.

Bourgeron, Jean-Pierre. *Les Reutlinger: Photographes à Paris 1850-1937*. Paris: Jean-Pierre Bourgeron, 1979.

Breward, Christopher. "The Actress: Covent Garden and the Strand, 1880-1914." In *Fashion: Critical and Primary Sources*. Volume 3, *The Nineteenth Century*, 78-105. Edited by Peter McNeil. Oxford: Berg, 2009.

Burke, Billie. "My Simple Rules for Beauty." *The Delineator* (June 1911): 510.

___. "Personal Reminiscences." *The Theatre* (September 1916): 122-25.

___. "The Actress and Her Clothes." *The Saturday Evening Post* (February 20, 1909): 12-13.

___. "Under My Own Vine and Fig Tree." *Harper's Bazar* (August 1913): 19, 45.

Burke, Billie, with Cameron Shipp. *With a Feather on My Nose*. New York: Appleton-Century-Crofts, 1949.

___. *With Powder on My Nose*. New York: Coward-McCann Inc., 1959.

C. de C. [Claire de Chancenay]. "Tournées Artistiques de Madame Jane Hading." *Le Théatre* (September 1898): inside front and back covers.

Capon, Gaston, and Robert Yve-Plessis. *Paris galant au dix-huitième siècle: La vie privée du Prince de Conty*. Paris: J. Schemit, 1907.

Carré, Albert. *Souvenirs du théâtre*. Paris: Plon, 1976.

Carter, Randolph. *The World of Flo Ziegfeld*. New York: Praeger Publishers, 1974.

Carter, Randolph, and Marjorie Farnsworth. *Ziegfeld Follies.* New York: G. P. Putnam's Sons, 1956.

Céran, Jane de. "L'Art de Rester Jeune." *Les Modes* (supplement?) (December 1909): n.p.

Cheek, Pamela. "The Mémoires secrets and the Actress: Tribadism, Performance, and Property." In *The Mémoires Secrets and the Culture of Publicity in Eighteenth-Century France*, 107-28. Edited by Jeremy Popkin and Bernadette Fort. Oxford: Voltaire Foundation, 1998.

Clermont, Camille. *Souvenirs des parisennes en temps de guerre.* Paris: Berger-Levrault, 1918.

Comœdia Illustré 5, no. 10 (1913): 460, 462.

Coolus, Romain. "Jane Hading: Notes d'Interview." *Le Théatre* (November 1900): 11-17.

Dale, Alan. "The Girl Who Made Good." *Cosmopolitan* (December 1911): 85-91.

Datta, Venita. *Heroes and Legends of Fin-de-Siècle France: Gender, Politics, and National Identity.* Cambridge: Cambridge University Press, 2011.

Daudet, Léon. *Memoirs of Léon Daudet.* Edited by Arthur Kingsland Griggs. New York: Dial Press, 1925.

Davis, Charles Belmont. "Having Risen from the Chorus." *Harper's Bazar* (December 1913): 40-41.

Davis, Tracy. *Actresses as Working Women: Their Social Identity in Victorian Culture.* London: Routledge, 1991.

Day, Roy. "Curtain Falls for Jane Hading; A Career Rivaling Bernhardt's." *New York Herald Tribune*, February 3, 1934.

DeBauche, Leslie Midkiff. "Testimonial Advertising Using Movie Stars in the 1910s: How Billie Burke Came to Sell Pond's Vanishing Cream in 1917." *Charm* (2007): 146-56.

Dene, Darracotte. "Paris Notes." *The Author* (May 1, 1899): 278-81.

Detmold, Rita. "Frocks & Frills." *The Play Pictorial* 18, no. 108 (1911).

Dieudonné, Robert. "En honneur de Madame Bartet." *Femina* (September 1, 1905): 396.

Dubeux, Albert. *Julia Bartet.* Paris: E. Sansot, 1938.

Duff Gordon, Lady (Lucile). *Discretions and Indiscretions.* London: Jarrolds Publishers; New York: Frederick A. Stokes Co., 1932.

Eaton, Walter Prichard. "Personality and the Player: The Matter of Individual Charm and Technical Efficiency." *Collier's* (October 22, 1910): 17, 34.

Elsie, Lily. "The Art of Gesture: II. The English View." *The Strand* (December 1910): 726-28.

Etherington-Smith, Meredith, and Jeremy Pilcher. *The "It" Girls: Lucy, Lady Duff Gordon, Couturière "Lucile," and Elinor Glyn, Romantic Novelist.* London: Hamish Hamilton, 1986.

Fashion Institute of Technology. *Designing the It Girl: Lucile and Her Style.* Exh. cat. New York: FIT, The School of Graduate Studies, 2005.

Featherstone, Mike. "The Body in Consumer Culture." In *The American Body in Context: An Anthology*, 83. Edited by Jessica R. Johnston. Wilmington DE: Scholarly Resources Inc., 2001.

Félix. "Les Toilettes de Félix." *Le Gaulois*, supplement (March 1, 1885): 2.

Foley, Susan K. *Women in France since 1789.* New York: Palgrave Macmillan, 2004.

Fouquier, Henry. "Some Recent French Plays." *The Anglo-American Magazine* (January 1902): 18-38.

___. "Théâtre de la Porte-Saint-Martin." *Le Théatre* (December 11, 1901): 20.

Fyles, Vanderheyden. "Clothes and the Actress." *Green Book Album* (June 1911): 1181.

Galtier, Joseph. "Les grandes artistes modernes: Bartet." *Je sais tout* (April 15, 1910): 370-72.

Gaudriault, Raymond. *La Gravure de mode féminine en France.* Paris: Editions de l'Amateur, 1983.

Giffard, Pierre. *Nos mœurs, La vie au théâtre.* Paris, 1888.

Glenn, Susan A. *Female Spectacle: The Theatrical Roots of Modern Feminism.* Cambridge MA: Harvard University Press, 2000.

Goncourt, Edmond and Jules de. *Journal. Mémoires de la vie littéraire.* Vol. 2. Edited by Robert Ricatte. Paris: Ernest Flammarion and Fasquelle, 1935.

Greer, Howard Kenneth. "The Psychology of Color." *Theatre Magazine* (December 1917): 374-76.

Grein, James Thomas. *Dramatic Criticism.* Vol. 5. London: Eveleigh Nash, 1903.

Griffith, Marie. *Born Again Bodies: Flesh and Spirit in American Christianity.* Berkeley: University of California Press, 2004.

Guiral, Pierre, and Félix Reynaud. *Les Marseillais dans l'histoire.* Paris: Ed. Privat, 1988.

Gutwirth, Madelyn. *The Twilight of the Goddesses: Women and Representation in the French Revolutionary Era.* New Brunswick NJ: Rutgers University Press, 1992.

Hargreaves, Roger. "Putting Faces to the Names: Social and Celebrity Portrait Photography." In Peter Hamilton and Roger Hargreaves, *The Beautiful and the Damned: The Creation of Identity in Nineteenth-Century Photography*, 17-55. Aldershot, Hampshire: Lund Humphries, 2001.

Hart, Jerome Alfred. *Sardou and the Sardou Plays.* Philadelphia: J. B. Lippincott Company, 1913.

Hayter-Menzies, Grant. *Mrs. Ziegfeld: The Public and Private Lives of Billie Burke.* Jefferson NC: McFarland & Company, 2009.

Heilgers, Louise. "Delightful Dresses at Daly's." *The Play Pictorial* 10 (1907): 106-7.

Hemmings, F. W. J. "Play-writers and Play-actors: the controversy over the comités de lecture in France, 1757-1910." *French Studies* (October 1989): 405-22.

___. *The Theatre Industry in Nineteenth-Century France.* Cambridge: Cambridge University Press, 1993.

Hervez, Jean. *Les femmes et la galanterie au XVIIe siècle.* Paris: H. Daragon, 1907.

Holmes, Diana, and Carrie Tarr, ed. *A 'Belle Epoque'?: Women in French Society and Culture, 1890-1914.* New York: Berghahn Books, 2006.

Hunter, Jane H. *How Young Ladies Became Girls: The Victorian Origins of American Girlhood.* New Haven and London: Yale University Press, 2002.

"In Her Latest Rôle: Miss Lily Elsie as a Member of Her Husband's Hunt." *The Bystander* (November 19, 1913): 405.

Isébor, Robert. "Le théâtre du grand couturier." *Femina* (December 15, 1911): 697.

Jahyer, Félix. "Jane Hading de la Renaissance." *Camées Artistiques* (November 27, 1880): n.p.

"Jane Hading at Home: A Visit to the French Actress." *Current Literature: A Magazine of Record and Review* (July-December 1895): 396. (This article was reprinted from *Harper's Bazar*.)

"Jane Hading: Former Favorite of Comedie Francaise Dies at 81." *New York Times*, February 19, 1941.

"Jane Hading's Wonderful [eyes] and how they were made." *The Atlanta Journal*, February 22, 1903.

Kaplan, Joel H., and Sheila Stowell. *Theatre and Fashion: Oscar Wilde to the Suffragettes.* Cambridge: Cambridge University Press, 1994.

Kelly, Veronica. "Beauty and the Market: Actress Postcards and their Senders in Early Twentieth-Century Australia." *New Theatre Quarterly* 78, no. 20, pt. II (2004): 99-116.

Kobbé, Gustav. "The Stage as a School of Costume." *The Delineator* (January 1905): 63.

Kracauer, Siegfried. *Orpheus in Paris: Offenbach and the Paris of his Time.* Translated by Gwenda David and Eric Mosbacher. New York: Alfred A. Knopf, 1938.

Lacour, Léopold. *Les premières actrices françaises.* Paris: Librairie française, 1921.

Lancey, Sybil de. "La Mode et Les Modes." *Les Modes* 10, no. 120 (1910): 28.

Landes, Joan. *Women in the Public Sphere in the Age of the French Revolution.* Ithaca NY: Cornell University Press, 1980.

Larchy, Lorédon, ed. *Documents inédits sur le règne de Louis XV, ou anecdotes galantes sur les actrices, demoiselles entretenues, grisettes, etc. formant le journal de Monsieur le lieutenant de police de Sartine.* Brussels: Parent, 1863.

Lecomte, L.-Henry, ed. *Un amour de Déjazet. Histoire et correspondance inédite, 1834-1844.* Paris: H. Daragon, 1908.

Lees, Frederic. "The Evolution of Paris Fashions: An Inquiry." *Pall Mall Gazette* (May-August 1902): 113-22.

Leslie, Amy. *Some Players: Personal Sketches.* Chicago and New York: Herbert S. Stone & Company, 1899.

"Les rats de l'Opéra." *La Vie parisienne* (September 19, 1891), 528-29.

"Le Théâtre Instantané." *Le Théâtre* (January 1898): 1.

Loring, Janet. "Costuming on the New York Stage from 1895 to 1915 with Particular Emphasis on Charles Frohman's Companies," PhD diss., State University of Iowa, 1960; Ann Arbor, MI, 1960.

Lowe, Margaret. *Looking Good: College Women and Body Image.* Baltimore: Johns Hopkins University Press, 2003.

Mackrell, Alice. *An Illustrated History of Fashion: 500 Years of Fashion Illustration.* New York: Costume & Fashion Press, 1997.

"Mademoiselle Duchesnois au Nord." *Le temps*, June 4, 1896.

"Manuel's Heart with Lily Elsie." *Philadelphia Inquirer*, December 5, 1909.

Marcosson, Isaac F., and Daniel Frohman. *Charles Frohman: Manager and Man.* New York and London: Harper & Brothers, 1916.

Marly, Diana de. *Costume on the Stage, 1600-1940.* Totowa NJ: Barnes and Noble, 1982.

___. *Worth: Father of Haute Couture.* London: Elm Tree, 1980. Reprint edition London and New York: Holmes & Meier, 1990.

Marra, Kim. "Elsie de Wolfe Circa 1901: The Dynamics of Prescriptive Feminine Performance in American Theatre and Society." *Theatre Survey* 35, no. 1 (1994): 100-20.

___. *Strange Duets: Impresarios and Actresses in the American Theatre, 1865-1914.* Iowa City: University of Iowa Press, 2006.

Marshall, Gail. "Cultural Formations: The Nineteenth-Century Touring Actress and her International Audiences." In *The Cambridge Companion to the Actress*, 52-73. Edited by Maggie B. Gale and John Stokes. Cambridge: Cambridge University Press, 2007.

Martin-Fugier, Anne. *La bourgeoise: Femme au temps de Paul Bourget.* Paris: B. Grasset, 1983.

___. *Comédiennes. Les actrices en France au XIXe siècle.* Paris: Seuil, 2001.

Mason, A. E. W. *Sir George Alexander and the St. James's Theatre.* London: Macmillan, 1935.

Masque de Velours. "La Vie Mondaine." *La Revue illustrée* (June-December 1886): 723-24.

Mayer, David. "The Actress as Photographic Icon: From Early Photography to Early Film." In *The Cambridge Companion to the Actress*, 74-94. Edited by Maggie B. Gale and John Stokes. Cambridge: Cambridge University Press, 2007.

McArthur, Benjamin. *Actors and American Culture, 1880-1920.* Philadelphia: Temple University Press, 1984; reprinted Iowa City: University of Iowa Press, 2000.

McCauley, Elizabeth Anne. *Industrial Madness: Commercial Photography in Paris 1848-1871.* New Haven and London: Yale University Press, 1994.

McManners, John. *Abbés and Actresses: The Church and the Theatrical Profession in the Eighteenth Century.* Oxford: Clarendon Press, 1984.

McPherson, Heather. "Sarah Bernhardt: Portrait of the Actress as Spectacle." *Nineteenth-Century Contexts* (March 1999): 409-54.

Mendes, Valerie D., and Amy de la Haye. *Lucile Ltd. London, Paris, New York and Chicago, 1890s-1930s.* London: V&A Publishing, 2009.

Mendès, Madame Catulle. "La mode au théâtre." *Femina* (November 15, 1906): 57-58.

___. "Robes de théâtre." *Femina* (October 15, 1908): 474-76.

"The Mind the Paint Girl." *The Playgoer and Society Illustrated* 5, no. 30 (1912): 185.

Mirecour, Marcelle de. "Les Succès de Redfern au Théâtre / The Theatrical Successes of Redfern." *Paris Review* (April 1902): n.p.

"Miss Lily Elsie: The Merry Widow." *Times* (London), December 18, 1962.

Mizejewski, Linda. *Ziegfeld Girl: Image and Icon in American Culture and Cinema.* Duke University Press, 1999.

Modern Girl around the World Research Group. *The Modern Girl around the World: Consumption, Modernity, and Globalization.* Durham NC: Duke University Press, 2008.

Monselet, Charles. "Compte rendue." *Le Monde illustré* (December 14, 1867): 362.

"Monsieur Dumas et les Comédiennes." *Le temps*, March 24, 1895.

Moore, Mary. *Charles Wyndham and Mary Moore.* Edinburgh: Privately printed, 1925.

Mordden, Ethan. *Ziegfeld: The Man Who Invented Show Business.* New York: St. Martin's Press, 2008.

Motte, Dean de la, and Jeannene M. Przyblyski, eds. *Making the News: Modernity & the Mass Press in Nineteenth-Century France.* Amherst: University of Massachusetts Press, 1999.

Nérode, Charles de. "Une heure chez Madame Jane Hading." *La Revue illustrée* (May 1, 1893): 347-53.

Noble, Mrs. Robert E. "Fascinating Fashions behind the Footlights at Daly's." *The Play Pictorial* 15, no. 88 (1909): 22-23.

North, Susan. "John Redfern and Sons, 1847-1892." *Costume* 42 (2008): 145-68.

___. "Redfern Limited, 1892 to 1940." *Costume* 43 (2009): 85-108.

Nye, Robert A. *Masculinity and Male Codes of Honor in Modern France.* New York: Oxford University Press, 1993.

"Our Gallery of Players. XXIV. Jane Hading." *The Illustrated American* (December 12, 1891): 179.

Paris correspondent. "What to Wear: Chit-Chat on Dress." *Cassell's Family Magazine* (June 1887): 439-41.

Patterson, Ada. "A Sunday Morning Chat with Billie Burke." *The Theatre* (November 1908): 300-304.

___. "The Lady of Burkeleigh Crest." *The Theatre* (January 1913): 28-30.

Peiss, Kathy. *Hope in a Jar: The Making of America's Beauty Culture.* New York: Metropolitan Books, Henry Holt, 1998.

Penniston, Benjamin H. *The Golden Age of Postcards: Early 1900s: Identification and Values.* Paducah KY: Collector Books, 2008.

Perrot, Michelle. "Women, Power, and History: The Case of Nineteenth-Century France." In *Women, State and Revolution: Essays on Power and Gender in Europe since 1789,* 44-59. Edited by Sian Reynolds. Brighton, UK: Wheatsheaf Books, 1986).

Pinero, Arthur. *The "Mind the Paint" Girl: A Comedy in Four Acts.* Teddington: The Echo Library, 2008.

"The Players." *Everybody's Magazine* (July-December 1908): 846.

Plunkett, John. "Carte-de-visite" and "Postcard." In *The Encyclopedia of Nineteenth-Century Photography.* Vol. 1, pp. 276-77, 1162-64. Edited by John Hannavy. London: Routlege, 2007.

Poiret, Paul. *My First Fifty Years.* Translated by Stephen Haden Guest. London: Victor Gollancz, 1931.

Porel, Jacques. *Fils de Réjane: Souvenirs, 1895-1920.* 2 volumes. Paris: Plon, 1951.

Postlewait, Thomas. "George Edwardes and Musical Comedy: the Transformation of London Theatre and Society, 1878-1914." In *The Performing Century: Nineteenth-Century Theatre's History,* 80-102. Edited by Tracy Davis and Peter Holland. Basingstoke: Palgrave Macmillan 2007.

"Probate, Divorce, and Admiralty Division (Before Mr. Justice Hill): Decree Nisi for Miss Lily Elsie." *Times* (London), July 16, 1929.

Remaury, Bruno, and Lydia Kamitsis, eds. *Dictionnaire inter-*

national de la mode. Paris: Éditions du Regard, 2004.

Ribeiro, Aileen. "Costuming the Part: A Discourse of Fashion and Fiction in the Image of the Actress in England, 1776-1812." In *Notorious Muse: The Actress in British Art and Culture, 1776-1812*, 104-27. Edited by Robyn Asleson. New Haven and London: Yale University Press, 2003.

Richardson, Genevieve. "Costuming on the American Stage, 1751-1901: A Study of the Major Developments in Wardrobe Practice and Costume Style." PhD diss., University of Illinois, 1953.

Ripert, Aline, and Claude Frère. *La carte postale: Son histoire, sa function sociale*. Paris: Centre National de la Recherche Scientifique, 2001.

Roberts, Mary-Louise. "Subversive Copy: Feminist Journalism in Fin-de-Siècle France." In Motte and Przyblyski, *Making the News*, 302-350.

___. "Acting Up: The Feminist Theatrics of Marguerite Durand." *French Historical Studies* (Fall 1996), 1, 103-38.

___. *Disruptive Acts: The New Woman in Fin-de-Siècle France*. Chicago: University of Chicago Press, 2002.

___. "Rethinking Female Celebrity: The Eccentric Stars of Nineteenth-Century France." In *Constructing Charisma: Celebrity, Fame, and Power in Nineteenth-Century Europe*, 103-18. Edited by Edward Berenson and Eva Giloi. New York: Berghahn Books, 2010.

Rochefort, Florence. "The French Feminist Movement and Republicanism, 1868-1914." In *Women's Emancipation Movements in Nineteenth-Century Europe: A European Perspective*, 77-101. Edited by Sylvia Paletshek and Bianca Pietrow-Ennker. Stanford CA: Stanford University Press, 2004.

Rogan, Bjarne. "An Entangled Object: The Picture Postcard as Souvenir and Collectible, Exchange and Ritual Communication." *Cultural Analysis* 4 (2005): 1-27.

Sagne, Jean. "All Kinds of Portraits." In *A New History of Photography*, 103-22. Edited by Michel Frizot. Cologne: Könemann, 1998.

Sarcey, Françisque. "In the World of Art and Letters: French Artists in America." *The Cosmopolitan* 18 (1894-April 1895): 752-55.

___. "Première Année." *Le Théatre* (December 1898): 1.

Sartoris, Mlle. "Madame Hading's Ideas on Dress Together with Fashions of the Month." *The Theatre* (October 1909): xvi-xx.

Saunders, Edith. *The Age of Worth*. London: Longmans, 1954.

Scanlon, Jennifer. *Inarticulate Longings: The Ladies' Home Journal, Gender, and the Promises of Consumer Culture*. New York: Routledge, 1995.

Schweitzer, Marlis. "'Darn That Merry Widow Hat': The On- and Offstage Life of a Theatrical Commodity, circa 1907-1908." *Theatre Survey* (November 2009): 189-221.

___. "'The Mad Search for Beauty': Actresses, Cosmetics, and the Middle-Class Market." In *Testimonial Advertising in the American Marketplace: Emulation, Identity, Community*, 123-50. Edited by Marlis Schweitzer and Marina Moskowitz. New York: Palgrave Macmillan, 2009.

___. "'The Mad Search for Beauty': Actresses' Testimonials and the 'Democratization' of Beauty." *Journal of the Gilded Age and Progressive Era* (July 2005): 255-92.

___. "Surviving the City: Press Agents, Publicity Stunts, and the Spectacle of the Urban Female Body." In *Performance and the City*, 133-51. Edited by D. J. Hopkins, Shelley Orr, and Kim Solga. Houndsmills and New York: Palgrave Macmillan, 2009.

___. *When Broadway Was the Runway: Theater, Fashion, and American Culture*. Philadelphia: University of Pennsylvania Press, 2009.

Scott, Virginia. "The Actress and Utopian Theatre Reform in Eighteenth-Century France: Riccoboni, Rousseau, and Restif." *Theatre Research International* (March 2002): 18-28.

Senelick, Laurence. "Eroticism in Early Theatrical Photography." In *Theatre History Studies* 9 (1991): 1-49.

Sherrow, Victoria. *For Appearance' Sake: The Historical Encyclopedia of Good Looks, Beauty, and Grooming*. Westport CT: Oryx Press, 2001.

Short, Ernest Henry, and Arthur Compton-Rickett. *Ring up the Curtain: Being a Pageant of English Entertainment Covering Half a Century*. London: Herbert Jenkins, 1938.

Silver, Kenneth E. "Celebrity, Patriotism, and Sarah Bernhardt." In *Constructing Charisma: Celebrity, Fame, and Power in Nineteenth-Century Europe*, 145-54. Edited by Edward Berenson and Eva Giloi. New York: Berghahn Books, 2010.

Slattery-Christy, David. *Anything But Merry!: The Life and Times of Lily Elsie*. London: Author House, 2008.

Smith, Leonard V., Stéphanie Audoin-Rouzeau, and Annette Becker. *France and the Great War*. Cambridge: Cambridge University Press, 2003.

Solomon-Godeau, Abigail. "The Other Side of Venus: The Visual Economy of Feminine Display." In *The Sex of Things: Gender and Consumption in Historical Perspective*, 113-50. Edited by Victoria de Grazia and Ellen Furlough. Berkeley: University of California Press, 1996.

Steinbrügge, Liselotte. *The Moral Sex: Women's Nature in the French Enlightenment*. Translated by Pamela Selwyn. New York: Oxford University Press, 1995.

Stone, Judith F. "The Republican Brotherhood: Gender and Ideology." In *Gender and the Politics of Social Reform in France, 1870-1914*, 28-58. Edited by Elinor A. Accampo, Rachel G. Fuchs, and Mary Lynn Stewart. Baltimore: Johns Hopkins University Press, 1995.

Tortora, Phyllis G. "The Evolution of the American Fashion Magazine as Exemplified in Selected Fashion Journals, 1830-1969." PhD diss., New York University, 1973.

Tracy, Louis. *The "Mind the Paint" Girl*. New York: Edward J. Clode, 1912.

Troy, Nancy J. *Couture Culture: A Study in Modern Art and Fashion*. Cambridge MA: Massachusetts Institute of Technology, 2003.

Vauzat, Guy. *Blanche d'Antigny, Actrice et demi-mondaine*. Paris: Lahure, 1933.

Violette. "Paris Fashions." *The Woman's World* (July 1889): 472-73.

"Wealthy Scot to Marry Lily Elsie: Favorite English Actress Will Retire from the Stage Before Long." *Philadelphia Inquirer*, November 12, 1911.

Westbrook, Virginia. "Role of Trade Cards in Marketing Chocolate During the late 19th Century." In *Chocolate: History, Culture, and Heritage*, 183-91. Edited by Louis Evan Grivetti and Howards-Yana Shapiro. Hoboken: John Wiley & Sons, 2009.

Wexler, Victor. "Made for Man's Delight: Rousseau as Antifeminist." *American Historical Review* 81 (April 1979): 266-91.

Ziegfield, Richard, and Paulette. *The Life and Times of Florenz Ziegfeld, Jr*. New York: Harry N. Abrams, 1993.

Zola, Émile. *Nana*. Translated by Douglas Parmée. New York: Penguin, 1992.

RESOURCES

Billie Burke scrapbooks, Part V, RLC, http://digitalgallery. nypl.org/nypldigital/dgkeysearchdetail.cfm?trg=1&strucID =672497&imageID=V86_046&parent_id=668001&word= &snum=&s=&notword=&d=&c=&f=&k=0&sScope=&sLe vel=&sLabel=&total=107&num=40&imgs=20&pNum=& pos=46, accessed May 24, 2011.

Lily Elsie scrapbooks, Robinson Locke Scrapbook Collection, New York Public Library for the Performing Arts.

Jane Hading file, Bibliothèque de la Comédie-Française, Paris.

Jane Hading scrapbooks, Bibliothèque nationale de France, (Rez de Jardin, François Mitterand), Paris, Rt 8095 and Rt 8096.

Jane Hading scrapbooks, Bibliothèque nationale de France (Arts du spectacle, Richelieu), Paris, 4- ICO PER- 11858 (1-5).

Jane Hading clipping file, New York Public Library for the Performing Arts.

Jane Hading photographs file, New York Public Library for the Performing Arts.

Florenz Ziegfeld Papers, New York Public Library for the Performing Arts.